STEALTH JIHAD

How Radical Islam
Is Subverting America
without Guns or Bombs

STEALTH JIHAD

How Radical Islam
Is Subverting America
without Guns or Bombs

ROBERT SPENCER

Since 1947
REGNERY
PUBLISHING, INC.
An Eagle Publishing Company • Washington, DC

Cataloging-in-Publication data on file with the Library of Congress

ISBN 978-1-59698-556-8

Published in the United States by
Regnery Publishing, Inc.
One Massachusetts Avenue, NW
Washington, DC 20001
www.regnery.com

Manufactured in the United States of America

10 9 8 7 6 5 4 3 2 1

Books are available in quantity for promotional or premium use. Write to Director of Special Sales, Regnery Publishing, Inc., One Massachusetts Avenue NW, Washington, DC 20001, for information on discounts and terms or call (202) 216-0600.

*To all those who recognize the danger of
the stealth jihad and are ready to resist*

CONTENTS

TERRORISM WITHOUT TERROR?

The name of this book is *Stealth Jihad: How Radical Islam Is Subverting America without Guns or Bombs*. For many people, the title itself will be nonsensical—it is tantamount to saying, "How the terrorists are winning without terrorism." Most Americans regard the terror threat as one that necessarily involves guns and bombs, and anti-terror efforts as consisting solely in finding terrorist cells and foiling their plans to blow up buildings and kill Americans.

If the terrorists have an ideology, many Americans assume that it is an extreme and perverted version of Islam that twists the peaceful teachings of the Qur'an into a license to kill. They further suppose that the ideological component is minor; they believe that Islamic terrorism is an activity engaged in primarily by the desperately poor, the ignorant, and the manipulated, and that it needs to be countered with education, compassionate hearts-and-minds initiatives, and financial incentives as much as with military or law enforcement action. Senator Joseph Biden (D-Delaware) summed up this point of view when he asserted that "to compare terrorism with an all-encompassing ideology like communism and fascism is evidence of profound confusion."[1]

Not only do many influential Americans deny the existence of, or minimize in importance, any common ideology that jihadists around the world may have, but they also have taken the recent disarray among terrorist groups (principally al Qaeda) as evidence that the jihad ideology is disintegrating—discredited by those who once had been its foremost proponents.

Lawrence Wright, author of *The Looming Tower: Al Qaeda and the Road to 9/11,* fostered this perception in a lengthy *New Yorker* article, "The Rebellion Within: An al Qaeda mastermind questions terrorism," in June 2008.[2] In it, Wright relates that one of al Qaeda's chief theorists has rejected terrorism. This news led to a cascade of both liberal and conservative voices rejoicing that the end of the war on terror is at hand.

Unfortunately, reality—as is usually the case—is not quite so comforting. The subject of Wright's piece, Sayyid Imam al-Sharif, also known as "Dr. Fadl," does not reject the idea that Muslims must strive to subjugate unbelievers under the rule of Islamic law. He simply advocates a change in strategy: less terrorism, more stealth jihad. This revelation shouldn't make Americans go back to sleep; it should spur them to become aware of the ways in which the jihadist agenda of Islamic supremacism is advancing without guns and bombs.

In one key passage, Montasser al-Zayyat, whom Wright identifies as an "Islamist lawyer," offends al Qaeda second-in-command Ayman al-Zawahiri by asserting that "jihad did not have to be restricted to an armed approach." This is indicative of the wishful thinking that so many have brought to their reading of Wright's article. Zayyat didn't reject the necessity of waging jihad against infidels; he just denied that it had to be restricted to an armed approach. But many readers mistakenly assumed he was denouncing jihad altogether.

"Zawahiri," says Wright, "became increasingly isolated. He understood that violence was the fuel that kept the radical Islamist organizations running; they had no future without terror."

That may be so for some organizations. Others, such as the Muslim Brotherhood, get along just fine without violence. In fact, the Brotherhood, as we shall see, is the key force behind the stealth jihad agenda, which aims to establish Islamic law in the West.

In any case, the Brotherhood, according to Wright, "wrote a series of books and pamphlets, collectively known as 'the revisions,' in which they formally explained their new thinking." Wright met with the Grand Mufti of Egypt, Sheikh Ali Gomaa, to ask him about this.

Wright calls Gomaa a "highly promoted champion of moderate Islam." This description in itself shows the inadequacy of speaking only of "terrorism," without recognizing the myriad ways in which the jihad agenda is advancing. Gomaa may indeed be a "highly promoted champion of moderate Islam," but he has also expressed support for the terrorist group Hizballah.[3] "Gomaa," Wright continues, "has also become an advocate for Muslim women, who he says should have equal standing with men." Yet he is also an "advocate for Muslim women" who has spoken positively of wife-beating.[4] "His forceful condemnations of extreme forms of Islam," says Wright, "have made him an object of hatred among Islamists and an icon among progressives, whose voices have been overpowered by the thunder of the radicals." Yet Gomaa's "forceful condemnations of extreme forms of Islam" have been accompanied by his denial of reports that he had rejected the traditional Islamic death sentence for apostates.[5]

In fact, Gomaa openly declares that all his "revisions" are only intended as temporary measures. He tells Wright, "We accept the revisions conditionally, not as the true teachings of Islam but with the understanding that this process is like medicine for a particular time."

In other words, the true teachings of Islam include the mandate to wage violent jihad against unbelievers. But jihad violence can temporarily be set aside for strategic reasons, as "medicine for a particular time." That is, different times call for different tactics, but the overall objective remains the same.

After outlining various reasons why, in Fadl's new view, today's global jihad is illegitimate, Wright informs us that "Fadl does not condemn all jihadist activity." To the contrary, Fadl says that "jihad in Afghanistan will lead to the creation of an Islamic state with the triumph of the Taliban, God willing," and that "if it were not for the jihad in Palestine, the Jews would have crept toward the neighboring countries a long time ago." As for September 11, Fadl asks, "what good is it if you destroy one of your enemy's buildings, and he destroys one of your countries? What good is it if you kill one of his people, and he kills a thousand of yours? . . . That, in short, is my evaluation of 9/11."

In other words, it was not morally wrong, just tactically stupid.

This is no rejection of jihad; it is just a change in tactics. It should make us all the more aware of, and on guard against, the stealth jihad.

THE STEALTH JIHAD

In this book, I offer evidence for the proposition that terror attacks involving bombings and shootings are not the sum total of terrorist aspirations, but are just one component of a larger initiative. The goal of that initiative is the imposition of jihadists' ideology over the world—over their fellow Muslims and non-Muslims alike. That ideology may be summed up by the phrase "radical Islam," although that term is used in many different ways. Some use it to suggest that the core teachings of Islam are essentially peaceful, and that it is only radicals—those who distort those teachings into "radical Islam"—who are responsible for violence committed in Islam's name.

I am not using the phrase in that way. Rather, I have long contended that Islam is unique among the major world religions in having a developed doctrine, theology, and legal system mandating warfare against and the subjugation of unbelievers. There is no orthodox sect or school of Islam that teaches that Muslims must coexist peacefully as equals with non-Muslims on an indefinite basis. I use the term "radical Islam" merely to distinguish those Muslims who are actively working to advance this subjugation from the many millions who are not, as well as to emphasize that the stealth jihad program is truly radical: it aims at nothing less than the transformation of American society and the imposition of Islamic law here, subjugating women and non-Muslims to the status of legal inferiors.

Those who are working to advance the subjugation of non-Muslims are not doing it solely by violent means. The common distinction between "radical" and "moderate" Muslims has generally been made between those who are engaged in blowing things up or are plotting to do so, and those who are not. However, the evidence presented in this book shows that the distinction ought to be placed elsewhere: between those Muslims who believe that Islamic law is the perfect system for human society and who are working by whatever means to impose that Islamic law, and those Muslims who support Western pluralistic governments and seek to live with non-Muslims as equals, under secular rule, on an indefinite basis.

Those who are working to advance the hegemony of Islamic law do so in innumerable ways, including by introducing it, bit by bit, into American society and demanding that Americans accommodate it; by shouting down any and all who dare to discuss the supremacist impulse within traditional and mainstream Islam; and by engaging in efforts to transform and control Western economies.

The West today faces the threat of stealth jihadists. By using this term, I am not implying that they operate in secret; to the contrary, one of the key characteristics distinguishing them from their violent counterparts is that they carry out their business openly, carefully constructing a facade of moderation. What is stealth about these operatives is their ultimate agenda—they are not seeking to protect Muslims' "civil rights" from the rampant "Islamophobia" that ostensibly plagues Western societies, as they claim. Rather, they are leading a full-scale effort to transform pluralistic societies into Islamic states, and to sweep away Western notions of legal equality, freedom of conscience, freedom of speech, and more.

The stealth jihadists have already made significant inroads into American life. They are well-funded, well-organized, and persistent. They will not be pacified by negotiations, compromises, or concessions; they cannot be bought off. And every day, they are advancing their agenda—while most Americans don't even know they exist.

In his controversial book *America Alone*, Mark Steyn suggests that Europe is falling to the Islamic jihad, and that only America will be left as a bulwark against Islamization. But it is unclear how much of a bulwark we will be if we allow our freedoms and way of life to be eroded in the name of "getting along." That is exactly what is happening today. The stealth jihadists are working energetically to wear away the very fabric of American culture.

It is happening right now, under our noses.

CHAPTER ONE

MUSLIMS TRYING TO TAKE OVER THE USA? YOU'VE GOT TO BE KIDDING . . . .

THE GRAND JIHAD

- The Muslim Brotherhood "must understand that their work in America is a kind of grand jihad in eliminating and destroying the Western civilization from within and 'sabotaging' its miserable house by their hands and the hands of the believers so that it is eliminated and Allah's religion is made victorious over all other religions."[1]

- "We reject the UN, reject America, reject all law and order. Don't lobby Congress or protest because we don't recognize Congress. The only relationship you should have with America is to topple it . . . . Eventually there will be a Muslim in the White House dictating the laws of sharia."[2]

- "Let us damn America, let us damn Israel, let us damn them and their allies until death."[3]

- "Very soon, Allah willing, Rome will be conquered, just like Constantinople was, as was prophesized by our Prophet Muhammad. Today, Rome is the capital of the Catholics, or the Crusader capital.... This capital of theirs will be an advanced post for the Islamic conquests, which will spread through Europe in its entirety, and then will turn to the two Americas."[4]
- "I have complete faith that Islam will invade Europe and America, because Islam has logic and a mission."[5]
- "Islam isn't in America to be equal to any other faith, but to become dominant. The Koran should be the highest authority in America, and Islam the only accepted religion on earth."[6]
- "I wouldn't want to create the impression that I wouldn't like the government of the United States to be Islamic sometime in the future."[7]
- "If only Muslims were clever politically, they could take over the United States and replace its constitutional government with a caliphate."[8]

Ravings of a lone crank? If only they were. In reality, these statements were made by eight separate speakers—including some of the most influential Islamic spokesmen and leaders in the United States.

Nor were they indulging in wishful thinking or empty braggadocio, however far they may be from actually attaining their goals. Rather, they were enunciating, in various ways, an agenda that many Muslims within the U.S. are pursuing today.

They envision not only a Muslim president, but that the United States Constitution be replaced or amended so as to comply in all particulars with Islamic sharia law. These would not simply be small or cosmetic changes that would leave America's foundations intact. Whether the United States has a Baptist president or a Methodist president or a Jewish president or a Catholic president would almost certainly make little difference in policy or law. But a Muslim president who began to institute Islamic law in the United States, as these men envision it, would make for a very large difference indeed.

Those who are advancing this agenda are striving for nothing less than an Islamic conquest of North America, after which not only the government will be Islamic, but so will society as a whole. Even if a majority of Americans do not convert to Islam, Islam will be dominant: Islamic perspectives will reign supreme, non-Muslims will have to cater to Islamic sensibilities, and Islamic law will govern not only Muslim communities, but non-Muslims as well. This will also include—most important of all—the Islamization of the mainstream media and the public sphere.

Yes, that can mean stonings for adultery and amputations for theft. But it means much more as well. Islamic law is an enormous complex of regulations governing every aspect of human existence—and it institutionalizes discrimination on the basis of gender and religion.

Could this ever happen here?

Of course not, most analysts confidently reply. In the minds of our academic, political, and media elites, the advent of sharia law in the U.S. is about as likely as a return to Prohibition or the Libertarian Party candidate being elected president.

And yet, while the groups advancing the Islamic agenda may be small, they are by no means powerless and in no sense discredited. In fact, they are in many cases extraordinarily well-financed and surprisingly influential. And even if one grants for the sake of argument that they will never be able to attain their goals in all their fullness, there is no doubt whatsoever that there are Muslims in the United States today, as well as outside it, who are working to accomplish exactly those goals.

One of the best weapons they have on their side is that very few, even among law-enforcement or government officials, are even aware that this agenda exists, or that anyone is advancing it, or by what means. For this is a jihad—a struggle to advance the cause of Islam, the cause of Allah—but it is a jihad without any of the signs that law enforcement officials are trained to recognize as indications of terrorist activity. There are no guns and bombs. No terrorist training manuals. No open glorification of blood-drenched thugs.

It is a jihad that advances without violent attacks at a time when almost all our "anti-terror" resources and energy are devoted to heading off another violent attack on American soil. Many American officials, and officials all over the Western world, persist in regarding the problem we face solely as a "terrorism threat," consisting entirely of the possibility of attacks against civilians and the work of preventing those attacks. During the 2008 presidential campaign we heard many candidates speak about the terrorism threat (or, in the case of failed Democratic hopeful John Edwards, the absence of such a threat), but no one dealt with the possibility that the terrorist agenda might be advancing through non-terrorist means. Most analysts inside and outside of government don't possess the knowledge necessary to understand, or to recognize the implications of the fact, that the jihadists might be laboring to advance their goals without any terror attacks at all.

It is a jihad, but one whose leaders work within American communities and organizations, and quite often have won the respect and gratitude of their non-Muslim colleagues and peers.

It is a jihad whose leaders enjoy the respect of the mainstream media, who often aid and abet their efforts to present themselves as benign civil rights advocates and conceal their actual agenda.

It is a jihad, but one that has a good chance to transform American society before most Americans have any idea of what's happening.

It should rightly be called a stealth jihad.

THE MAIN PLAYER

As we'll see, the work that many Muslims in the United States today are undertaking to advance this stealth jihad is already doing significant damage to our legal systems, our financial systems, and our sense of ourselves as a society. Even if the United States never becomes an Islamic state—and it may seem fanciful that it ever would—this damage will not be easily repaired.

Are all Muslims in the United States involved in such an effort? Of course not. To say that some Muslims in this country are working to advance a supremacist agenda that would subvert the Constitution doesn't mean that all are. There is a spectrum of belief, knowledge, and fervor among Muslims as there is among devotees of every belief system, religious or not. And so there are innumerable Muslims in this country today who are happy to live in a pluralistic society in which there is no established religion.

But it is no less true that there are also untold numbers of Muslims within the United States who are working today to make the U.S., someday, into an Islamic state. Although they often have links to jihad terrorist organizations, they don't need any terror attack to advance their agenda. In fact, many of them would regard one, if it does come, as an actual hindrance to their efforts.

The chief player in this stealth jihad in America today is the shadowy international organization known as the Muslim Brotherhood.

The Brotherhood (in Arabic, *Al-Ikhwan Al-Muslimun*) is an international Islamic organization that has, in the course of its tumultuous eight decades of existence, given rise to the jihad terror groups Hamas and al Qaeda. An earnest and pious Muslim named Hasan al-Banna founded the group in Egypt in 1928 in part as a response to the establishment of a secular, non-Islamic government in Turkey and the abolition of the caliphate, the office of the successor of Muhammad that had stood for centuries as the symbol of Islamic unity and political power. With his Brotherhood, al-Banna wanted to revive the political aspects of Islam that had retreated with the decline of the Ottoman Empire and the advent of Western colonialism; he decried the separation of "the state from religion in a country which was until recently the site of the Commander of the Faithful."[9] His Islam was inherently and essentially political:

> We summon you to Islam, the teachings of Islam, the laws of Islam and the guidance of Islam, and if this smacks of "politics" in your eyes, then it is our policy.... Islam does have a policy embracing the happiness of this world.... We believe that Islam is an all-embracing concept which regulates every aspect of life, adjudicating on every one of its concerns and prescribing for it a solid and rigorous order.[10]

Al-Banna wrote in 1934 that "it is a duty incumbent on every Muslim to struggle towards the aim of making every people Muslim and the whole world Islamic, so that the banner of Islam can flutter over the earth and the call of the Muezzin can resound in all the corners of the world: God is greatest [*Allahu akbar*]!"[11] He further instructed his followers, "Islam is faith and worship, a country and a citizenship, a religion and a state. It is spirituality and hard work. It is a Qur'an and a sword."[12]

The Brotherhood was no ragtag gathering of marginalized kooks. It grew in Egypt from 150 branches in 1936 to as many as 1,500 by 1944. In 1939 al-Banna counted "100,000 pious youths from the Muslim Brothers from all parts of Egypt," although the foremost historian of the Brotherhood movement, Brynjar Lia, believes he was exaggerating then. Nevertheless, by 1944 membership was estimated at between 100,000 and 500,000.[13] By 1937 the Brotherhood had expanded beyond Egypt, setting up "several branches in Sudan, Saudi Arabia, Palestine, Syria, Lebanon, and Morocco, and one in each of Bahrain, Hadramawt, Hyderabad, Djibouti, and," Lia adds portentously, "Paris."[14] These many thousands, dispersed around the world, heard al-Banna's call to "prepare for jihad and be lovers of death."[15]

But the Brotherhood's modus operandi involves much more than blood and death and terror. Scholar Martin Kramer notes that the Brotherhood had "a double identity. On one level, they operated openly, as a membership organization of social and political awakening. Al-Banna preached moral revival, and the Muslim Brethren engaged in good works. On another level, however, the Muslim Brethren created a 'secret apparatus' that acquired weapons and trained adepts in their use."[16]

That double identity has in America today become the instrument for conducting the stealth jihad. It takes the form of groups that appear outwardly to be moderate, but advance the jihadist agenda through various non-violent initiatives—even while the groups themselves and many of those involved in them have ties to violent jihadist organizations.

THE PLAN

"I have complete faith that Islam will invade Europe and America, because Islam has logic and a mission." Muhammad Mahdi Othman 'Akef made that statement in 2004 when he took over leadership of the Muslim Brotherhood. But he didn't mean an invasion of armies, or even of bomb-wielding terrorists: "The Europeans and the Americans," he explained, "will come into the bosom of Islam out of conviction."[17]

Forming that conviction in the minds of European and American non-Muslims would take a concerted effort spanning years and comprising many fronts. But the ultimate goal of the stealth jihad is clear: the elimination of Western civilization. This was unequivocally enunciated in a 1982 Muslim Brotherhood document that detailed a twelve-point strategy to "establish an Islamic government on earth." Instead of advocating terrorism, the document advises avoiding "confrontation with our adversaries, at the local or the global scale, which would be disproportionate and could lead to attacks against the dawa [Islamic proselytizing] or its disciples."[18] Instead, according to terror analyst Patrick Poole, the Brotherhood would use "deception to mask the intended goals of Islamist actions."[19]

Those goals were described in detail by a top Brotherhood operative in this country, Mohamed Akram, who explained that the Muslim Brotherhood "must understand that their work in America is a kind of grand jihad in eliminating and destroying the Western civilization from within and 'sabotaging' its miserable house by their hands and the hands of the believers so that it is eliminated and Allah's religion is made victorious over all other religions."[20]

Akram's directive came in a Muslim Brotherhood memorandum from May 22, 1991 entitled "An Explanatory Memorandum on the General Strategic Goal for the Group in North

America." The document came to light during the 2007 trial of what had been the largest Islamic charity in the United States, the Holy Land Foundation for Relief and Development, which was accused of funneling charitable donations to the jihad terror group Hamas. The case ended in a mistrial on most charges and the defendants, who are pleading not guilty, are now being retried.[21]

In the memorandum, Akram lays out a plan to do nothing less than conquer and Islamize the United States. The Brotherhood's success in America would ultimately further the even larger goal of establishing "the global Islamic state."[22]

Akram seems to be aware of how fantastical his goal might sound—even to his fellow Muslim Brothers. He claims his plans are not "abundant extravagance, imaginations or hallucinations which passed in the mind of one of your brothers, but they are rather hopes, ambitions and challenges that I hope that you share some or most of which with me."

Arguing that those hopes and ambitions can become reality, Akram says that he perceives a "glimpse of hope" that "we have embarked on a new stage of Islamic activism stages [sic] in this continent." A new stage, yes, but not a new plan: the plan he is elucidating, he explains, is "not strange or a new submission without a root, but rather an attempt to interpret and explain some of what came in the long-term plan which we approved and adopted in our council and our conference in the year [1987]."

Akram states that the Brotherhood's 1987 blueprint was designed to bring about the "Enablement of Islam in North America" by means of a six-point plan:

1. Establishing an effective and stable Islamic Movement led by the Muslim Brotherhood.

2. Adopting Muslims' causes domestically and globally.

3. Expanding the observant Muslim base.

4. Unifying and directing Muslims' efforts.

5. Presenting Islam as a civilization alternative.

6. Supporting the establishment of the global Islamic State wherever it is.

That "effective and stable Islamic Movement led by the Muslim Brotherhood" would, of course, be in the United States. It would agitate for Islamic causes, try to get Muslims to become more observant, unify the disparate activities of Islamic groups in the country, and present Islam as a "civilization alternative"—that is, an alternative to Western constitutional government and Western civilization in general. The Brotherhood's efforts in the United States would aid the worldwide Islamic jihad, which aims for a supranational unity among Muslims under the rule of Islamic law—which they would then work to impose upon the non-Muslim world as well.

ABSORPTION, NOT TERROR

In America, Islam would not be "enabled" through terror attacks. Rather, explains Akram, the Brotherhood's priority would be to "settle" Islam and the Brotherhood movement in the United States, so that the Islamic religion will be "enabled within the souls, minds and the lives of the people of the country in which it moves."

How will this be accomplished? Through the establishment of "firmly-rooted organizations on whose bases civilization, structure and testimony are built." That is, American civilization will give way to Islamic civilization; Islamic law will supplant the American Constitutional legal structure; and from these new bases

Muslims in the United States will bear testimony to Islam, in order to bring more Americans into the faith itself.

According to Akram, this plan requires a number of shifts in the thinking and strategy of Muslims in the United States. These include an increase of cooperation among U.S.-based Muslim groups in order to ensure that everything is devoted to the goal of Islamizing America: "All of our priorities, plans, programs, bodies, leadership, monies and activities march towards the process of the settlement"—that is, the spread and ultimate dominance of Islam in the United States.

Crucially, Akram argues that this strategy will succeed only if Muslims discard the idea that they will inevitably become locked in conflict with non-Muslims in the U.S. They must "shift from the collision mentality to the absorption mentality."[23] America could be conquered and Islamized through a slow and steady process of "absorption"—a kind of reverse assimilation in which Muslim immigrants and converts in the United States gradually impose their values, and, ultimately, their laws, upon the larger population.

WINNING MUSLIMS TO THE CAUSE

Akram reminds the Muslim Brothers that the Islamic "process of settlement" in the United States is a "'Civilization-Jihadist Process' with all the word means." They must understand that their core task—"eliminating and destroying the Western civilization from within"—is not negotiable, as it is part of the basic duty of every Muslim: "Without this level of understanding, we are not up to this challenge and have not prepared ourselves for Jihad yet. It is a Muslim's destiny to perform Jihad and work wherever he is and wherever he lands until the final hour comes."

The Muslim Brotherhood's role in the Grand Jihad involves "initiative, pioneering, leadership, raising the banner and pushing people in that direction. They are then to work to employ, direct and unify muslims' efforts and powers for this process." Again, Akram insists that cooperation among U.S.-based Muslims will be key: "In order to do that, we must possess a mastery of the art of 'coalitions,' the art of 'absorption' and the principles of 'cooperation.'"

"Absorbing" Muslims means winning them over to the Brotherhood's vision—persuading them "with all of their factions and colors in America and Canada" that they ought to be pursuing the Brotherhood's "settlement project, and making it their cause, future and the basis of their Islamic life in this part of the world."

As to the likelihood of finding recruits, Akram optimistically notes that "the U.S. Islamic arena is full of those waiting." Once Muslims understand the urgency of their task in the U.S., "if we ask for money, a lot of it would come, and if we ask for men, they would come in lines." Resources are not lacking, either domestically or among the friends of the Muslim Brothers in other countries: "If we examined the human and the financial resources the Ikhwan [Brotherhood] alone own in this country, we and others would feel proud and glorious. And if we add to them the resources of our friends and allies, those who circle in our orbit and those waiting on our banner, we would realize that we are able to open the door to settlement and walk through it seeking to make Almighty God's word the highest."

That is not just a pious statement; making "Almighty God's word the highest" in this context means establishing Islamic law as the law of the land in America.

WORKING THROUGH ORGANIZATIONS

Akram calls upon Muslim Brotherhood operatives in the U.S. to establish various organizations to further the Islamic cause.

Creating these organizations is touted as a sound strategy for the bureaucratically minded U.S.: "We must say that we are in a country which understands no language other than the language of the organizations, and one which does not respect or give weight to any group without effective, functional and strong organizations." And indeed, Akram notes that many organizations useful for this Grand Jiihad have already been established: "All we need is to tweak them, coordinate their work, collect their elements and merge their efforts with others and then connect them with the comprehensive plan we seek."

This plan would be truly comprehensive, encompassing not just the spreading of Islam but attempts to influence every aspect of American life. "For instance," Akram expains, "we have a seed for a 'comprehensive media and art' organization." He then lists some things that "we own," including "a print advanced typesetting machine," an "audio and visual center," "magazines in Arabic and English," "photographers," "producers," "programs anchors," and, most notably, "journalists."

Consolidation was essential. "The big challenge that is ahead of us," he concludes, "is how to turn these seeds or 'scattered' elements into comprehensive, stable, 'settled' organizations that are connected with our Movement and which fly in our orbit and take orders from our guidance." Although this would not mean total centralization, it would entail the coordination of organizations devoted to education, proselytizing, finance and investments, youth, women, charity, political action, legal action, and more.

The conquest of America would not happen overnight, but Akram envisions a day when Muslims in the United States would own their own television station and have their own political party, as well as a daily newspaper, weekly, monthly, and seasonal magazines, radio stations, and television programs to be featured on other networks. He also foresees an Islamic Central bank and an organization to provide sharia-compliant interest-free loans, as well as an Islamic university, Islamic schools, centers to train teachers, and a body for the writing and development of Islamic curricula. There would also be an "organization for Islamic thought and culture," a "publication, translation and distribution house for Islamic books," an "Islamic Organization to Combat the Social Ills of the U.S. Society," an "Islamic houses project," and "an advanced communication network."

Finally, the Brotherhood would ultimately establish "a Central Jurisprudence Council," a "Central Islamic Court," a "Muslim Attorneys Society," an "Islamic Foundation for Defense of Muslims' Rights," and the like.

"And success," Akram maintains, "is by God."

THE PARTNERS

The Brotherhood memorandum includes "a list of our organizations and the organizations of our friends," with the appended note: "Imagine if they all march according to one plan!!!"

Among these organizations are some of the most prominent "moderate Muslim" organizations in the U.S. today, including the Islamic Society of North America (ISNA); the Muslim Students Association (MSA); the North American Islamic Trust (NAIT); the Muslim Arab Youth Association (MAYA); the Islamic Association for Palestine (IAP), out of which emerged in 1994 the most prominent Muslim group in the United States, the Council on American-Islamic Relations (CAIR); the Islamic Circle of North America (ICNA); the International Institute for Islamic Thought (IIIT); and many others.

The statements of Islamic supremacism, conquest, and dominance that began this chapter all came from spokesmen affiliated with groups within or linked to this web. Most of them were made in the United States by American Muslim leaders. Leaving aside the statements from Brotherhood members 'Akef and Akram already described, the first declaration, which calls for the "toppling" of America and predicts that a Muslim president will institute sharia law in the U.S., was made by a speaker at a chapter of the MSA, a campus Muslim group that has chapters at hundreds of colleges and universities all over the United States—and is one of the groups named as part of this stealth jihad effort in the Muslim Brotherhood memorandum.

The next two statements come from Muslims affiliated with jihadist groups in the Middle East. The speaker who damned America and Israel "until death" was Sami Al-Arian, a leader of the terrorist organization Palestinian Islamic Jihad, which is a spinoff from the Muslim Brotherhood. Al-Arian conducted his activities on behalf of the stealth jihad for several years while working as a professor at the University of South Florida. There, he amassed a national reputation as a moderate Islamic leader while engaging in activities to aid terror operations against Israel. Today, upon serving out a prison sentence after pleading guilty to a charge of conspiracy to aid Palestinian Islamic Jihad, he is awaiting trial for refusing to testify against a group of Muslim organizations suspected of having links to terrorism. Nevertheless, segments of the American Left still laud him as a hero and a martyr to the Republican, Bush-led war on terror.[24]

The prediction that Muslims would conquer Rome and use it as a base to take over Europe and the Americas came from a Palestinian Islamic cleric affiliated with another Palestinian jihad terror group, Hamas. And the last three statements came from prominent

Islamic spokesmen in the United States who have enjoyed wide-spread respect as moderates, and yet are affiliated with the Council on American-Islamic Relations (CAIR), a group that has been named an unindicted co-conspirator in a terrorism case involving funding for Hamas.[25] Omar Ahmad, co-founder and former board chairman of CAIR, insisted that Islam become dominant in the U.S. and "the only accepted religion on earth" (Ahmad now denies having made this statement, although the journalist who reported it stands by her account);[26] CAIR spokesman Ibrahim Hooper declared his desire for an Islamic government here; and CAIR Advisory Board member and prominent Muslim speaker Siraj Wahhaj lamented that Muslims could take over America and establish Islamic rule if only they were more politically astute.

What's more, CAIR co-founders Omar Ahmad and Nihad Awad helped establish CAIR after working at the Islamic Association for Palestine (IAP), where Awad was public relations director. Former FBI counterterrorism official Oliver Revell has called the IAP "a front organization for Hamas that engages in propaganda for Islamic militants."[27] Awad himself declared in 1994, "I am in support of the Hamas movement."[28] Hamas, in turn, styles itself in its 1988 charter as "one of the wings of the Muslim Brothers in Palestine."[29]

Thus, every one of the statements of Islamic supremacism and dominance that began this chapter come from people linked in one way or another to the Muslim Brotherhood.

The crucial question is this: Was Akram's memorandum just an elaborate exercise in wishful thinking—in building castles in the air? Or is the Brotherhood, and its present-day allies and friends, really working to forward the "grand jihad," using stealth tactics to subvert Western civilization from within and to transform the U.S. into an Islamic state?

DENIAL

Many will find it hard to believe that the Muslim Brotherhood would be involved in such an effort. Recently the idea that the Brotherhood has reformed and become a force for moderation in the Islamic world has gained considerable currency—even in the U.S. State Department. *Foreign Affairs*, the influential publication of the Council on Foreign Relations, included in its March-April 2007 edition an article by Robert S. Leiken and Steven Brooke entitled "The Moderate Muslim Brotherhood," which contended that "jihadists loathe the Muslim Brotherhood...for rejecting global jihad and embracing democracy. These positions seem to make them moderates, the very thing the United States, short on allies in the Muslim world, seeks."[30]

This followed an April 2005 article in the Egyptian newspaper *Al-Sharq Al-Awsat* reporting that the U.S. State Department thought it would be a "historical mistake" to isolate or marginalize the Brotherhood, and was interested in initiating talks and finding common ground with Brotherhood representatives. The paper, citing unnamed Western diplomatic sources, even said that the State Department was considering pressuring the Egyptian government to relax restrictions on the Brotherhood, which has been officially outlawed in Egypt since 1954, but still retains significant political influence and popular support.[31] Two years later came reports that the Bush administration, resigned to the fact that the Middle East was "going Islam," had quietly established contacts with Brotherhood officials.[32]

The British government was interested in following suit. In a Summer 2007 report, the House of Commons Select Committee on Foreign Affairs stated, "As long as the Muslim Brotherhood expresses a commitment to the democratic process and nonviolence, we recommend that the British Government should engage with it and seek to influence its members."[33]

Although the belief is now spreading that the Brotherhood rejects jihad and embraces democratic pluralism, it is hard to see how anyone got this idea in the first place; perhaps it's an indication of the power of wishful thinking, even, or perhaps especially, in official Washington. Nevertheless, notwithstanding the moderate face they now present to gullible Westerners, Brotherhood officials continue to proclaim their goal of bringing the entire world under Islamic rule. In January 2007, a Muslim Brotherhood official and member of Egypt's parliament, Mohammed Shaker Sanar, declared unequivocally that the Brotherhood has no interest in democracy: "The organization was founded in 1928 to reestablish the Caliphate destroyed by Ataturk," he explained, while insisting that the movement's goal had not changed: "With Allah's help [the Muslim Brotherhood] will institute the law of Allah."[34]

What's more, as of November 2007 the Brotherhood declared on its website that it regarded its mission as universal: "We want a Muslim individual, a Muslim home, a Muslim people, a Muslim government and state that will lead the Islamic countries and bring into the fold the Muslim Diaspora and the lands robbed from Islam and will then bear the standard of jihad and the call [da'wah] to Allah. [Then the] world will happily accept the precepts of Islam....The problems of conquering the world will only end when the flag of Islam waves and jihad has been proclaimed." The goal was nothing less than "the establishment of a world Islamic state."[35]

However, not everyone was as forthright. Leiken and Brooke's impression that the Brotherhood was a moderate, democratically inclined group may have been formed at least in part by the genial, unthreatening face of Brotherhood operatives in the U.S. Spokesmen connected with Brotherhood affiliates, including organizations named in Akram's memorandum, have been quick to deny that there is any stealth jihad at all designed to eliminate and destroy Western civilization from within. No Muslim group in the U.S., they insist, is pursuing any such agenda.

Esam Omeish, president of the Muslim American Society (MAS), which was identified in a 2004 *Chicago Tribune* exposé as the name under which the Muslim Brotherhood currently operates in the U.S., has said that documents such as Akram's memorandum that came to light during the Holy Land Foundation trial are not to be understood as revealing any Brotherhood plan for America. Rather, they are loaded with "abhorrent statements and are in direct conflict of the very principles of our Islam."[36]

Instead, he said that "the Muslim community in America wishes to contribute positively to the continued success and greatness of our civilization. The ethics of tolerance and inclusion are the very tenets that MAS was based on from its inception." In fact, he denied that MAS had any ties to the Brotherhood at all, insisting that "MAS is not the Muslim Brotherhood." Rather, it "grew out of a history of Islamic activism in the U.S. when the Muslim Brotherhood once existed but has a different intellectual paradigm and outlook."[37]

Mahdi Bray of the Muslim American Society's Freedom Foundation was similarly dismissive: "If those documents talk about the establishing of sharia law in America, I'm saying that's a lot of hype: wishful thinking from an immigrant perspective....It doesn't reflect [a] genuine American perspective in terms of where we're heading."

It's interesting in itself that any Muslims in America, whether immigrants or not, think of a sharia state being imposed here as something desirable. And indeed, Bray conceded that some members of MAS still thought in these terms: "I wouldn't be candid if I didn't say there weren't some old-timers who want to hold onto the old way, who say that this is the way the Ikhwan [i.e. the Brotherhood] did it, this should be our model. We said, 'So what? It doesn't work here.' We've been very adamant about that."

Bray completely ruled out any intention of replacing the U.S. Constitution with Islamic law, blaming (oddly, in light of his acknowledgment of the "wishful thinking" of Muslim "old-timers") American opponents of the global jihad for the notion that any Muslims might think otherwise: "Those on the right and many of those who I would classify as Islamophobes, many of them have failed to realize that there is an authentic American Muslim organization here and movement in America that wants to integrate. We believe the ballot is an appropriate place to be." In fact, Bray even claimed he "liked the Bill of Rights"![38]

Unfortunately, however, these denials ring hollow. When I appeared on Laura Ingraham's radio show along with MAS president Esam Omeish in August 2007, he avowed that he would be happy to see sharia rule in the U.S.—as long as, he was quick to add, Americans voted it in!

In September 2007, Virginia governor Tim Kaine appointed Omeish to Virginia's Commission of Immigration, but accepted Omeish's resignation after videos surfaced of the MAS leader telling a crowd of Palestinian Arab Muslims in Washington that "you have learned the way, that you have known that the jihad way is the way to liberate your land." He was also seen congratulating Palestinian jihadists for dying for Allah's sake (that is, in suicide bombings) and making inflammatory statements about Israel.[39]

If jihad violence for the sake of establishing a sharia state is acceptable in the Middle East, one may legitimately wonder whether Omeish is really all that deeply committed to republican, non- sharia rule here.

And Bray?

Terrorism expert Steven Emerson notes that when Abdurrahman Alamoudi of the American Muslim Council, who is now serving a twenty-three-year prison sentence for a terrorism financing conviction,[40] encouraged a Muslim crowd at a rally in October 2000 to declare their support of the jihad terror groups Hamas and Hizballah, "MPAC's Political Advisor, Mahdi Bray, stood directly behind Alamoudi and was seen jubilantly exclaiming his support for these two deadly terrorist organizations." This was just three weeks after Bray "coordinated and led a rally where approximately 2,000 people congregated in front of the Israeli Embassy in Washington, D.C." Emerson reports that "at one point during the rally, Mahdi Bray played the tambourine as one of the speakers sang, while the crowd repeated: 'Al-Aqsa [Mosque] is calling us, let's all go into jihad, and throw stones at the face of the Jews.'"[41]

Of course, while it is noteworthy that two Brotherhood-linked Muslims in America would turn out to be less moderate than they wish to appear, this doesn't mean that the stealth jihad is actually in full swing. Even if Esam Omeish and Mahdi Bray aren't exactly true-blue American patriots, the stealth jihad delineated in the Brotherhood memorandum may still be just a pipe dream, a Mittyesque bit of grandiosity, rather as if a group of Minnesota Rotarians had a few too many and started drawing up plans to invade North Dakota.

Maybe. But there is abundant evidence to the contrary—evidence that has been given short shrift by most analysts simply because they don't understand the significance of what has been going on right before their eyes. Legal endeavors, civil rights initiatives, media campaigns—all these and more are the weapons of the stealth jihadists, chosen precisely because without other pieces of the puzzle, they don't appear to be weapons at all, or part of any cumulative effort.

The bottom line is this: there is a concerted effort in America today by Islamic organizations to further a series of initiatives that are outwardly quite different in their stated purposes, and are being advanced by different groups of people. However, they are all geared toward the same set of goals: to encourage Americans to downplay anti-terror initiatives, accommodate Muslim practices, and make special exceptions for Islamic law—while being cowed by cries of "bigotry" into dropping all resistance to these phenomena.

The result, if things continue in this vein, would be an America completely subjugated under Islamic law—just the way the Brotherhood memorandum envisions it. An America in which non-Muslims must humble themselves before Muslims, not daring to say or do anything that they find offensive.

This stealth jihad is advancing steadily and quietly, and most Americans have no idea it is happening at all.

CHAPTER TWO

FORGET "WHY DO THEY HATE US?" THE REAL QUESTION IS "WHAT DO THEY WANT?"

THE "WHY DO THEY HATE US?" INDUSTRY

After September 11, media analysts and government officials frequently wondered in public why so many Muslims harbor such an animus toward the United States. The overwhelming majority of the answers had one thing in common: they posited that they hate us because of something we ourselves had done. Even the question itself has a certain self-accusing, hand-wringing air about it.

No one agreed, and no one agrees today, on what exactly we might have done to make them hate us enough to incinerate almost 3,000 office workers one September morning, but there is a remarkable unanimity on the idea that it is ultimately we who are responsible for the fact that they hate us, and it is we who have it within our power to make them stop hating us and start liking us.

One of the most common suggestions has been that many Muslims hate us because of our political power and the ways we have used it to impose our will upon the Islamic world—by defending the State of Israel; by (since 2003) toppling Saddam Hussein and attempting to export democracy to Iraq and Afghanistan; and by our alliances with autocrats such as Egypt's Hosni Mubarak and Pakistan's Pervez Musharraf. Others, such as the noted conservative writer Dinesh D'Souza, have posited that "they hate us" because of our cultural hegemony, which has spread our degenerate pop culture of Madonna, McDonald's and bare midriffs into the dignified and traditionally minded homes of the overwhelming majority of Muslims.

Still, flying jetliners into high-rises because Britney Spears is a trollop might strike people as something of an overreaction, and cooler heads than D'Souza's—including many at high levels in the State Department and Pentagon—believe instead that they hate us simply because they don't know us well enough to love us. They have been taught to hate us, you see, by sinister, anti-American, Islamic jihad preachers. Americans have tried to counter this by directing U.S. soldiers in Iraq and Afghanistan to conduct initiatives to win Muslim hearts and minds, initiatives ranging from handing out candy to children to building roads, schools, and hospitals.

This too assumes that they hate us because of something we can control. It further presupposes that two can play at this public relations game, and that Americans can offset this negative impression by showing Muslims that we are not in fact anti-Muslim at all, contrary to what the imams say, and are actually terrific folks—humanitarian, generous, and kind.

There's one consideration missing from all this: it just may be that there's little or nothing we can do to change the mindset of those who hate us, because they hate us for their own reasons, reasons that have nothing to do with what we have or haven't done, or can or cannot do. All the analyses, and the attendant pre- scriptions, of the vast "Why do they hate us?" industry fail to con- sider the very real possibility that they may hate us for reasons that cannot be resolved through our own actions. This is a dis- turbing prospect, for it implies that they will not stop hating us no matter what we do or what acts of kindness and generosity we display. The unexamined possibility is that they hate us for rea- sons embedded within their core assumptions about who we are, who they are, and what their rightful role in the world is.

The founder of the Muslim Brotherhood is one of the foremost modern exponents of that view of the world and those core assumptions.

AL-BANNA'S VISION

Hasan Al-Banna, founder of the Muslim Brotherhood, dedi- cated his life to defending and restoring to prominence within the Islamic world the fundamental proposition that Islam is a total program for every aspect of life. "Islam," he declared, "is a com- prehensive system which deals with all spheres of life. It is a coun- try and homeland or a government and a nation. It is conduct and power or mercy and justice. It is a culture and a law or knowledge and jurisprudence. It is material and wealth or gain and prosper- ity. It is Jihad and a call or army and a cause. And finally, it is true belief and correct worship."

The Brotherhood's task, Al-Banna explained, was to work to impose this total way of life first over Egyptian society, liberat- ing "the homeland from all un-Islamic or foreign control, whether political, economic, or ideological," and "reforming the

government so that it may become a truly Islamic government.... By Islamic government I mean a government whose
officers are Muslims who perform the obligatory duties of Islam,
who do not make public their disobedience, and who enforce the
rules and teachings of Islam."

But it wouldn't end with Egypt. The Brotherhood would then
work to rebuild "the international prominence of the Islamic
Umma [international community] by liberating its lands, reviving
its glorious past, bringing closer the cultures of its regions and ral-
lying under one word. Until once again the long awaited unity and
the lost Khilafah [Caliphate] is returned." This would involve
"guiding the world by spreading the call of Islam to all corners of
the globe 'until there is no more tumult or oppression and the
Religion of Allah prevails.'" The quotation comes from the
Qur'an (2:193).

To this end, Muslims must wage jihad, for jihad is a "divinely
ordained obligation," and "whoever dies without struggling in the
Way of Allah, or wishing to do so, dies a Pre-Islamic Jahiliya
death"—that is, he dies as an unbeliever and will not enter Paradise. Al-Banna points out that a Muslim can wage jihad in numerous ways. One form of jihad is "the heart's abhorrence of evil."
This is the non-violent "interior spiritual struggle" that Islamic
apologists in the West so often characterize as the beginning and
end of jihad. Al-Banna, however, defines this as the "weakest
degree" of jihad. The "highest degree," in contrast, is the more
aggressive component—"fighting in the Way of Allah." Additionally, according to Al-Banna, "between these two degrees are
numerous forms of jihad, including struggling with the tongue,
pen, or hand, and speaking a word of truth to a tyrannical ruler."

Al-Banna instructs that jihad is—or should be—an all-con-
suming endeavor for every believer. Muslims should give them-

selves, as well as their "wealth, time, energy, and everything else for the cause of Islam."[1]

SAME GOAL AS BIN LADEN

One prominent Muslim who shares these goals—the waging of jihad to establish the rule of Islamic law throughout the world—is none other than Osama bin Laden. In his "Letter to the American People" of October 6, 2002, he stated, "The first thing that we are calling you to is Islam."

Bin Laden continued that the United States was "the worst civilization witnessed by the history of mankind," for "you are the nation who, rather than ruling by the shariah of Allah in its Constitution and Laws, choose to invent your own laws as you will and desire." He went on to castigate Americans for separating religion from politics and refusing to accept Allah's "Absolute Authority."[2]

The objective, then, for Osama is not simply to wreak havoc, as his minions did on September 11, 2001; "terror" is not an objective to be pursued for its own sake. The point of it all is to extend the hegemony of Islamic law over the world, and to compel the United States to accept the laws of Islam in preference to the U.S. Constitution.

This objective has deep roots in traditional Islam.

A REVIVAL OF TRADITIONAL ISLAM

Many analysts would hasten to assure you that the vision of Hasan al-Banna and Osama bin Laden is at variance with traditional and mainstream Islam, which is peaceful and harbors no supremacist designs on non-Muslims. Whether or not this assertion is true is an extraordinarily important question whose answer goes a long way toward explaining why "they" hate us.

Al-Banna's exhortation to jihad is a call to revive traditional Islamic understandings regarding warfare against and the subjugation of unbelievers, which are rooted in a cluster of Qur'anic verses that contain general and open-ended commands to fight non-Muslims. These include:

- "O ye who believe! Fight the unbelievers who gird you about, and let them find firmness in you: and know that Allah is with those who fear Him" (9:123).
- "O Prophet! Strive hard against the unbelievers and the hypocrites, and be firm against them. Their abode is Hell, an evil refuge indeed" (9:73). The Arabic word translated here as "strive hard" is *jahidi*, a verbal form of the noun *jihad*.

The command applies first to fighting those who worship other gods besides Allah: "Then, when the sacred months have passed, slay the idolaters wherever ye find them, and take them (captive), and besiege them, and prepare for them each ambush. But if they repent and establish worship and pay the poor-due, then leave their way free." (9:5). In plain English, this means that "idolaters" are to be killed, unless they convert to Islam and begin following Islamic laws such as paying alms ("the poor-due.")

However, Muslims must fight Jews and Christians as well, although the Qur'an recognizes that as "People of the Book" they have received genuine revelations from Allah: "Fight those who believe not in Allah nor the Last Day, nor hold that forbidden which hath been forbidden by Allah and His Messenger, nor acknowledge the religion of Truth, (even if they are) of the People of the Book, until they pay the Jizya [the special tax on non-Muslims] with willing submission, and feel themselves subdued" (9:29).

JIHAD AND THE SUBJUGATION OF THE UNBELIEVERS IN ISLAMIC LAW

The words mean what they appear to mean. The noted Qur'anic commentator Ibn Juzayy says that Qur'an 9:29 is "a command to fight the People of the Book." Another respected mainstream Qur'anic commentary, the *Tafsir al-Jalalayn,* notes that when verse 9:29 says that Muslims must fight against those who "follow not the Religion of Truth," it means those who do not follow Islam, "which is firm and abrogates other deens [religions]."[3]

All four principal Sunni schools of jurisprudence, the Shafi'i, Maliki, Hanafi, and Hanbali schools, agree on the importance of jihad warfare against non-Muslims who refuse to convert to Islam. Ibn Abi Zayd al-Qayrawani (d. 996), a Maliki jurist, declared that "it is preferable not to begin hostilities with the enemy before having invited the latter to embrace the religion of Allah except where the enemy attacks first. They have the alternative of either converting to Islam or paying the poll tax (*jizya*), short of which war will be declared against them."[4] Ibn Taymiyya (d. 1328), a Hanbali jurist who is a favorite of bin Laden and other modern-day jihadists, explained that the aim of jihad was "that the religion is God's entirely and God's word is uppermost, therefore according to all Muslims, those who stand in the way of this aim must be fought."[5]

The other schools echo these teachings. The Hanafi school stipulates, "If the infidels, upon receiving the call [to convert to

Islam], neither consent to it nor agree to pay capitation tax, it is then incumbent on the Muslims to call upon God for assistance, and to make war upon them...the Prophet, moreover, commands us so to do."[6] Likewise, the Shafi'i scholar Abu'l Hasan al-Mawardi (d. 1058) taught that once infidels refuse the invitation to convert to Islam, "war is waged against them and they are treated as those whom the call has reached."[7]

In other words, "Let me make you an offer you can't refuse."

A Hanafi legal manual explains that the fight against unbelievers can sometimes take non-violent forms: "Jihad in the language is exerting effort. In the understanding of the sharia, it is exerting effort and energy in fighting fi sabeel lillah [in the path of Allah] by nafs [spiritual struggle], finance, tongue or another."[8] Indeed, in traditional Islam, *jihad bil sayf* (jihad with the sword) or combat (*qitaal*) is only one means of jihad. Other forms of jihad include *jihad bil mal* (waging jihad by means of one's wealth); *jihad bil lisan* (waging jihad through persuasion); *jihad bil yad* (waging jihad by taking action, but not necessarily arms, against injustice).

But all these various forms of jihad—both violent and non-violent—are directed toward the same end: the Islamization of the world and the imposition of Islamic law over unbelieving societies. Majid Khadduri (1909-2007), an internationally renowned Iraqi scholar of Islamic law, explained in his 1955 book *War and Peace in the Law of Islam* that Islam had embedded within it an expansionist and supremacist imperative:

> The Islamic state, whose principal function was to put God's law into practice, sought to establish Islam as the dominant reigning ideology over the entire world. It refused to recognize the coexistence of non-Muslim communities, except per-

haps as subordinate entities, because by its very nature a universal state tolerates the existence of no other state than itself.... The jihad was therefore employed as an instrument for both the universalization of religion and the establishment of an imperial world state.[9]

Imran Ahsan Khan Nyazee, Assistant Professor on the Faculty of Shari'ah and Law of the International Islamic University in Islamabad, quotes the twelfth-century Maliki jurist Ibn Rushd: "Muslim jurists agreed that the purpose of fighting with the People of the Book...is one of two things: it is either their conversion to Islam or the payment of *jizyah*." Nyazee concludes, "This leaves no doubt that the primary goal of the Muslim community, in the eyes of its jurists, is to spread the word of Allah through jihad, and the option of poll-tax [jizya] is to be exercised only after subjugation" of non-Muslims.[10]

But if this is so, why hasn't the worldwide Islamic community been waging jihad on a large scale up until relatively recently? Writing in 1994, before the worldwide jihadist effort had reached the strength it enjoys today, Nyazee said it is only because it has not been able to do so: "The Muslim community may be considered to be passing through a period of truce. In its present state of weakness, there is nothing much it can do about it."[11]

THE OBJECT OF THE WAR

What is the point of this existential battle against non-Muslims? In fact, the ultimate goal is not to force unbelievers to become Muslims. Rather, the jihad is fought in order to bring non-Muslims into the Islamic social order. The Qur'anic verse that explicitly directs Muslims to make war against Jews and Christians directs them not to convert the Jews and Christians to Islam, but to make them "pay the jizya with willing submission, and feel themselves subdued" (9:29). In Islamic law, this condition of submission is known as the *dhimma*, the protection of the Muslims, and those within it are *dhimmis*, protected (or guilty) people. The classical Islamic scholar As-Sawi specifies that the payment of the *jizya* signifies that non-Muslims are "humble and obedient to the judgments of Islam."

The verse also specifies that non-Muslims should assume a "state of abasement." The Bedouin commander al-Mughira bin Sa'd spelled this out when he met the Persian warrior Rustam. Said al-Mughira, "I call you to Islam or else you must pay the jizya while you are in a state of abasement."

Rustam replied, "I know what jizya means, but what does 'a state of abasement' mean?"

Al-Mughira explained, "You pay it while you are standing and I am sitting and the whip is hanging over your head."[12]

How tolerant!

Renowned Qur'anic commentator Ibn Kathir (1301-1372), whose writings are still influential today, bluntly explained that the dhimmis must be "disgraced, humiliated and belittled. Therefore, Muslims are not allowed to honor the people of Dhimmah or elevate them above Muslims, for they are miserable, disgraced and humiliated."[13]

The renowned and influential Egyptian Islamic scholar Imam Jalaluddin Al-Suyuti (1445-1505 AD) observed that the jizya is "not taken from someone in a state of hardship"; however, that stipulation was at times honored in the breach.[14] For example, a contemporary account of the Muslim conquest of Nikiou, an Egyptian town, in the 640s, related that "it is impossible to describe the lamentable position of the inhabitants of this town, who came to the point of offering their children in exchange for the enormous sums that they had to pay each month."[15]

Tolerant and multicultural, too!

Although the jizya has not been collected on a formal basis in the Islamic world since the mid-nineteenth century, jihadists hope to revive the practice along with the other features of the dhimma. In a recent Friday sermon preached in Islam's holiest city, Mecca, Sheikh Marzouq Salem Al-Ghamdi said this about Jews and Christians in Muslim lands:

> If the infidels live among the Muslims, in accordance with the conditions set out by the Prophet—there is nothing wrong with it provided they pay *Jizya* to the Islamic treasury. Other conditions are...that they do not renovate a church or a monastery, do not rebuild ones that were destroyed, that they feed for three days any Muslim who passes by their homes...that they rise when a Muslim wishes to sit, that they do not imitate Muslims in dress and speech, nor ride horses, nor own swords, nor arm themselves with any kind of weapon; that they do not sell wine, do not show the cross, do not ring church bells, do not raise their voices during prayer, that they shave their hair in front so as to make them easily identifiable, do not incite anyone against the Muslims, and do not strike a Muslim.... If they violate these conditions, they have no protection.[16]

In sum, the infidels must *humble themselves before the Muslims.*

This brings us back to our central question: Why do they hate us? Even this short study of Islamic theology reveals the answer: they hate us not because of anything we have done, but because fundamental Islamic imperatives command them to do so.

These imperatives are put forth in the obligation to wage jihad against unbelievers in order to spread Islamic rule. The object of both the classical and the contemporary jihad is not the mass conversion of Westerners to Islam, although that is something jihadists would welcome, but the chastened subservience of non-Muslim states, groups, and individuals, and their recognition of the superiority and hegemony of Islam.

This imperative is and always has been an integral part of Islamic sharia law, and that law enjoys wide support among Muslims even in the United States. A 2004 survey conducted by a Muslim group asked Muslims in Detroit whether or not they agreed with the statement: "Shari'iah should be the law of the land in Muslim countries." Eighty-one percent said they did, with 59 percent agreeing "strongly."[17]

And would they also want to see sharia in the United States? The survey didn't ask that question, but it is noteworthy that Ihsan Bagby, a University of Kentucky professor of Islamic Studies who conducted the study, strongly suggested in the late 1980s that he himself preferred sharia rule to constitutional government and thought other Muslims should think likewise. He declared, "Ultimately we can never be full citizens of this country, because there is no way we can be fully committed to the institutions and ideologies of this country."[18]

STEALTH JIHAD VS. TERRORISM

But how can Islamic rule be spread in a world in which infidel polities have overwhelming military superiority over every Muslim state? Note what Siraj Wahhaj said was the prerequisite for an Islamic government in the United States: Muslims must be politically astute.

It may indeed be absurd to think that the Brotherhood and its partners could ever attain their goal of "settling" Islam in the United States and transforming it into an Islamic state, at least through "coalitions," "absorption," and "cooperation" alone, without ultimately resorting to violence. But in the short-term, the absence of violence—combined with a bit of political savvy—allows the stealth jihadists to do their work more effectively. This is one of the lessons that some jihadists learned from September 11: attack America, and it tends to strike back; but quietly undermine America from within, and there's a lot less resistance. In fact, people tend not even to notice.

This tactical, temporary rejection of violence is the current strategy employed in the United States by Hizballah, the Lebanese Shi'ite jihadist group. Its leader, Hassan Nasrallah, made clear in 2002 on Hizballah's satellite television station, Al-Manar, that the group ultimately wants to see the destruction the United States: "Let the entire world hear me. Our hostility to the Great Satan [America] is absolute.... Regardless of how the world has changed after 11 September, 'Death to America' will remain our reverberating and powerful slogan: 'Death to America.'"[19] Yet despite this hostility, Thomas Fuentes, the FBI's special agent in charge of the International Operations, noted in 2007 that Hizballah is reluctant to launch violent attacks on U.S. soil because it would hinder their overall operations: "They want to maintain a low profile by engaging in criminal activity [but] not direct attacks.... They've not been enthusiastic about doing it on U.S. soil because of the attention and reaction that would occur."[20]

Other jihadists have come to the same conclusion—that it's politically astute at this time to refrain from acts of violence in the United States. But that doesn't mean they aren't pursuing their supremacist agenda in America by other means. To the contrary, their low profile enables the smooth progress of activity that is oftentimes legal, but is nonetheless aimed at the stealth jihadist goal of destroying U.S. constitutional rule and establishing an Islamic state here. This agenda is now advancing through a quiet program designed to avoid unwelcome attention from government or law enforcement officials.

THE AMERICA THEY ENVISION

An America in which sharia supremacists succeeded in their goal of "settling" Islamic law as the supreme law of the land would look very different from the America of today—to say nothing of the America of the Founding Fathers.

What would such an America look like? Remember that the only states anywhere in the world today that claim to implement full sharia are Iran, Saudi Arabia, and Sudan. And besides sharia, or perhaps because of it, they have something else in common as well: each has an abysmal human rights record, and each is currently a hotbed of jihadist activity and support networks.

In April 2008, the Pakistani jihadist group Lashkar-e-Islam offered a glimpse of its perfect Islamic society when it listed its preferred policies for governing the Khyber Agency, a Pakistani tribal area. Some of these are specific to the situation in that region, but many would be features of any sharia regime. These included:

- "Eradicating all shirk [polytheism/idolatry], bid'at [innovation in the religious principles of Islam] and all un-Islamic practices from Khyber Agency"—which would involve severe restrictions on non-Muslim religious practice, in accord with the classic dhimmi laws

- Permitting "only Islamic-style graves"—that is, graves that face Mecca
- Enforcing "a total ban on the sale of wine" and on gambling
- Prohibiting the charging of interest in all business transactions
- Ensuring "that women are modestly dressed according to Islamic norms when attending school"
- Banning wedding music. This prohibition would likely extend beyond weddings; the Lashkar-e-Islam leader notes, "According to the local tradition, singing and dancing are not permitted. People are fined for listening to music because this is a habit of the English [Westerners]"
- Forbidding women from visiting a doctor or hospital without being accompanied by a male relative[21]

Note that some of these practices have already made inroads in Western countries. In 2006, a British cemetery began facing all its graves, for Muslims and non-Muslims alike, toward Mecca—in a spirit of accommodation, of course.[22] Likewise, numerous sharia finance initiatives are already helping Muslims in the West to get around the Islamic prohibition on usury.

Other measures are already enforced by local Islamic vigilantes. For example, Christian women have been horse-whipped in Nigeria for not dressing according to Islamic standards.[23]

Islam's Western apologists argue that this oppressive vision of sharia is confined to a small extremist fringe. It's instructive, then, to note the tenets of Islamic law outlined by Al-Azhar University in Cairo, Egypt. The foremost authority in Sunni Islam, Al-Azhar is led by a grand sheikh whom the BBC calls "the highest spiritual authority for nearly a billion Sunni Muslims."[24] In 1991, Al-Azhar certified a manual of Islamic law as conforming "to the practice and faith of the orthodox Sunni Community."[25] That manual includes the following laws:

- "When a person who has reached puberty and is sane voluntarily apostatizes [i.e. converts] from Islam, he deserves to be killed"[26]
- "Circumcision is obligatory." While Islamic scholars agree that this applies to men, there is some dispute about the need for female circumcision. (Commonly known as "female genital mutilation," this procedure removes part of the clitoris.) Some Islamic authorities believe female circumcision is obligatory, while others argue it is a courtesy to the husband and a traditional accepted practice but not an obligatory one.[27]
- "The husband may forbid his wife to leave the home"[28]
- "Musical instruments of all types are unlawful"[29]
- "The caliph . . . makes war upon Jews, Christians, and Zoroastrians . . . until they become Muslim or else pay the non-Muslim poll tax"[30]

In a stunning testament to Western self-delusion, shortly after September 11 the *New York Times* upheld Al-Azhar as a beacon of Islamic moderation, reporting that the institution "has sought to advise Muslims around the world that those who kill in the name of Islam are nothing more than heretics. It has sought to guide, to reassure Westerners against any clash of civilizations."[31]

Most Americans are completely unaware that such elements of Islamic law even exist. Lulled by the soothing assurances of our media, academic, and political leaders that Islam is a religion of peace, they have little notion of the true, oppressive nature of Islamic law, as dictated by the highest spiritual authorities in the Islamic world—or that domestic Islamic groups are now working to get these laws adopted in the United States.

SINAI, THE SERMON ON THE MOUNT... AND THE QUR'AN?

Some of the nation's highest authorities have helped to ensure Americans' obliviousness to the true tenets of Islamic law. In his Second Inaugural Address on January 20, 2005, President George W. Bush spoke of "integrity, and tolerance toward others, and the rule of conscience in our own lives." He asserted that "that edifice of character is...sustained in our national life by the truths of Sinai, the Sermon on the Mount, the words of the Koran, and the varied faiths of our people."[32]

His conflation of Biblical and Islamic values is a rhetorical slight employed by many U.S.-based Islamic activists. Just the year before, in 2004, Agha Saeed of the American Muslim Alliance recommended that U.S. government and media figures begin speaking of "Judeo-Christian-Islamic values" rather than "Judeo-Christian values," and should do so "in all venues where we normally talk about Judeo-Christian values, starting with the media, academia, statements by politicians and comments made in churches, synagogues and other places."[33]

As is clear from the preceding discussion, however, Judeo-Christian values are in fact dramatically different from Islamic ones. Thomas Jefferson, who is often described as a non-Christian, once wrote, "The philosophy of Jesus is the most sublime and benevolent code of morals ever offered to man. A more beautiful or precious morsel of ethics I have never seen."[34] It is hard to see how such words can be applied with equal accuracy to a creed that, instead of telling people to love their enemies (Matthew 5:44) tells them to be "harsh" or "ruthless" to those who do not believe (Qur'an 48:29).

And indeed, not only do Christianity and Islam differ markedly in moral and ethical as well as dogmatic content, but Islam, as we have seen, contains a supremacist impulse that rejects the very notion of equal coexistence with non-Muslim value systems; it must dominate. Jefferson and John Adams noted this tendency back in 1786, after their meeting with Sidi Haji Abdul Rahman Adja, Tripoli's ambassador to Britain. While trying to negotiate a settlement to end raids on American ships by Barbary pirates, Adams and Jefferson asked the ambassador how he could justify such attacks. Adja replied, as they explained in their report to the Continental Congress, "that it was founded on the Laws of their Prophet, that it was written in their Koran, that all nations who should not have acknowledged their authority were sinners, that it was their right and duty to make war upon them wherever they could be found, and to make slaves of all they could take as Prisoners, and that every Musselman who should be slain in Battle was sure to go to Paradise."[35]

Americans must realize that at its core sharia entails the negation of freedom, for the only freedom that sharia recognizes is the freedom to obey Islamic law, a "freedom" enforced by the power of the state. And many Muslims today are working to advance that notion of "freedom" in America, though not by means of terrorism. As the September 11 attacks retreat farther and farther into memory, and politicians and public officials increasingly revert to what is now known as a September 10 mentality, the Muslim Brotherhood and other Islamic groups in service of the stealth jihad remain active across the country. As we shall see, many of them are furthering various initiatives for "Muslim accommodation," often under the guise of civil rights, that are in fact far removed from the spirit of American constitutionalism and the U.S. civil rights movement that they disingenuously invoke as inspiration. In reality, they are part of this "grand jihad" aimed at destroying U.S. constitutional government and establishing an Islamic autocracy in this country.

Distracted by foreign wars and the prospect of domestic terror attacks, Americans pay little heed to the true agents of intolerance in their midst. The stealth jihad advances largely unopposed because it is largely unrecognized.

CHAPTER THREE

SILENCING THE CRITICS

TELLING THE TRUTH = HATRED

One of the most effective tactics employed by Islamic jihadists throughout the world is to intimidate their opponents into silence. Death threats, murders, acts of mass terrorism, beheadings broadcast over the Internet—all these actions are obviously useful to minimize resistance to the jihadists' agenda. Naturally, the number of people who repudiate Islamic supremacism becomes less significant when such dissidents are afraid to express their opposition in any way.

Threats of violence are indeed effective in silencing criticism of jihadists or even simple mockery of any aspect of Islam, as we shall see in chapter four. Stealth jihadists, however, do not employ this approach. Groups such as the Council on American-Islamic Relations (CAIR) and the Muslim-American Society (MAS) have learned from the past mistakes of many U.S.-based Islamic leaders that aggressive public pronouncements and threats uttered against Islam's perceived enemies bring unwelcome attention and undermine their pretensions of being mainstream civil rights organizations. So they've adopted a different strategy to silence critics of jihadism and Islamic supremacism: they label them as "bigots," "hatemongers," and "Islamophobes."

In the U.S., playing the race card can in some ways be even more effective than death threats. If a U.S.-based Islamic group announced a death fatwa against an American writer, that organization would be denounced in the media as "extremist" and possibly trigger a police investigation. But if the group cries "racism" against the same writer, liberal as well as conservative media figures hop to shun and denounce the accused "racist," for bigotry and racism are the cardinal sins of the U.S. public square.

Islamic groups in the U.S. skillfully play the race card against those who publicize uncomfortable truths about Islam: criticism of Islamic supremacist impulses or of the organizations themselves is frequently met with indignant cries of "racism." These groups deliberately conflate race with religion, exploiting the fact that most Muslims in the country are either black or Arab and Pakistani immigrants. The fact that Islam is a religion and not a race is apparently irrelevant, and journalists almost never challenge these groups on their confusion of the two.

CAIR in particular has become expert at bandying about allegations of bigotry and racism to silence its critics or quash even fictional representations that it deems offensive to Muslims. In 2001, when Tom Clancy's novel *The Sum of All Fears* was being made into a movie, CAIR launched a successful campaign to pressure the filmmakers into changing the Islamic terrorists of the story into some other kind of villain. (Ultimately they became neo-Nazis—apparently the Aryan Nations doesn't have CAIR's clout.) There can be little doubt that the filmmakers were simply bullied into making the change by the prospect of CAIR publicly denouncing them as racists. Film director Phil Alden

Robinson wrote abjectly to CAIR, "I hope you will be reassured that I have no intention of promoting negative images of Muslims or Arabs, and I wish you the best in your continuing efforts to combat discrimination."[1] America got a dramatic reminder of the fact that there really are Islamic terrorists, and they're not just the figments of bigoted imaginations, on September 11, 2001, but by then filming on *The Sum of All Fears* had already been completed.

I myself have been a target of this intimidation campaign for years. On August 1, 2007, a lawyer for CAIR, former Democratic National Committee staff counsel Joseph E. Sandler, sent a letter about me to Ron Robinson, president of the Young America's Foundation (YAF), a conservative youth outreach organization. The letter said that I was a "well-known purveyor of hatred and bigotry against Muslims," with a "history of false and defamatory statements." Sandler threatened to "pursue every appropriate legal remedy" if I were allowed to address YAF's annual conference in Washington the following day as scheduled.[2] The topic of my talk, not coincidentally, was, "The Truth About the Council on American-Islamic Relations."

One can hardly blame CAIR for resorting to these tactics, since they work so well against filmmakers and many other targets. Robinson and YAF refused to be intimidated, however, and my talk went on as scheduled; YAF's Jason Mattera defiantly told reporters, "CAIR can go to hell and take their seventy-two virgins with them."[3]

And as it turned out, CAIR did indeed "pursue every appropriate legal remedy" after I addressed the conference: they did nothing.

That was not the first or last time, however, that CAIR had threatened or undertaken legal action against people who said things they didn't like. The organization has sued former Representative Cass Ballenger (R-NC), Anti-CAIR website proprietor Andrew Whitehead, and others for saying things about CAIR that the organization found objectionable. Interestingly enough, CAIR dropped most of its complaints against Whitehead, who had alleged that CAIR was founded by Hamas supporters, seeks to implement sharia law in America, and supports terrorist groups, after Whitehead's lawyers asked a series of questions about CAIR's funding and operations during the discovery process that CAIR didn't want to answer. The group later settled with Whitehead, who never withdrew his allegations, and the case was dismissed with prejudice. [4]

Islamic groups in the U.S. have employed the race card innumerable times in myriad contexts in order to intimidate and silence their opponents. To give credit where credit is due, it has proven to be an excellent strategy for deflecting attention from the reality of jihadist sentiments and jihadist activity among American Muslims.

For example, in February 2003 I appeared on MSNBC's *Nachman* show with Ibrahim Hooper of CAIR. (Incidentally, the show's guest host was none other than Keith Olbermann, before he morphed into a leftwing blowhard.) In the course of the discussion, I referred to Sheikh Muhammad Hisham Kabbani's 1999 statement at a State Department Open Forum that 80 percent of American mosques were under the control of extremists.

Kabbani, a Muslim himself, told the State forum that "the most dangerous thing that is going on now in these mosques . . . is the extremist ideology. Because [Islamic jihadists] are very active they took over the mosques; and we can say that they took over more than 80 percent of the mosques that have been established in the U.S. And there are more than 3000 mosques in the U.S. So it means that the methodology or ideology of extremist [sic] has been spread to 80 percent of the Muslim population, but not all of them agree with it."[5]

When I referred to Kabbani's assertion on the MSNBC show, Hooper bristled. "It's just a falsehood. It's one of those standard lines put out by hatemongers like Mr. Spencer." When asked again about the "80 percent figure," Hooper replied,

> It's a bunch of baloney.... When people don't have information about the real Islam, the real experience of the American-Muslim community, when somebody comes to them and makes the false claim that 80 percent of mosques are extremist, they go: "Well, really? I don't know about Islam, so maybe that's true." But if they have some contact with Muslims, if they know about Islam, if they understand what's really happening and they understand the agenda of those who are putting forward this hate and this misinformation, they can make a reasoned decision. But if they don't have that information, again, they're vulnerable to this.[6]

Hooper, you'll note, offered no substantive refutation of Kabbani's assertion. In fact, he ignored the fact that it came from Kabbani altogether and replied as if I myself, out of some irrational hatred and ignorance of Islam, had fabricated the statistic. It never seems to occur to Muslim spokesmen like Hooper how odd it is to claim that things like this spring from an irrational hatred in the first place. No one ever seems to develop an irrational hatred of, say, Buddhism, or to bother to make up lies about how Buddhist extremists are congregating in monasteries and plotting the downfall and subjugating of the non-Buddhist social order. No, it's only poor Islam that gets picked on in this way. And yet for all the smoke of jihad activity, overt and stealthy, all over the world, you're a "hatemonger" if you conclude there must be a fire somewhere.

Contrary to Hooper's characterization of anyone crazy enough to imagine that extremists control most American mosques, Kabbani is not unacquainted with "the real Islam, the real experience of the American-Muslim community." In fact, he made his estimate after visiting 114 mosques around the country. He reported that "ninety of them were mostly exposed, and I say exposed, to extreme or radical ideology."

This long-ago TV appearance was my personal introduction to a phenomenon I have witnessed hundreds of times since: when non-Muslims point out that Islamic jihadists commit acts of violence and justify them by reference to the Qur'an, apologists for jihad, including many U.S.-based Islamic leaders who are widely known as "moderates," respond by claiming that the one who is pointing out all this is committing an act of "hatred," "bigotry," "Islamophobia," and the like. In much the same way that CAIR representatives have targeted me, they have likewise vilified the radio personality Paul Harvey, Representative Virgil Goode (R-VA), terrorism expert Daniel Pipes, columnist Cal Thomas, talk show host Michael Graham, *National Review* magazine, FOX's drama *24*, and many others for statements about Islam and terrorism that they found offensive.

The stealth jihadists malign their opponents even when such people are simply stating incontrovertible facts. The accuracy of their statements, in fact, is seldom at issue. In 2006, John Casson, a British psychotherapist and gay rights campaigner, was shocked when Arshad Misbahi, Imam at the Manchester Central Mosque, told him that homosexuals should be executed "for the common good of man." Misbahi did not deny saying this, but in the ensuing controversy he and his supporters put the onus on Casson to prove that he wasn't an anti-Islamic bigot. Massoud Shadjareh of the Islamic Human Rights Commission complained that "Muslims are being put under a magnifying glass. I think that this is part of demonising Muslims."[7] He didn't explain how it could be demonizing Muslims to report accurately what an imam said— but that was par for the course. Some Muslim spokesmen are so intent on covering up the calls to violence and supremacism in Islamic texts and teachings that they actively lie about this material when non-Muslims bring it to light. I've been on the receiving end of this tactic, too.

SPENCER LIED, MUSLIMS CRIED

Or did I?

In March 2008, the Al-Arabiya news channel denounced my book *The Truth about Muhammad,* claiming that it contained "lies and hate." Its article quoted the Islamic apologist Karen Armstrong as saying that the book was "written in hatred" and contains "basic and bad mistakes of fact."[8]

The jihad terror group Hamas soon joined in the denunciation, thundering that my book was not just full of "lies," but was actually part of a "campaign by Western extremists against the religion of Islam and values that are sacred to Moslems," and was "another in a series of actions designed to distort the image of Islam in the public eye."[9]

Only two problems with all this: there was (and is) no campaign to "distort the image of Islam in the public eye," and neither Al-Arabiya nor Hamas (nor Karen Armstrong, for that matter) actually demonstrated that anything in the book was false. This is an important point, for all too often we hear that not just

I but many others who speak about Islamic violence are lying, jim-mying the data in some way, or playing fast and loose with the facts. But those who are manipulating the facts are all too often the ones making the charges, and that is itself fraught with impli-cations.

Uncharacteristically, Al-Arabiya tried valiantly to point out inaccuracies in my book, asserting, "The book claims that Muhammad said terrorism made him victorious and that he used to tempt people with paradise so they would crush his enemies." But is this really untrue? Examining the veracity of such claims offers a glimpse of the ways in which the stealth jihad advances by obfuscating the truth about Islam and vilifying critics who point it out.

Did I really make any false claims about Muhammad? No. "I have been made victorious with terror"—so says Muhammad not according to me, but according to the hadith collection *Sahih Bukhari*, that is, the collection of traditions of Muhammad that Muslims themselves consider most reliable.[10]

And what about Muhammad guaranteeing Paradise to his war-riors? In another Islamic tradition recorded by Bukhari, one of Muhammad's warriors approached him on the day of the momen-tous Battle of Uhud, fought between the Muslims and the pagan Arabs. The warrior asked his prophet: "Can you tell me where I will be if I should get martyred?" Muhammad replied: "In Para-dise." We are then told that "the man threw away some dates he was carrying in his hand, and fought till he was martyred."[11]

Al-Arabiya tried again with this: "The author also accuses Muhammad of treason, breaching the Treaty of Hudaybiya with the Meccan tribe of Quraish, and instigating Muslims to kill Jews."

The Treaty of Hudaybiya was an extremely significant agree-ment Muhammad made with his pagan enemies in the year 628—

a treaty that had an enormous influence on the formation of Islamic law. According to Muhammad's earliest biographer, Ibn Ishaq, the Treaty of Hudaybiya contained this provision: "If anyone comes to Muhammad without the permission of his guardian he will return him to them; and if anyone of those with Muhammad comes to Quraysh they will not return him to him."[12]

That is, those fleeing the Quraysh and seeking refuge with the Muslims would be returned to the Quraysh, while those fleeing the Muslims and seeking refuge with the Quraysh would not be returned to the Muslims. Muhammad, aware of the weakness of the Muslims before the Quraysh, readily agreed to this. But as the Muslims gained strength, the situation changed. Some time after the treaty was signed, a woman of the Quraysh, Umm Kulthum, joined the Muslims in Medina; her two brothers came to Muhammad, asking that she be returned "in accordance with the agreement between him and the Quraysh at Hudaybiya." But Muhammad refused because Allah forbade it. Allah then conveniently gave Muhammad a new revelation: "O ye who believe! When there come to you believing women refugees, examine and test them. Allah knows best as to their faith: if ye ascertain that they are believers, then send them not back to the unbelievers" (Qur'an 60:10).

In refusing to send Umm Kulthum back to the Quraysh, Muhammad broke the treaty. Although Muslims have claimed throughout history that the Quraysh broke it first, this incident came before all those by the Quraysh that Muslims point to as treaty violations—as even Islamic apologist Yahiya Emerick acknowledges in his own CAIR-endorsed biography of Muhammad.[13]

And as for the claim that Muhammad told his followers to kill Jews, the earliest biographers of Muhammad, Ibn Ishaq and Ibn

Sa'd, both zealous Muslims, record his telling his followers at a certain point: "Kill any Jew that falls into your power."[14] This was not a blanket command for genocide, but a specific directive for a particular circumstance; nevertheless, Muhammad said it—not according to me, but according to Islamic texts that Muslims generally accept as reliable.

Finally, Al-Arabiya made one last attempt: "Spencer, the director of the Jihad Watch and Dhimmi Watch websites, also claims that the prophet encouraged Muslim men to take women captive to control them."

So apparently it was I who wrote into the Qur'an the permission for Muslim men to have sexual relations with women "whom your right hands possess" (4:24). This locution refers to women taken as spoils of war after a victorious battle.

"Lies and hate"? Not in what I wrote about Muhammad— unless the "lies and hate" are to be found in the Islamic texts that I quote.

The implications of this are larger than just my book. With Al-Arabiya and Hamas denouncing an accurate portrayal of Muhammad as he is depicted in Islamic texts, it's clear that in their view, non-Muslims are not to be permitted to examine those texts and investigate how jihadists use them to justify violence and Islamic supremacism. In other words, non-Muslims are not to be allowed to investigate the motives and goals of those who would destroy them.

The stealth jihadists employ this kind of obfuscation to great effect. Their immediate goal is not to overpower America directly through combat, but rather to convince Americans that there is nothing at all to fear from Islamic theology, and that anyone who argues otherwise is an Islamophobe motivated solely by hate. With the population lulled into complacency, they can go about their work of forcing Western "accommodation" to Islamic practices. This is meant to set the stage for Islam eventually to emerge supreme.

PLAYING THE INCITEMENT CARD

The vilification of anti-jihadists as bigots and hatemongers is part of a larger effort by U.S.-based Muslim groups that are advancing the sharia by means of the stealth jihad. Along with their allies and dupes, such groups seek to portray themselves as victims of the "Islamophobia" these "hatemongers" purvey—so as to deflect criticism and unwanted scrutiny. Those who dare in today's politically correct atmosphere to raise questions about stealth jihad activity will likely be targeted not only with charges of racism and bigotry, but with claims that they are inciting violence against Muslims. CAIR for a long period even had a running feature on its website entitled "Incitement Watch" devoted to exposing what it represented as inflammatory statements that put Muslims in danger of being victimized by vigilante attacks.

More often, however, the "incitement" was a simple statement of fact, such as columnist Charles Krauthammer's observation that it was ironic that prisoners at Guantanamo were given Qur'ans, since the Qur'an had inspired them to engage in anti-infidel violence in the first place: "That we should have provided those who kill innocents in the name of Islam with precisely the document that inspires their barbarism is a sign of the absurd lengths to which we often go in extending undeserved humanity to terrorist prisoners."[15] CAIR headed its "Action Alert" on this item "Incitement Watch: Krauthammer Says Qur'an 'Inspires Barbarism,'" as if the Qur'anic verses cited by Osama bin Laden, Ayman al-Zawahri, and other jihad terrorists to justify violence had been cooked up by Krauthammer rather than originating in Islam's holiest book.[16]

Groups like CAIR are savvy in employing allegations of incitement to manipulate the media into deflecting attention from uncomfortable developments. For example, in late 2007, critics such as myself began to charge that a charter school in Minnesota, the Tarek ibn Ziyad Academy [TIZA], was an Islamic school improperly supported with public funding. As the school came under heightened media scrutiny for blurring the line between mosque and state, CAIR inserted itself in the case, asking the FBI to investigate alleged death threats against the school's director.[17] The AP reported that a CAIR spokesman said that it was " 'a sad reflection' of the level anti-Muslim feeling has reached in U.S. society that the column [a newspaper column questioning whether the academy promotes Islam] has apparently resulted in 'hatred directed at innocent students.' Identifying the threats as possible hate crimes makes it clear that prejudice could have prompted them, and 'we wanted to bring that to light in case that wasn't already obvious to people,' he said."[18]

And just like that, the focus of the story's coverage changed from allegations that the academy was illegally promoting Islam to claims that the school had received death threats, as well as the widespread "anti-Muslim feeling" that supposedly permeates U.S. society overall. The alleged death threats were dutifully chronicled by the Minneapolis-St. Paul *Star-Tribune*, the local Fox news channel, and others.[19] Charles C. Haynes, a senior scholar at the First Amendment Center in Washington, penned an article lamenting that discussion about the school's practices had so quickly become poisoned: "TIZA may have crossed a First Amendment line.... But it should go without saying that in a nation committed to the rule of law, even the most egregious First Amendment violation doesn't justify hate mail and death threats."[20]

Whose fault was this? Mine, evidently: Haynes wrote that "a longtime critic of Islam, Robert Spencer, suggested that TIZA might be part of a 'grand jihad' bent on undermining Western civilization. Not surprisingly, TIZA now receives what the school's director describes as 'numerous death threats, harassing e-mails, [and] harassing phone calls.' "

Of course, I never called for anyone's death, nor did I encourage such threats in any way.

If the school really did receive death threats—and it's possible that it did—these threats were deplorable, as evil as they were idiotic and contemptible.

However, if the culprit were ever found, school officials may wish to slip him a thank-you note as the FBI hauls him away; for if there really were threats, they worked only to the advantage of CAIR. This is the group's modus operandi—trumping up and exaggerating hate crimes, deflecting attention away from anything Muslims are doing that might cause non-Muslims concern, and doing everything possible to portray Muslims as victims who need a special protected status.[21] The suddenly sympathetic turn of media coverage, I believe, played a key role in influencing the Minnesota Department of Education's report on the school, which brushed aside critics' main objections to the academy's operation and found only minor infractions of laws separating religion and state.

THE GOVERNMENT BAN ON "JIHAD"

In the past, the Bush administration has shown undue respect for U.S.-based stealth jihadist organizations, feting them, currying favor with them, and listening closely to their advice on Islam-related issues. One would have thought that President Bush's embarrassment at posing for a photograph in 2000 with Sami Al-Arian, who cofounded the World Islamic Study Enterprise and other jihadist front organizations and was later imprisoned for his activities in support of the terror organization Palestinian Islamic Jihad, would have been enough to dissuade the administration from maintaining connections with such groups. If not that, surely federal prosecutors' naming of CAIR, the Islamic Society of North America (ISNA), and the North American Islamic Trust as unindicted co-conspirators in a terrorism funding trial should have done the trick. But no, somehow CAIR and Co.'s advice keeps finding its way into official U.S. policies.

And the advice such groups give the government is predictable: don't do anything to offend Muslims, and don't admit to any connection between Islam and terrorism—even when the terrorists proclaim it themselves.

At the behest of these and other U.S.-based Muslim organizations, the Bush administration has continually softened its rhetoric about our conflict with the jihadists in order to cater to Islamic sensitivities. This process began almost immediately after the September 11 attacks, when the military named its imminent campaign against the Taliban in Afghanistan "Operation Infinite Justice." The name lasted less than two weeks before the administration changed it in order to avoid offending Muslims, as Secretary of Defense Donald Rumsfeld freely admitted.[22] As Salon's Jake Tapper reported, the ball got rolling on this issue when an article appeared in the *San Francisco Chronicle* in which Aly Abu Zaakouk, executive director of the American Muslim Council, protested that the name "Infinite Justice" was "offensive to some in the Muslim community."[23]

In the immediate aftermath of September 11, the Bush administration got plenty of hints that U.S.-based Islamic organizations had a more extreme agenda than they were letting on. For example, just three days after the attacks, President Bush attended a remembrance ceremony at the National Cathedral that the ISNA imam, Muzammil Siddiqi, was invited to address. Siddiqi's remarks raised some eyebrows, including those of Charles Krauthammer, who noted that the imam declined to denounce the attacks on the World Trade Center as being contrary to Islam. Soon after, it emerged that this kind of vagueness on questions of Islam and violence was nothing new for Siddiqi—when a *Los Angeles Times* reporter had asked him in 1989 if he supported the Ayatollah Khomeini's longstanding fatwa calling for the murder of writer Salman Rushdie for blasphemy, "Siddiqi was non-committal, saying that would have to be determined in the due process of Islamic law."[24]

In light of the near-complete absence of genuine "moderate" Islamic organizations in the U.S., the government relies on the voice of groups like ISNA for the "Islamic perspective" on U.S. policies. Of course, the fact that these groups and the enemy we are fighting share the same goal—the Islamization of the Western world—casts some doubt on the utility of the advice we receive from them.

Recently, the signs that these groups harbor an Islamic supremacist agenda have become so overwhelming that the Bush administration has finally taken some steps toward distancing itself from them. But still, the recommendations of these groups continue to find their way into official U.S. policies, where they serve to silence those in the government who dissent from the myopic view of Islam as a religion of peace.

For example, the Pentagon declined to renew the contract of Major Stephen Coughlin, formerly its lone specialist on Islamic law. As we shall see in greater detail in chapter ten, Coughlin was apparently cashiered after he declined to soften his presentation of the elements of Islamic teaching that jihadists use to justify violence.[25] He was a forceful proponent of the necessity of speaking clearly about the nature of the threat we face: in his thesis, " 'To Our Great Detriment': Ignoring What Extremists Say About *Jihad*," submitted to the National Defense Intelligence College in July 2007, he argued that the politically correct refusal to name the enemy was placing the United States at a strategic disadvantage:

> The Current Approach stands for the proposition that the WOT [War on Terrorism] can be successfully prosecuted without reference to a substantive understanding of the enemy. In this, the Current Approach purposefully violates Sun Tsu's first rule of war: to know the enemy. Never understanding the enemy means never being able to generate an effective strategy to defeat him. At the operational level, this means never having the ability to convert tactical successes into strategic victories. The cost of not understanding the enemy has been high and is getting higher everyday. It will increasingly be measured by news stories that narrow in on senior leaders' inability to answer basic questions about the nature of the enemy and his environment. It will also manifest itself in official responses to terrorist attacks that become progressively less reality-based.[26]

In April 2008 the perspectives Coughlin criticized were codified as official U.S. policy: the State Department, the Department of Homeland Security, and the National Counter Terrorism Center issued new guidelines forbidding personnel from using the words "jihad" or "jihadist" in reference to Islamic terrorism and its perpetrators.[27]

A Homeland Security report tellingly entitled "Terminology to Define the Terrorists: Recommendations from American Muslims" explained that this initiative stemmed from a concern not to offend moderate Muslims. By calling the terrorists "jihadists," U.S. officials could be "unintentionally portraying terrorists, who lack moral and religious legitimacy, as brave fighters, legitimate soldiers or spokesmen for ordinary Muslims."

The report argued that using the term "jihad" may not be "strategic." Why not? "Because it glamorizes terrorism, imbues terrorists with religious authority they do not have and damages relations with Muslims around the world." U.S. officials, the report cautioned, "should not concede the terrorists' claim that they are legitimate adherents of Islam."

As previously noted, the sanction of violent jihad to spread Islam is not some fringe view, as the Bush administration insists, but rather is the interpretation put forward by many of the most prominent scholars of Islamic law throughout history—including today.

It is short-sighted and foolish to refrain from studying those elements of Islamic tradition—a study that can reveal a great deal about the motives and goals of modern-day Islamic jihadists—in order to avoid offending Muslims. Yet the government chooses to shut its eyes to this inconvenient fact, dismissing officials like Coughlin who simply point it out.

So who is responsible for the misguided, politically correct recommendations that found their way into the Homeland Security report? The memorandum cites the contribution of "American Muslims." But which ones? The guidelines do not name them.

However, we get a hint at who stood behind these policies from the founder and president of the influential TrueSpeak Institute, Jim Guirard, who contributed significantly to the new guidelines.

TrueSpeak is a lobbying group dedicated to influencing government policy on these matters; Guirard has briefed, among others,
Pentagon PsyOp officials, a Senior Advisory Committee to the
Secretary of Homeland Security, the U.S. Army's World Conference on Public Affairs, a NORAD-Northcom Conference on the
Global War On Terror, and the National Defense University. The
new State Department and Homeland Security recommendations
closely reflect Guirard's thinking—for years now he has been
arguing that U.S. officials should stop using the word "jihad" for
reasons similar to those outlined in the Homeland Security report.

Guirard explains that he developed his proposals for a new
nomenclature after consulting with a number of "moderate" Muslim scholars. Coughlin, however, notes that Guirard's advisers
included Muqtedar Khan, Akbar Ahmed, Anthony Sullivan,
Robert Crane, Asma Afasaruddin, and Layla Sein—all of whom
have multiple links to Brotherhood organizations. Khan, Ahmed,
Sullivan, Asfaruddin, and Sein are members of the Association of
Muslim Social Scientists (AMSS). Khan, Ahmed, Sullivan, Crane,
and Sein are members of the International Institute of Islamic
Thought (IIIT). Crane is also a member of the United Association
for Studies and Research (UASR).

Guirard also lists as a "moderate" consultant Taha Jabir al-
Awani, the Chairman of the Fiqh Council of North America and
a co-founder and President of IIIT; Sherman Jackson, a trustee of
the North American Islamic Trust (NAIT) and the Muslim Stu-
dents Association (MSA); Jeremy Henzell. Executive Director of
AMSS; and Sayed Syeed, president of the MSA, cofounder of
ISNA, General Secretary of AMSS, and Director of Academic
Outreach for the IIIT.[28]

All these groups—AMSS, IIIT, UASR, NAIT, MSA, and
ISNA—are listed in the 1991 Muslim Brotherhood "grand jihad"

memorandum as being among "our organizations and the organizations of our friends."

As if that weren't enough to taint the TrueSpeak enterprise, Guirard also consulted with Sheikh Yusuf al-Qaradawi, a U.S.-designated supporter of terrorism who has justified suicide attacks against Israeli civilians—and is one of the leaders of the Muslim Brotherhood.[29]

Guirard's entire conceptual apparatus rests on his authorities. Coughlin notes that "when Mr. Guirard 'cites' to authority for the terms and definitions he uses, it is to these individuals and not to reviewable published authoritative sources. This is hearsay."[30]

And yet Guirard cannot be sure that the individuals whom he invokes as authority, with all their connections to the Muslim Brotherhood, are not using his Orwellian effort to soft-pedal jihad as part of the Brotherhood's explicit "grand jihad in eliminating and destroying the Western civilization from within."

Those within the government who oppose Guirard-style policies are forced to express their dissent off-the-record in order to preserve their jobs. A source who has extensive experience throughout the U.S. Central Command area of operations offered me this overview of the situation within the U.S. government in June 2008: "There is, without a doubt, not only a real tendency, but a maximum effort to ensure that Islamic dissimulation and . . . disinformation are given priority over any other views of Islam in the United States Government."

The source says that this doesn't apply only to Central Command "which is actually probably the most sane amongst the various government entities that are involved in this. That said, there is nearly a sense of desperation to ensure that 'both sides' are always represented in U.S. Government analyses. The problem is, in the fight against jihad, there are not two sides. The views of moderate Muslims have no bearing whatsoever when grappling with attempting to get our commanders to understand jihad in Islamic apocalyptic and salvation history. The government agencies have *voluntarily* deferred their responsibility to understand the traditional obligation to violent jihad in Islam to Islamic apologists."

He terms the new State Department and Homeland Security guidelines "ridiculous," and notes that "for no other reason than to proactively demonstrate that they are engaging in outreach, for its own sake, our government agencies make great efforts to exclude the deep traditions of violent jihad in Islam from the picture."[31]

THE LARGER GOAL

Fantasy-based policymaking is never wise. But that is what the Bush administration reaffirmed in these directives—yet again, years after the president proclaimed Islam a "religion of peace." The formulation of such platitudes as the basis of U.S. security policy certainly satisfies the U.S.-based Muslim groups who recommend them, as well as our politically correct media. But in doing so, the administration has greatly encumbered the identification of the enemy and the intelligent study of their motivation and methods. The losers in all this will be the American people, who are lulled into complacency as stealth jihadists continue their campaign to encourage America's ever-greater accommodation to Islamic law.

It is no coincidence that all these varied efforts to silence voices critical of Islamic supremacism recall one of the most important laws by which dhimmis must abide within the Islamic state: according to traditional Islamic law, non-Muslims must not speak about Islam in a manner that Muslims consider offensive. The manual of Islamic law certified by Cairo's Al-Azhar University, the foremost authority in the Sunni Islamic world, stipulates that a dhimmi who lives under the rule of the Muslims forfeits the "protection" he receives from the Muslims, and his life, if he "mentions something impermissible about Allah, the Prophet...or Islam."[32]

Thus non-Muslims in a society in which Islam reigns supreme should become, and remain, submissive and quiet—particularly about Islam.

And that is precisely what the outcome will be if U.S.-based stealth jihadist groups have their way. They have become adept at generating sympathetic media coverage, deflecting attention away from stories about Islamic supremacy, and silencing their critics by vilifying them as racists and worse. This is all bad enough when it takes place in the realm of public opinion, but the fact that this campaign has been successfully extended to the U.S. government is cause for grave concern.

CHAPTER FOUR

THE INTERNATIONAL JIHAD AGAINST FREE SPEECH

CRIMINALIZING DISCUSSION OF ISLAM

In April 2008 the British newspaper the *Telegraph* reported that "David Davis, the shadow home secretary, has accused Muslims of promoting a kind of 'voluntary apartheid' by shutting themselves in closed societies and demanding immunity from criticism."[1]

The demand for legal protection from criticism is part of an international agenda agreed upon at the March 2008 meeting in Senegal convened by the world's most powerful Islamic organization, the Organization of the Islamic Conference (OIC), which is comprised of fifty-seven governments of Muslim-majority states (including the reified "State of Palestine"). At that convocation the OIC developed what the Associated Press called "a battle plan" to defend Islam—but not from the terrorists who, as we hear all the time, have "hijacked" their religion. Rather, the OIC declared its intention to craft a "legal instrument" to fight against the threat to Islam they perceived "from political cartoonists and bigots."[2]

The OIC was referring, of course, to the "notorious" Danish cartoons of Muhammad that appeared in 2005, touching off riots and murders all over the Islamic world. "Muslims are being targeted by a campaign of defamation, denigration, stereotyping, intolerance and discrimination," explained Ekmeleddin Ihsanoglu, the OIC's secretary general. The AP reported that OIC "delegates were given a voluminous report by the OIC that recorded anti-Islamic speech and actions from around the world. The report concludes that Islam is under attack and that a defense must be mounted."

The offensive would take the form of a "legal instrument" that would criminalize what the OIC and other Islamic entities perceive as criticism of Islam. "Islamophobia," Ihsanoglu declared, "cannot be dealt with only through cultural activities but (through) a robust political engagement." This is a careful euphemism calling for restrictions on freedom of speech. Abdoulaye Wade, the President of Senegal and chairman of the OIC, made this point explicit: "I don't think freedom of expression should mean freedom from blasphemy. There can be no freedom without limits."[3]

The OIC kicked off its international campaign against free speech when *Fitna*, a short film by Dutch MP Geert Wilders that connects acts of violence by Muslims to violent passages in the Qur'an, appeared on the Internet shortly after the OIC's Senegal conference. The organization condemned the film in "the strongest terms," claiming that Wilders' movie was "a deliberate act of discrimination against Muslims" intended only to "provoke unrest and intolerance."[4]

Iran and Pakistan added to the OIC's efforts by lodging formal complaints against *Fitna* with the European Union and the Dutch Ambassador to Islamabad, respectively.[5] Other Islamic states and organizations also expressed outrage over the film.

Perhaps more disquieting, even greater indignation came from non-Muslim leaders, especially top officials from the United Nations. UN Secretary-General Ban Ki-moon dubbed the film "offensively anti-Islamic" and regurgitated the OIC's core argument that free speech rights do not protect criticism of Islam: "There is no justification for hate speech or incitement to violence. The right of free expression is not at stake here."[6]

The UN High Commissioner for Human Rights, Louise Arbour, on the other hand, saw precisely that the "right of free expression" was at stake—and she came down squarely against it. After seconding Ban Ki-moon's condemnation of the film, she urged international lawmakers to prohibit race and religious hatred and incitement, further imploring legislators to "offer strong protective measures to all forms of freedom of expression, while at the same time *enacting appropriate restrictions*, as necessary, to protect the rights of others"[7] [emphasis added]. The "rights of others" that need protection, clearly, refers to the new rights of Muslims not to be offended.

With woolly logic, Jorge Sampaio, UN High Representative for the Alliance of Civilizations, urged the world not to overemphasize extremism, for to do so would only create extremism: "We should indeed beware of overemphasizing it, because extremism anywhere is extremism everywhere, thanks to new media technologies. Few people think of themselves as extremists, but many can be pushed towards an extreme point of view, almost without noticing it, when they feel that the behavior or language of others is extreme. We therefore deeply regret this offensive film."[8]

In essence Sampaio told non-Muslims to avoid pointing out the evil that Muslim "extremists" were committing, or risk pushing moderate Muslims into the extremist camp. Passive acquiescence would seem to be the only appropriate response to acts of Islamic extremism.

And that was precisely the aim of the OIC's campaign, which was quickly embraced by the United Nations.

STEALTH JIHAD VICTORY AT THE UN HUMAN RIGHTS COUNCIL

The OIC's campaign against free speech met with its first big success at the UN Human Rights Council. In June 2008, the AP reported that "Muslim countries have won a battle to prevent Islam from being criticised during debates by the UN Human Rights Council." Council President Doru-Romulus Costea explained that religious issues can be "very complex, very sensitive and very intense.... This council is not prepared to discuss religious matters in depth, consequently we should not do it." Henceforth only religious scholars would be permitted to broach such sensitive issues.[9]

"While Costea's ban applies to all religions," the AP explained, "it was prompted by Muslim countries complaining about references to Islam." The ban came after a heated session in which David G. Littman, speaking for several non-governmental organizations (NGOs), denounced the practices of female genital mutilation (FGM), execution by stoning, and child marriage as sanctioned by Islamic law. Egypt, Pakistan, and Iran angrily protested, interrupting Littman over a dozen times and eventually forcing the proceedings to be suspended. In the course of this contentious discussion, representatives from Islamic countries made numerous revealing statements that are well worth examining in light of the ongoing campaign by Islamic nations and organizations against free speech in the West.

Pakistani representative Imran Ahmed Siddiqui echoed the common refrain of Islamic apologists in the West, complaining that Littman's initiative on genital mutilation, stoning, and child marriage amounted to an "out-of-context, selective discussion on the sharia law." He then asked Costea, the council's president, to prohibit Littman from further speaking on the topic. The representative from Slovenia mildly protested against the attempt to silence Littman, insisting that any NGO representative had the right to speak about topics on the council's agenda.

The representative from Egypt then responded, "I would humbly and kindly ask my colleague from Slovenia to reconsider." He further warned, "We will not take this lightly. . . . This is not about NGOs and their participation in the Council. This is about the sharia law." Pakistan's Siddiqui added, "I would like to state again that this is not the forum to discuss religious sensitivity." Why not? Because to do so, Siddiqui argued, would spread hatred: "It will amount to spreading hatred against certain members of the Council. I mean, it has happened before also that selective discussions were raised in the Council to demonize a particular group." He then asked Costea to "bar any such discussion again, at the Council."

Eventually Littman was allowed to proceed. After noting that "almost 90 percent of the female population in the north of Sudan undergo FGM which, in many cases, is practiced in its most extreme form known as infibulation," Littman declared, "We believe that only a fatwa from Al-Azhar Grand Sheikh Sayyed Tantawi—replacing the ambiguous fatwas of 1949, 1951 and 1981—will change this barbaric, criminal practice, which is now growing even in Europe."

At this point Egypt interrupted, complaining that "this is an attempt to raise a bad traditional practice to Islam. Sheikh Al-Azhar

[Sayyed Tantawi] is the president of the largest and the biggest and the oldest Islamic university in the world." He exclaimed, "My point is that Islam will not be crucified in this Council. That's why we are challenging this ruling [which allowed Littman to continue speaking.]"

Taken aback by that emotional declaration, the representative from Germany asked Costea to confirm the wording of the statement about Islam not being "crucified" in the council, and enquired whether Costea considered it appropriate. The Egyptian delegate ignored the question and requested that the references to the fatwa of Sheikh Al-Azhar be deleted from the meeting's official transcript.[10]

Littman then resumed his speech, noting that "the stoning of women for alleged adultery still occurs regularly in Iran, Sudan, and other countries. In Iran, they are buried up to their waists in pits and blunt stones are used thereby increasing their agony in death." Soon thereafter he was interrupted by the Iranian delegate, who denounced Littman's report of the stoning of women in Iran as "completely false."

Littman's arguments, in fact, were irrefutable. The Islamic legal manual endorsed by Al-Azhar, the most influential Sunni Muslim institution in the world, indeed mandates circumcision "for both men and women."[11] According to Geneive Abdo, author of *No God But God: Egypt and the Triumph of Islam*, Al-Azhar has praised female circumcision as "a laudable practice that [does] honor to women."[12] As for Iran, Amnesty International reports that despite the regime's approval in 2002 of a moratorium on executions by stoning, "Sentences of death by stoning in Iran are still being passed and, on occasion, carried out." In fact, Amnesty International launched a campaign to save eleven people in Iran awaiting execution by stoning.[13]

As part of the new campaign against free speech in the West, Islamic representatives may sometimes challenge the accuracy of statements like Littman's, which they're seeking to criminalize. But that's not the point. As demonstrated by the discussion in the UN Human Rights Council, the goal is not to ban inaccurate criticism of Islam, but *all* criticism of Islam. And as far as the UNHRC goes, the campaign was a complete success. With council president Costea ultimately prohibiting all discussion of "religious issues" from council meetings, the Islamic delegates can rest assured that there will be no more discussion of the fact that Islamic theology provides the basis for human rights outrages ranging from female genital mutilation to stonings. Thus, an international body ostensibly dedicated to promoting human rights voluntarily renounced any study of one of the leading sources of international human rights violations.

Shortly after this incident, Ekmeleddin Ihsanoglu, Secretary General of Organization of the Islamic Conference, declared victory in clearly supremacist terms: Muslims had dictated to the West the "red lines that should not be crossed," and the West was complying. He said that OIC initiatives against "Islamophobia" had resulted in "convincing progress at all these levels, mainly the UN Human Rights Council in Geneva, and the UN General Assembly." And indeed he is right: both the UN Human Rights Council and the UN General Assembly now annually approve resolutions condemning the "defamation of religions." Notably, though, Ihsanoglu didn't refer to these resolutions as applying to "defamation of religions," but rather, to "defamation of Islam."

He added, "In confronting the Danish cartoons and the Dutch film 'Fitna', we sent a clear message to the West regarding the red lines that should not be crossed. As we speak, the official West and its public opinion are all now well-aware of the sensitivities of these issues. They have also started to look seriously into the question of freedom of expression from the perspective of its inherent responsibility, which should not be overlooked."[14]

The Senegalese diplomat Doudou Diène, currently the United Nations Special Rapporteur on contemporary forms of racism, racial discrimination, xenophobia and related intolerance, took the campaign against Islam's critics one step further. In an August 2007 report to the UN Human Rights Council, he suggested that merely quoting the Qur'an in the context of criticizing Islam was an act of bigotry:

> The ideological dimension of Islamophobia is directly con-
> nected to its intellectual legitimization as currently reflected
> in a number of so-called intellectuals and political and social
> commentators that put forward openly Islamophobic state-
> ments, including explicit defamation of Islam. In particular,
> one may note that a number of Islamophobic statements have
> been falsely claimed to be scientific or scholarly, in order to
> give intellectual clout to arguments that link Islam to violence
> and terrorism. Furthermore, the manipulation and selective
> quoting of sacred texts, in particular the Koran, as a means
> to deceptively argue that these texts show the violent nature
> of Islam has become current practice.[15]

So-called "Islamophobes" are not the ones responsible for this. But they are the ones Diène aspires to silence. His words were ominous, given that Diène supports the OIC's call for all govern-ments to outlaw "defamation of religions"—which is a euphe-mism for blasphemy of Islam.

The attempt to compel Western states to ban insults to Islam is quickly picking up speed, and bodes ill for the ability of those states to defend themselves against the global jihad in all its forms—since Islamic supremacists and their allies routinely characterize all investigation of the Islamic roots of the jihadist agenda as "hate speech."

This campaign represents the international dimension of the stealth jihad. It does not consist of attacking Western countries with guns or bombs, or even threatening to do so. Instead, we're pressured to accommodate Islam by placing the religion off-limits to critical discussion. It's presented as an act of "tolerance," but the deliberate result is the erosion of core Western concepts of free expression. Think about the extent to which that single value defines Western civilization: for one thing, it is an indispensable foundation of the American Revolution and the American system of republican government. And we are surrendering it, gradually and voluntarily, to those who seek to impose on us a value system that elevates the sanctity of Islam over freedom.

One would have never thought that Westerners would give up free speech of their own accord, but we are now in the process of carving out a major exception for Islam. Yet the freedom to criticize religion, of course, is the very cornerstone of the right to free expression. Once we surrender that right, can the surrender of freedom of religion be far behind?

A BACKDROP OF VIOLENCE—THE DANISH CARTOONS

The international stealth jihad operates in a similar way to its U.S.-based counterparts. As we have seen, Islamic representatives to the UN and other international forums put forward their demands and argue within those bodies for the West to sign on to various conventions outlawing "defamation of religions"—in other words, blasphemy. None of the countries threaten to attack the U.S. if we don't go along, but that doesn't mean that the threat of violence is absent from the discussion. To the contrary, Islamic diplomats involved in this offensive shrewdly exploit the violence that inevitably erupts throughout the Islamic world whenever a perceived slight of Islam in the West gains sufficient media exposure.

As previously noted, the international Islamic campaign to outlaw blasphemy was spurred largely by two events—the publication of the Danish Muhammad cartoons and the release of the movie *Fitna*. The first of these events sparked rioting and killings in numerous Islamic countries, while the second was accompanied by all kinds of threats of violence, although thankfully not much actual violence occurred. Both these cases provide important examples of how international stealth jihadists, while eschewing violence themselves, exploit the ever-present threat of violence to forward their campaign of intimidating the West into adopting elements of sharia such as blasphemy laws.

Let's begin with a recent example related to the Muhammad cartoons. On June 2, 2008, a suicide attack against the Danish Embassy in Pakistan killed six people. Two days later, a web posting claiming to be from al Qaeda declared that the bombing was fulfillment of Osama bin Laden's vow to exact revenge for the publication of the Muhammad cartoons.[16]

Pakistan's ambassador to Denmark responded to these events with the following remark addressed to the Danish people: "It isn't just the people of Pakistan that feel they have been harassed by what your newspaper has begun. I'd like to know if your newspaper is satisfied with what it has done and what it has unleashed? Danes know that they have insulted people around the world by printing and reprinting the Mohammed cartoons, which were done in poor taste."[17]

The statement was emblematic of how Islamic diplomats are trying to turn the world's moral sensibility on its head. After jihadist thugs and murderers in Pakistan killed six innocent people because of cartoons published in a newspaper half a world away, Pakistan's ambassador blamed the violence of his own people on the intended victims—the Danes—because they allowed the exhibition of cartoons "in poor taste."

One would reasonably think she would have felt more "harassed" by the murders of six people (who, incidentally, had nothing to do with the cartoons) than by any verbal or visual affront. She might legitimately have regarded the Danish cartoonists as boors, or fools, or insensitive people. But if people cannot differ in good faith about what is true and good without killing each other or intimidating one another into silence, pluralistic societies are not long for this world.

Pakistan, which is leading the international campaign for blasphemy laws, has clearly established its position on this issue: Muslim rioting is the inevitable response to Western slights of Islam. Since Muslims will always respond in this way, it is incumbent upon us, in the West, not to offend Muslims and make them riot. This was made clear just six days after the Danish embassy was bombed in Pakistan, when the Pakistani government reacted by sending a delegation to the EU to request that European nations limit free speech rights to avoid offending Muslims.[18]

This twisted morality was again evident during a July 2008 briefing on Capitol Hill about the attempt by Islamic countries to force blasphemy laws on the West. In arguing for the adoption of blasphemy laws, Pakistani Embassy representative Asma Fatima declared, "The ideal of freedom of speech is precious to you, but it's not value-neutral. You don't have to hurt people's sentiments and bring them to the point where they have to react in strange ways."[19]

"React in strange ways," of course, refers to violent rioting. But note the preceding phrase, "they *have to* react." It's not that Muslims *might* react violently, you see. They really have no choice in the matter. They just *have to* do it.

The respected international terrorism analyst, Rohan Gunaratna, illuminated the violent threat hanging over discussion of the Muhammad cartoons. "There is still a lot of dissatisfaction here about the cartoons," he noted, "as well as the fact that the Danish government still has not condemned them or the people that were responsible for them. As long as that hasn't happened, Denmark will be under the constant threat of militant Muslims."[20]

Of course, Muslim leaders, in Pakistan and elsewhere, wanted to foster exactly that perception, because it coalesced neatly with the Islamic supremacist agenda. The underlying assumption is that Muslims may do whatever they wish; it is up to Western non-Muslims to adjust and adapt however they must, in order to placate them. And that includes everything up to and including abandoning freedom of speech in favor of the chastened silence prescribed for dhimmis in Islamic law.

THE FIT OVER *FITNA*

"Fitna" is Arabic for discord or upheaval; it is also the name of a sixteen-minute film by Dutch politician Geert Wilders that appeared in March 2008 and almost immediately created… *fitna*. The Dutch government feared that the film's release would spark a violent reaction by Muslims whose core objection, ironically, was that the film linked Islam with violence. Dutch prime minister Jan Peter Balkenende tried to mollify Muslims by publicly disavowing the connection between Islam and violence. "We reject this interpretation," he declared. "The vast majority of

Muslims reject extremism and violence."[21] Many Muslims, however, did not appear to embrace Balkenende's benign interpretation of their religion; the film's release sparked protests in Muslim
nations during which demonstrators demanded that Wilders be
killed.[22]

But was Wilders really responsible for the connection of Islam
with violence? The answer can be found in the film itself. Here
again, it is worthwhile to examine the assertions made by the
Islam critic in detail, in order to see if those who complain that the
film is an exercise in demonization have a case. The main part of
Fitna features a series of quotations from the Qur'an, followed by
scenes of violent acts committed by Muslims. The key question is
whether or not the violent acts are really related to the Qur'an
quotes.

Most of Wilders' detractors claim they are not, but Wilders
accounted for this objection in the film itself. For example, the
first verse of the Qur'an presented in *Fitna* is 8:60: "Against them
make ready your strength to the utmost of your power, including
steeds of war, to strike terror into the hearts of the enemies of
Allah and your enemies." Wilders follows this with heart-rending
scenes from September 11 and the 2004 Madrid train bombings,
as we hear two women, among the many victims, calling for help
on those days. The women are indeed terrified, but what does this
have to do with Qur'an 8:60? An Islamic preacher—not Wilders
or any other non-Muslim—soon appears in the film to answer this
question, stating in terms that clearly recall that verse of the
Qur'an: "Annihilate the infidels and the polytheists, your (Allah's)
enemies and the enemies of the religion. Allah, count them and kill
them to the last one."

Later, *Fitna* quotes Qur'an 47:4: "Therefore, when ye meet the
Unbelievers (in fight), smite at their necks; at length, when ye have

thoroughly subdued them, bind a bond firmly (on them)." Wilders
follows this with images of two unbelievers whose necks were
struck by the warriors of jihad: Theo van Gogh, the Dutch filmmaker who was shot, stabbed, and had his throat slit after making
a movie that criticized Islam's treatment of women, and Nick Berg,
the U.S. contractor who was kidnapped and decapitated in Iraq.

The statements of the perpetrators make it clear that they
believed themselves to be acting in accord with Islamic imperatives. Mohammed Bouyeri, the murderer of van Gogh, clutched a
Qur'an as he told a Dutch court in 2005, "What moved me to do
what I did was purely my faith. I was motivated by the law that
commands me to cut off the head of anyone who insults Allah and
his prophet."[23] And the late jihadist Abu Musab al-Zarqawi
invoked Muhammad's example to justify the beheading of Berg:
"Is it not time for you [Muslims] to take the path of jihad and
carry the sword of the Prophet of prophets? ... The Prophet, the
most merciful, ordered [his army] to strike the necks of some prisoners in [the Battle of] Badr and to kill them.... And he set a good
example for us."[24]

Here again, the Islamic justification for these acts of barbarism
comes not from Wilders, but from Muslims.

Next comes Qur'an 4:89: "They but wish that ye should reject
Faith, as they do, and thus be on the same footing (as they): But
take not friends from their ranks until they flee in the way of Allah
(From what is forbidden). But if they turn renegades, seize them
and slay them wherever ye find them; and (in any case) take no
friends or helpers from their ranks." Wilders again illustrates this
with Muslims calling for the deaths of those who convert from
Islam. One would think also that the case of Abdul Rahman, the
Afghan Muslim who was put on trial for his life in 2006 for converting to Christianity before being spirited away to safety in Italy,

would be enough to demonstrate that many Muslims take the traditional Islamic death penalty for apostasy seriously—and that penalty was not invented by Geert Wilders.

Finally, the film reproduces Qur'an 8:39: "And fight them on until there is no more tumult or oppression, and there prevail justice and faith in Allah altogether and everywhere." This is followed by scenes of Islamic preachers and other Muslims (including Iranian President Mahmoud Ahmadinejad) asserting that Islam will soon conquer the West and rule the entire world.

This demonstrates the odd myopia of virtually all the objections to *Fitna*. Does Wilders possess Zionist black arts to cast material into the Qur'an and other Islamic texts? Do I, and do others who point out passages in the Qur'an that Muslim spokesmen in the West would prefer that non-Muslims not know about? It was not Wilders, but the many Muslims he shows in his film, who link Islam with violence. And that link has already been made innumerable times around the world—by Islamic jihad warriors, not by non-Muslim "Islamophobes." Omar Bakri, once the leading jihadist in Britain but now banned from setting foot in that country, went so far as to say that with a few small edits, *Fitna* "could be a film by the Mujahideen."[25]

And that's the problem: Islamic groups that profess to oppose today's global jihad should have been supportive of *Fitna* and other attempts to show the elements of Islamic teaching that jihadists use to make their case in the Islamic world. After all, one can only reform what one admits needs reforming, and thus any genuinely reformist entity within Islam should have welcomed these presentations of the elements of Islam that need updating: the supremacist teachings and those that justify a violence that makes it impossible for Muslims to coexist peacefully with non-Muslims as equals on an indefinite basis.

With the *Fitna* controversy, we see that while claiming to eschew violence themselves, the diplomats leading Islam's international stealth jihad benefit from the constant threat of violence that hangs over Western attempts to critique Islam. Such diplomats are not going to threaten Wilders with death for insulting Islam—they know that many others will do that spontaneously. Instead, these officials work, all too successfully, to have such critics condemned for "provoking" violence, ostracized from the public debate, and in the future, preemptively silenced through blasphemy laws.

EMBRACING DHIMMIHOOD

Even if stealth jihadists do not employ or publicly endorse violence themselves, they know that physical attacks are effective in stifling opposition to their agenda. And of course, violence against Islam's critics is not, by any means, confined to Islamic countries. Such attacks are frequently carried out in the West, resulting in self-censorship by Westerners on topics related to Islam. This ever-present fear makes Western commentators and media figures much less resistant to the adoption of formal blasphemy laws.

The most brutally efficient way to get rid of critics, of course, is through murder. An Islamic supremacist killed filmmaker Theo van Gogh on an Amsterdam street in 2004 in revenge for van Gogh's film criticizing the mistreatment of women in Islam. Similarly, the artists who drew the Danish Muhammad cartoons in 2005 received numerous death threats, and some were forced into hiding. As recently as February 2008, Danish authorities arrested two Tunisians for plotting to strangle to death one of the cartoonists, seventy-four-year-old Kurt Westergaard. [26]

Violence works. When free speech advocates called upon newspapers in Europe and America to reprint the Muhammad cartoons as a reaffirmation of free expression, nearly all refused. Many editors and publishers professed a newly-found respect for religion that they had never shown when a crucifix dipped in urine and a dung-encrusted portrait of the Virgin Mary were publicly displayed as works of art. That strange new deference clearly had other derivations: most Christians, of course, are not in the habit of attacking and killing people to avenge insults to their faith.

Violence against Western "blasphemers" of Islam has been part of the public landscape at least since 1989, when the Ayatollah Khomeini called for the murder of Salman Rushdie after he published a book that Khomeini deemed "blasphemous to Islam." Rushdie is still alive today, but Iran never rescinded the fatwa on his head. Although he spent a decade in hiding, Rushdie must be considered lucky—one of his translators was murdered and several others attacked.

The death sentence passed on Rushdie elicited shock and revulsion in the West when it was first publicized. But today, nearly twenty years later, all too many Westerners placidly acknowledge violence as an acceptable element of the cultural landscape. When the Swedish artist Lars Vilks drew Muhammad as a dog in 2007 as a gesture in defense of artistic freedom, al Qaeda put a $100,000 bounty on his head. Incredibly, CNN's Paula Newton reacted by condemning *Vilks*, arguing that he "should have known better because of what happened in Denmark in 2005, when a cartoonist's depictions of the prophet sparked violent protests in the Muslim world and prompted death threats against that cartoonist's life." She registered no such disapproval of those who actually issued the threats.[27]

The same dynamic of fear was exhibited by Lawrence O'Donnell, Jr., MSNBC's senior political analyst and a panelist on *The McLaughlin Group*, who gained national attention late in 2007 for an emotional attack on Mormonism. Radio host Hugh Hewitt asked him, "Would you say the same things about Mohammed as you just said about Joseph Smith?" In reply O'Donnell expressed with unusual candor what many other journalists were undoubtedly thinking: "Oh, well, I'm afraid of what the . . . that's where I'm really afraid. I would like to criticize Islam much more than I do publicly, but I'm afraid for my life if I do."[28]

John Voll, associate director of the Prince Alwaleed bin Talal Center for Muslim-Christian Understanding at Georgetown University, also seemed quite ready to condemn those who insulted Muslims—while raising no complaint against Muslims who engaged in violent threats and intimidation. In May 2008 in the Netherlands, the Iranian avant-garde artist Sooreh Hera exhibited a series of photographs that included depictions of Muhammad and his son-in-law Ali, the hero of Shi'ite Islam, in provocative homosexual poses. Death threats followed, forcing the cancellation of the exhibition. Hera's "art" might justly have been deplored or condemned, but that was no justification for threatening her life. Still, Voll chided her for provoking the threats. "Can you imagine," he asked, "what would happen if John McCain used the n-word about Obama while campaigning? There are consequences. Free speech is not absolute."

Yet if McCain really had done such a thing, he probably wouldn't have been killed or even threatened with death. The consequences would have been condemnation and electoral defeat. Voll, however, went farther, essentially suggesting that threats of violence in such circumstances were perfectly justifiable.[29]

The violence unleashed by Muslims throughout the world in response to perceived Western slights of their religion has softened up Western cultural elites, making them more conducive to accept the limits on free speech demanded by Islamic diplomats. Indeed,

with commentators such as Lawrence O'Donnell, Jr., already cen-
soring themselves out of fear, the adoption of international conventions outlawing blasphemy of Islam would just legally enshrine
restrictions that many frightened Westerners already observe.
With potential critics intimidated into silence by the knowledge
that voicing their concerns about Islam will likely result in
ostracism on charges of "bigotry" at best or physical violence at
worst, very few commentators are left who are willing to stand up
publicly to the full scope of the jihadists' efforts.

STIFLING "RACE HATE"—OR STIFLING FREE SPEECH

Perhaps the most disturbing aspect of the international campaign against free speech is that many Western governments
already enforce it on their own people. In fact, international conventions against blasphemy would be largely redundant in many
Western countries, where governments preemptively silence critics of Islam in the name of fighting racial hatred.

In June 2002 Muslims in Switzerland targeted the fearless Italian journalist Oriana Fallaci for her passionate post-September 11
book, *The Rage and the Pride*, in which she argued that Europe
was being colonized by Muslims. Citing Swiss laws against
racism, the Islamic Center of Geneva called for the book to be
banned. Hani Ramadan, brother of the controversial European
Muslim spokesman Tariq Ramadan, declared that "Fallaci is
insulting the Muslim community as a whole with her shameful
words." The Center called on Swiss authorities not only to ban
the sale of her book, but to prosecute those who distributed it.[30]
Swiss officials moved into action, unsuccessfully attempting to
have Fallaci extradited to face trial.[31] This move turned out to be

unnecessary, as the Italian government itself indicted Fallaci in May 2005 for allegedly writing a book that "defames Islam."[32]

The campaign against the author spread to France, where a group calling itself the Movement Against Racism And For Friendship Between Peoples (MRAP) also filed racism charges against Fallaci, arguing that "Freedom of expression is and will remain a fundamental right... but when this great writer resorts to outrageous stigmatization of Islam, the limits of what is tolerable are breached."[33] In the end, Fallaci escaped prosecution only because she had left Europe and moved to New York. Shortly before she died in 2006, she predicted that when the case came to trial, she would be found guilty.[34]

The guardians of "tolerable" speech had better luck against Sixties screen siren Brigitte Bardot, who has been convicted five times in her native France for "inciting racial hatred"—in every case for remarks considered denigrating to Muslims. In June 2008, a court fined the seventy-three-year-old Bardot 15,000 euros (around $23,000) as punishment for writing that the Islamic community in France was "destroying our country and imposing its acts."[35] The court apparently didn't consider the possibility that imposing Islamic law was precisely what many Muslims in France had in mind.

Such prosecutions have already come to North America. On February 14, 2006, a Canadian magazine, the *Western Standard*, became one of the few publications in the Western world to reprint the Danish Muhammad cartoons. The Islamic Supreme Council of Canada and the Edmonton Muslim Council complained that the *Standard*'s publisher, Ezra Levant, was inciting hatred against Muslims, sparking an investigation of Levant by the Alberta Human Rights and Citizenship Commission. After Levant delivered a ringing defense of freedom of speech during his interrogation by a commission investigator, the Islamic Supreme Council—facing a groundswell of righteous indignation and support for Levant—withdrew its complaint.[36] The same public anger was surely behind the Alberta Human Rights and Citizenship's Council's later decision to dismiss a near-identical complaint filed against Levant by another Muslim group.

Even higher in profile was the case in Canada against *Maclean's* magazine for running an excerpt from *America Alone*, a book by the popular columnist Mark Steyn. Charging that Steyn's "flagrantly Islamophobic" writing subjected Canadian Muslims to "hatred and contempt," the Canadian Islamic Congress (CIC) filed complaints against *Maclean's* with three separate Human Rights Commissions.[37] Although widespread ridicule and mounting calls to reduce the commissions' powers have forced two of them to dismiss the complaints, an investigation by a third commission is still ongoing.

To be sure, Steyn's excerpt was pretty strong stuff, taken from a book arguing that Europe is destined for an Islamic takeover. Characteristic of the CIC's complaints was its objection to Steyn's contention that in Europe, "the number of Muslims is expanding like mosquitoes."[38]

"Expanding like mosquitoes!" No wonder the CIC was upset. And not just the CIC; writer Jim Henley, whose articles have appeared in *The New Republic* and *The American Spectator Online*, quoted that line before labeling Steyn a "racist."[39]

There is just one problem: the line did not originate with Steyn. He was quoting Mullah Krekar, a jihadist who continues to reside in Norway, despite longstanding efforts to deport him.

And Krekar's prediction of an Islamic demographic conquest of Europe is hardly original in the Muslim world. Algerian leader Houari Boumédienne declared at the United Nations way back in

1974, "One day, millions of men will leave the Southern Hemisphere to go to the Northern Hemisphere. And they will not go there as friends. Because they will go there to conquer it. And they will conquer it with their sons. The wombs of our women will give us victory."[40]

It was not Steyn who said that "Islam will return to Europe as a conqueror and victor," or that "The conquest this time will not be by the sword but by preaching and ideology." Those sentiments were uttered by Al-Jazeera's Sheikh Yusuf Al-Qaradhawi, who is widely hailed as a "moderate" reformer in the West and is a close friend of former London Mayor Ken Livingstone.[41] Did Steyn say that Muslims "will control the land of the Vatican; we will control Rome and introduce Islam in it"? No again: that one comes from a Saudi Sheikh, Muhammad bin Abd Al-Rahman Al-'Arifi, imam of the mosque of King Fahd Defense Academy.

With the CIC, we see the great lengths to which Western-based Muslim advocacy groups will go to silence public discussion of jihadists' self-stated goals. The CIC doesn't file complaints against the jihadists who actually advocate an Islamic conquest of Europe; they just go after publications such as *Maclean's* that allow people to report these exhortations—as if it is somehow an act encouraging "hatred and contempt" to reveal the unpleasant reality that comprises mainstream Islamic rhetoric.

And the jihadists' campaign is assisted by their cringing, apologizing enablers in the Canadian "human rights" commissions. In this they are energetically helping the stealth jihad. There is no indication that the commissions have done a thing to investigate the possibility that some Muslims in Canada might hold the views of Mullah Krekar, Boumédienne, Qaradhawi and Sheikh Muhammad. If the commissions truly wanted to combat racial incitement, they should have investigated the CIC president, Mohamed Elmasry, who proclaimed on a television show in 2004 that all Israelis over age eighteen were legitimate military targets. Israelis, however, apparently don't fit into the commissions' racial paradigm for groups that should be accorded protected minority status.

In light of their willingness to prevent their own citizens from criticizing Islam, it should come as no surprise to see Western governmental officials bending over backward to avoid offending Muslims in their own rhetoric and policies. We saw in the previous chapter that U.S. officials are instructed not to refer to Islamic terrorists as "jihadists." The British government has adopted this approach but taken it one Orwellian step further, calling for Islamic terrorism to be renamed "anti-Islamic activity." Home Secretary Jacqui Smith explained, "As so many Muslims in the UK and across the world have pointed out, there is nothing Islamic about the wish to terrorise, nothing Islamic about plotting murder, pain and grief. Indeed, if anything, these actions are anti-Islamic."[42]

The move came in January 2008, after the British government had already decided to admonish top officials not to refer to the "war on terror." According to the *Daily Mail*, "Officials were concerned it [the phrase "war on terror"] could act as a recruiting tool for al Qaeda, which is determined to manufacture a battle between the values of Islam and the West."[43] The U.S. followed suit in May 2008 when Charles Allen, the senior intelligence official at the Department of Homeland Security, recommended that Americans also drop the phrase "war on terror." He explained that this "has nothing to do with political correctness. It is interpreted in the Muslim world as a war on Islam and we don't need this."[44]

The British and U.S. governments have somehow failed to notice that a battle between Western and Islamic values already exists, and that the terminology of Western officials has not provoked it. This battle plays out every time a Westerner refrains from criticizing or lampooning Islam for fear of being prosecuted or physically attacked, or simply vilified as a racist and bigot. British officials should ask the Danish Mohammad cartoonists, Mark Steyn, Geert Wilders, and Salman Rushdie whether there's a conflict between Islamic and Western values. Unfortunately, it's too late to ask Theo van Gogh.

THE LEGAL JIHAD

Stealth jihadists, backed by their violent counterparts, have made great strides in silencing Islam's critics. But they find it intolerable that here and there, a few people are still willing to speak out publicly about the connection between Islam and terrorism. With intimidation failing, they've adopted another method to suppress these recalcitrants—getting the courts to do the silencing for them. Rachel Ehrenfeld, founder and director of the American Center for Democracy, stands today as one of the primary targets of the legal jihad.

Billionaire Saudi financier Khalid Salim bin Mahfouz sued Ehrenfeld for libel after she wrote in her book *Funding Evil* that he was involved in funding Hamas and al Qaeda. Bin Mahfouz denied that he had knowingly given any money to either. However, he didn't sue her in the United States, where her book was published. Rather, taking advantage of British libel laws that place the burden of proof on the defendant rather than the plaintiff, bin Mahfouz sued Ehrenfeld in Britain. Neither he nor Ehrenfeld live there; his entire case depended upon a handful of copies of her book sold in that country mostly through special orders from Amazon.com, and the appearance of one chapter of the book on the Internet—where it may have been read by British readers.

If this looks like legal thuggery, it's because that's exactly what it is. Bin Mahfouz wasn't the first public figure to use British law as an easy means to suppress his critics: Britain's libel laws have given rise to the phenomenon of wealthy "libel tourists" (or "libel terrorists"), who sue there on the slimmest British connection in order to ensure a favorable ruling. In the Ehrenfeld case, bin Mahfouz had the good fortune of having the case heard by Judge David Eady, who has a long history of strange rulings in libel cases—rulings that generally ran in favor of censorship and against free speech. In connection with another of these rulings in May 2007, British journalist Stephen Glover wrote, "Mr Justice Eady is beginning to worry me. Is he a friend of a free Press? There are good reasons to believe that he isn't."[45]

In May 2005 Justice Eady ruled that Ehrenfeld had to apologize to bin Mahfouz and pay over $225,000. This fine remains uncollected, and Ehrenfeld sees no reason to say she's sorry. However, now she cannot travel to Britain, and her writing and research work has of course been banned there—thus preventing important information from reaching the public.

Ehrenfeld countersued in New York, asking the Second Circuit Court of Appeals for a declaration that the British judgment was contrary to the First Amendment and hence unenforceable on a U.S. citizen. The court agreed, and efforts to give U.S. writers protection from legal intimidation went farther still: on April 30, 2008, New York Governor David Paterson signed The Libel Terrorism Protection Act, which has also come to be known as "Rachel's Law" in honor of Ehrenfeld. The act, according to the Governor's office, "offers New Yorkers greater protection against libel judgments in countries whose laws are inconsistent with the freedom of speech granted by the United States Constitution."

Paterson explained: "New Yorkers must be able to speak out on issues of public concern without living in fear that they will be sued outside the United States, under legal standards inconsistent

with our First Amendment rights. This legislation will help ensure
the freedoms enjoyed by New York authors." He called upon the
other states and the Federal Government to follow suit:
"Although New York State has now done all it can to protect our
authors while they live in New York, they remain vulnerable if
they move to other states, or if they have assets in other states. We
really need Congress and the President to work together and enact
federal legislation that will protect authors throughout the country against the threat of foreign libel judgments."[46]

Ehrenfeld has not been bin Mahfouz's only victim. In August
2007, after legal threats from bin Mahfouz, the Cambridge University Press withdrew from publication and destroyed all copies
of another book that examined the alleged money trail between
bin Mahfouz and the jihadists: *Alms for Jihad: Charity And Terrorism in the Islamic World* by J. Millard Burr and Robert O.
Collins. The Press asked bookstores to return their copies, and
even requested that libraries remove the book from their shelves.
Lawyers for the Press wrote to bin Mahfouz, unctuously declaring his innocence: "Throughout the book there are serious and
defamatory allegations about yourself and your family, alleging
support for terrorism through your businesses, family and charities, and directly. As a result of what we now know, we accept and
acknowledge that all of those allegations about you and your family, businesses and charities are entirely and manifestly false."[47]

However, even the Bin Mahfouz Information website, a pro-bin
Mahfouz outlet that aims "to provide accurate information for
accredited journalists, governments and NGOs about Khalid Bin
Mahfouz and his immediate family," acknowledges that bin Mah-
fouz was initially the "principal donor" to the Muwafaq ("Blessed
Relief") Foundation,[48] an Islamic charity that the Treasury
Department identified in October 2001 as "an al Qaeda front that

receives funding from wealthy Saudi businessmen."[49] Bin Mahfouz insists that he had no involvement in Muwafaq's operations, and that may well be true; however, to discover links between his money and the global jihad is not as gratuitous and far-fetched as his libel adventures might suggest.

Meanwhile, there came to light in late June 2007 a September 13, 2001, note from France's foreign intelligence agency, the General Directorate of External Security (DGSE). The French news site Geopolitique.com obtained the note, and has revealed that already in 1996 Mr. bin Mahfouz was known as one of the architects of a banking scheme constructed for the benefit of Osama bin Laden. Moreover, the report claims that both U.S. and British intelligence services knew this.[50]

This is just the latest addition to the mountain of evidence from which Ehrenfeld constructed her case in *Funding Evil*, and Burr and Collins constructed theirs in *Alms for Jihad*. Even if this evidence is all mistaken, the immediate capitulation of Cambridge University Press and the British libel judgment against Ehrenfeld appear all the more fantastic and unjustifiable in light of the fact that French intelligence agents had documents causing them to come to the same conclusions that the authors did.

This demonstrates that if Saudis or others who have indeed supported the global jihad are able to cover their tracks using British libel laws to silence investigators, the only winners are the jihadists. "The British legal and political leadership's constant appeasement of the jihadists," says Ehrenfeld, "facilitated the rise of terrorism." She sees consequences for both the United States and Britain in her legal struggle: "My fight against bin Mahfouz is not only to prevent the extension of that influence here—to defend our First Amendment from British laws. My success here would deter other jihadists from using the British courts to silence

U.S. writers and publishers especially since it would—in similar situations—render U.K. court decisions useless."[51]

Fortunately, U.S. political leaders have taken notice of this pressing threat to free speech. In mid-2008, both the House and the Senate introduced bills to prohibit the judgments in these kinds of foreign libel cases from being enforced in U.S. courts.

While the approval of these bills is crucial for the protection of free expression in the United States, libel tourism is just one part of the larger legal jihad in the West. Stealth jihadists will use—and are using—all available legal channels to silence criticism of their agenda, their activities, and of Islam in general. By turning to the courts, stealth jihadist organizations maintain their carefully constructed facade of moderation—after all, suing somebody these days is as American as apple pie. However, when combined with media assaults by these groups on their critics, and working against a backdrop of violent threats against them, a broader campaign of intimidation emerges.

Islam is a religion of peace, we are told. And anyone who argues otherwise better watch out.

CHAPTER FIVE

THE FACE OF ISLAMIC MODERATION? CAIR, MPAC, AND OTHER "MODERATE" MUSLIM GROUPS

As we have seen, the U.S. government refuses to address the connection between jihadist terrorism and the theological tenets of Islam. In the government's view, the jihadists' argument that the Qur'an and other fundamental Islamic texts justify terrorism and Islamic supremacism is an anomaly, or even a heresy, in the Islamic world at large. U.S. policy dictates that the government work to marginalize the ostensibly small number of "extremists," and form connections instead with representatives of the "moderate" majority of Muslims who offer a viable alternative to the "extreme" interpretation of Islam proffered by Osama bin Laden and other jihadists.

Unfortunately, the "moderate" groups to which the government turns are hardly the mainstream organizations they claim to be. When we scratch the "moderate" surface of groups such as the Council on American-Islamic Relations (CAIR) and the Muslim Public Affairs Council (MPAC), we find links to terrorist organizations and exhortations to Islamic supremacism.

Though pursing a radical agenda, these organizations realized that extremist pronouncements and activities would be counterproductive, resulting in negative media attention and even criminal investigations. So they've adopted a new modus operandi—the stealth jihad. Instead of publicly proclaiming the inevitable arrival of sharia in the United States, they attempt to Islamize the United States quietly, through a long-term strategy aimed at undermining national security, forcing ever greater accommodation of Islamic practices, and minimizing any criticism whatsoever of Islam or of virtually any Muslim individual.

THE TWO FACES OF CAIR

CAIR has clearly emerged as the leading advocacy group for Muslims in the United States. When government officials and journalists need a Muslim perspective, they are likely to turn to CAIR, which they assume is a prime example of a moderate, patriotic American Muslim organization, the very existence of which proves that the overwhelming majority of American Muslims are perfectly happy in a pluralistic republic ruled by a non-Islamic government.

CAIR, in turn, uses its connections in elite society to bolster its pretenses of being moderate and mainstream. The organization's website features the following paeans to CAIR from congressmen and senators of both parties, as well as security and military officials:[1]

- "This outstanding event offers an opportunity to gather and recognize the true value of the contributions CAIR provides to its members and the entire community."—Sen. John Warner (R-VA)

- "I applaud CAIR's mission to enhance understanding and build coalitions that promote justice and mutual understanding."—Sen. Paul Sarbanes (D-MD)
- "Throughout its decade of existence, CAIR-LA has been instrumental in promoting cultural and religious understanding of the Muslim community....I commend CAIR-LA for playing a vital role in the integration of the Muslim community into American society in an effort to promote patriotism and pride in their home country."—Rep. Gary Miller (R-CA)
- "In a difficult environment, CAIR has much to be proud of. On the key civil rights issues of our time, CAIR has been out front. Energetic, quick to enter the debate, vigilant, CAIR has earned a reputation as a force to be reckoned with. Good thing, as the stakes could not be higher."—Rep. Dennis J. Kucinich (D-OH)
- "Since the tragic events of September 11, 2001, the Los Angeles FBI has worked closely with CAIR, and a multitude of other community based organizations, to develop and foster relationships that encourage an open exchange of ideas and concerns relative to the FBI's mission."—J. Stephen Tidwell, assistant director in charge, Los Angeles, California Field Office of the FBI
- "[CAIR-Chicago's] commitment to maintaining a dialogue leading to the frank and honest exchange of ideas, concerns and recommendations on issues affecting the communities we mutually serve is laudable."—Weysan Dunn, Special Agent in Charge, Springfield, Illinois Office of the FBI

- "The efforts of the Council on American-Islamic Relations (CAIR) in improving cross cultural communications is commendable."—Brigadier General Mark Wheeler, Chairman Senior National Representatives Coordination Group, United States Central Command.

The government places a high degree of trust in CAIR, which has conducted "sensitivity training" to teach government officials and law enforcement officers how to interact with Muslims. What's more, CAIR officials have been granted access to vital security procedures, such as airport security protocols. In June 2006, U.S. Customs and Border Protection agencies gave CAIR officials a tour of security operations at Chicago's O'Hare International Airport. According to CAIR's Chicago office, "the group walked through Customs and Borders operations beginning at the point of entry for passenger arrival to customs stations, agricultural screening, and the interview rooms. The agents described the 'Passenger Lookout Override' system that was implemented two months ago, in which a passenger who has the same or a similar name as a person with a suspicious record can be distinguished from the actual suspected person."[2]

CAIR presents itself as a mainstream civil rights organization for Muslims. According to CAIR spokesman Ibrahim Hooper, "We are similar to a Muslim NAACP."[3] The group says its mission is "to enhance understanding of Islam, encourage dialogue, protect civil liberties, empower American Muslims, and build coalitions that promote justice and mutual understanding."[4]

This mainstream image, however, is a carefully constructed facade behind which lies a more ambitious—and sinister—agenda. The "moderate" public statements of CAIR spokesmen may fool some politicians and a large number of gullible reporters, but the group's radical nature is constantly being exposed by government prosecutors and terrorism experts. And the evidence compiled from CAIR officials' own actions and words indicate beyond any doubt that CAIR is a stealth jihadist organization that ultimately seeks the imposition of Islamic law in the United States.

Perhaps the biggest blow to CAIR's moderate facade came on June 4, 2007, when the Justice Department named CAIR an unindicted co-conspirator in the Holy Land Foundation jihad terror funding case. Identifying CAIR as a present or past member of "the U.S. Muslim Brotherhood's Palestine Committee and/or its organizations," federal prosecutors stated that CAIR was a participant in a criminal conspiracy on behalf of the jihad terror group Hamas, which allegedly received funding from the Holy Land Foundation for Relief and Development (HLFRD), a now-defunct charity that was supported by CAIR.[5]

CAIR not only facilitated donations to the HLFRD, but also received half a million dollars from it. When confronted with this fact by terrorism analyst Steven Emerson in 2003, CAIR cofounder Nihad Awad vehemently denied the allegation: "This is an outright lie. Our organization did not receive any seed money from HLFRD. CAIR raises its own funds and we challenge Mr. Emerson to provide even a shred of evidence to support his ridiculous claim." Emerson duly produced the canceled check.[6]

CAIR's very establishment was rooted in the jihadist movement. It arose in 1994 as a spinoff of a Hamas front group, the Islamic Association for Palestine (IAP). Founded in 1981 by Hamas operative Mousa Abu Marzook, the IAP was shut down after a jury in a terrorism-related civil suit in December 2004 found that the organization, along with other Islamic fundraisers, had funded Hamas—a ruling that an appellate court later reversed.[7] According to an August 14, 2001, report from the

Immigration and Naturalization Services, the IAP was dedicated to "publishing and distributing HAMAS communiqués printed on IAP letterhead[s], as well as other written documentation to include the HAMAS charter and glory records, which are tributes to HAMAS' violent 'successes.'" The same report also stated that IAP had received "approximately $490,000 from [Mousa Abu] Marzook during the period in which Marzook held his admitted role as a HAMAS leader."[8]

Emerson referred to the IAP as Hamas's "primary voice in the United States," while a former chief of the FBI's counter-terrorism department, Oliver Revell, called the IAP "a front organization for Hamas that engages in propaganda for Islamic militants."[9]

This was the organization that gave birth to CAIR, whose cofounders, Nihad Awad and Omar Ahmad, served as IAP's president and public relations director, respectively.[10]

Since then, CAIR's current and former leaders are continually forced to explain the tremendous gap between the radical statements they made and the ties to jihadist groups they maintained in the past, and the "moderate" face that CAIR struggles to project today. These statements include the declarations discussed in chapter one, such as Ahmad's assertion that "Islam isn't in America to be equal to any other faith, but to become dominant," as well as Hooper's own stated preference for "the government of the United States to be Islamic sometime in the future." Today, Ahmad denies uttering the quote, while Hooper, in his prolific television appearances, now refrains from such direct utterances of support for Islamic supremacism.

Awad has shown the same tendency. In 1994 at Barry University in Florida, Awad proclaimed, "I'm in support of [the] Hamas movement more than the PLO"[11]—an unsurprising statement coming from the former president of a Hamas front group. However, Awad's open support for Hamas became a liability in 2006, when a Muslim candidate for Congress, Keith Ellison (D-MN), came under fire for his ties to CAIR. So Awad conveniently moderated his position, declaring, "I don't support Hamas today. My position and CAIR's position is extremely clear—we condemn suicide bombings. We are mainstream American Muslims."[12]

A final example is provided by the prominent U.S. Muslim spokesman Siraj Wahhaj, who is a former member of CAIR's advisory board. In the early 1990s he sponsored talks in New York City and New Jersey mosques by Sheikh Omar Abdel Rahman, the "blind sheikh" now imprisoned for conspiring to blow up the World Trade Center in 1993. In fact, Wahhaj was designated a "potential unindicted co-conspirator" in the case.[13] This is all consistent with Wahhaj's stated political and religious views, which include a warning that the United States will fall unless it "accepts the Islamic agenda."[14]

But soon after September 11, Wahhaj began singing a new tune. He pledged his efforts against the ideology of those who brought down the twin towers: "I now feel responsible to preach, actually to go on a jihad against extremism."[15] Gone are the assertions of Islamic supremacism—at least, they're gone from the statements he makes in public. Having completely overhauled his image, Wahhaj is now often trotted out by the media as a spokesman for "moderate" Muslims.

CAIR's ties to the stealth jihad are manifold. It was connected to the notorious "Flying Imams" lawsuit, in which six Muslim clerics sued US Airways in 2007 after they were removed from a flight for suspicious behavior. Their lawyer was Omar T. Mohammedi, a former president of CAIR's New York chapter.[16] The imams also initially sued the anonymous passengers who reported them, before House Republicans pushed through a measure protecting whistleblowers in such circumstances.[17] If successful, this effort would have been an immensely important contribution to the stealth jihad, for it would have essentially placed Muslims beyond the pale of security-related scrutiny; anyone who reported suspicious behavior by a Muslim in an airport or airplane would have faced a real risk of being sued for discrimination.

With such a record, it should come as no surprise that CAIR has financial ties to the virulently supremacist Islamic Wahhabi sect promoted by Saudi Arabia. According to its Form 990 filings for 2003, CAIR invested $325,000 from its California offices with the North American Islamic Trust (NAIT). According to a September 2002 *Newsweek* report, "NAIT money has helped the Saudi Arabian sect of Wahhabism—or Salafism, as the broader, pan-Islamic movement is called—to seize control of hundreds of mosques in U.S. Muslim communities."[18] NAIT also shows up among the allied organizations listed in the 1991 Muslim Brotherhood "grand jihad" memorandum on its strategy in the United States—along with the Islamic Association for Palestine (IAP), CAIR's predecessor.

The Muslim Brotherhood itself is extremely uncomfortable answering questions about its relationship with CAIR; Brotherhood officials don't want to undermine CAIR by acknowledging a close relationship, but they're also reluctant to deny outright their tight connection with a friendly organization. Their discomfort in discussing this topic becomes almost comical, as evident in this interview by an Egyptian blogger with Mohamed Habib, the second highest-ranking Brotherhood official:

Is there a Muslim Brotherhood in the U.S.?

Mohamed Habib: I would say yes. There are Muslim Brotherhood members there....

This is naturally very important. Who represents you in the US?

Mohamed Habib: Well, there are there those who do represent us, who do that role.

But it's not CAIR, right? The Council for American Islamic Relations? Many people say that they are your front. Other people say that its ISNA. But back to CAIR, some people from the Muslim Brotherhood have denied having a connection with CAIR. Do they really represent you?

Mohamed Habib: Ehh, this is a sensitive subject, and it's kind of problematic, especially after 9/11 ...

For them to say that there is a relationship between you two?

Mohamed Habib: Yes. You can say that.[19]

And Habib is right; it *is* problematic for CAIR, an organization presenting itself as a "mainstream" civil rights group, to admit to a relationship with an Islamic fundamentalist organization that aims, in its own words, to undertake "a kind of grand jihad in eliminating and destroying the Western civilization from within." One might begin to suspect that CAIR has some hidden agenda.

Despite its careful image makeover, the evidence of CAIR's real, radical agenda is so overwhelming that some security experts have been warning about the group for years. For example, Steven Emerson has for years called CAIR "a radical fundamentalist front group for Hamas,"[20] while Steven Pomerantz, the FBI's former chief of counterterrorism, stated long before CAIR was named as an unindicted co-conspirator in the Holy Land Foundation case that "CAIR, its leaders, and its activities effectively give aid to international terrorist groups."[21]

And politicians are catching on as well. According to Senator Richard Durbin (D-IL), CAIR is "unusual in its extreme rhetoric and its associations with groups that are suspect." Senator Charles Schumer (D-NY) has asserted that CAIR "has ties to terrorism" and "intimate links with Hamas."[22] Congressman Bill Shuster (R-PA) has bemoaned the fact that "time and again the organization has shown itself to be nothing more than an apologist for groups bent on the destruction of Israel and Islamic domination over the West."[23]

Finally, CAIR's role in the stealth jihad is well known to American victims of terrorism. The family of former FBI counterterrorism chief John P. O'Neill, Sr., who was killed on September 11 in the World Trade Center, has named CAIR in a lawsuit as having "been part of the criminal conspiracy of radical Islamic terrorism" responsible for the September 11 atrocities. The lawsuit charges that CAIR has "actively sought to hamper governmental anti-terrorism efforts by direct propaganda activities aimed at police, first-responders, and intelligence agencies through so-called sensitivity training. Their goal is to create as much self-doubt, hesitation, fear of name-calling, and litigation within police departments and intelligence agencies as possible so as to render such authorities ineffective in pursuing international and domestic terrorist entities." Although judges have thrown out a section of the lawsuit that seeks to hold Saudi Arabia's leaders responsible for the September 11 attacks, the courts have not yet ruled on the remainder of the suit.[24]

The charges contained in the lawsuit point to the seamlessness between CAIR's non-violent civil activities and the violent jihad.

While eschewing violence themselves, CAIR officials work to hinder the fight against Islamic terrorism. They aim to accomplish this by placing Muslims beyond legal scrutiny through the denunciation of citizens, analysts, officials, and prosecutors who voice concerns about any Muslims as "Islamophobes." While the campaign that was most potentially damaging to national security—the Flying Imams lawsuit—was largely neutralized by Congressional action, CAIR has not abandoned its fight to place Muslims above the law.

THE CAIR ARRESTS

Perhaps Nihad Awad and fellow CAIR cofounder Omar Ahmad left the IAP and formed CAIR because they had renounced IAP's "extremism" and had become moderates. If they did, however, they evidently still had some trouble distinguishing moderates from extremists, as shown by the arrest records of people they welcomed into their new organization.

For example, take Randall Todd ("Ismail") Royer, who began working with CAIR in 1997 and served as CAIR's communications specialist and civil rights coordinator. He was part of the "Virginia jihad network," which was indicted on forty-one counts of "conspiracy to train for and participate in a violent jihad overseas" in association with Lashkar-e-Taiba, a jihad terrorist group. Said a prosecutor about the group, "Ten miles from Capitol Hill in the streets of northern Virginia, American citizens allegedly met, plotted, and recruited for violent jihad." Of the eleven Muslim men charged in the case, six pleaded guilty, three were convicted at trial, and two were acquitted. The group's spiritual leader, Ali al-Timimi, received a life sentence. Matthew Epstein of the Investigative Project has said that Royer helped recruit the other member of the group to the jihad while he was working for CAIR.[25]

Royer was also among those charged in a separate indictment alleging that the group conspired to help al Qaeda and the Taliban fight against U.S. troops in Afghanistan. And Royer admitted to a grand jury that he had already waged jihad warfare in Bosnia—and that his commander took orders from Osama bin Laden.

According to Daniel Pipes, "Royer eventually pleaded guilty to lesser firearms-related charges, and the former CAIR staffer was sentenced to twenty years in prison."[26]

In a statement on its website, CAIR reminds readers twice in two sentences that Royer did not plead guilty to any terror charge: "In January 2004, Royer pleaded guilty to weapons charges and did not plead guilty to any charge of 'terrorism.' Notwithstanding the fact that any criminal action to which he pleaded guilty was done when Royer was no longer employed with CAIR and not at CAIR's direction, it is important to note that the only crimes that he pleaded guilty to were weapons charges, not charges of terrorism."[27]

The statement sounds the most resonant left-liberal notes in associating reports about the arrests of the officials with McCarthyism and the attempts to smear Martin Luther King: "This is probably the most widely recycled example of McCarthy-like attempts to portray CAIR as guilty by association. Such efforts evoke memories of attempts to smear Dr. Martin Luther King, Jr. as a communist or womanizer." Furthermore, "When Aldrich Ames (CIA) and Robert Hanssen (FBI) admitted to being spies for foreign governments, it did not automatically associate the CIA or FBI with being complicit in any of these criminal activities."

And CAIR, an organization that so frequently travels in defamation and ad hominem smears of its opponents, couldn't resist characterizing criticism of its employment of jihadist criminals such as Royer as a bigoted attack against all Muslims, charging that "only Islamophobes will assign guilt to Muslims by such false associations. These smears against CAIR are disseminated by agenda-driven extremists who seek to marginalize and disenfranchise the American Muslim community and its leaders."[28]

But is it really equivalent to blaming the CIA and FBI for Ames and Hanssen to see in Royer's actions an indictment of CAIR? The key difference is that the CIA and FBI did not preach the philosophy that Ames and Hanssen acted upon in their espionage; they were, in fact, transgressing against the principles they had promised to uphold when they took their agency jobs. But wasn't Royer transgressing against CAIR's avowed purpose of building bridges between Muslims and non-Muslims, encouraging dialogue, and condemning terrorism? Certainly; but he was not at all transgressing against the principles of Hamas, with which CAIR is so closely entwined, or against the Islamic supremacist principles that Ahmad and Hooper have enunciated.

Another CAIR official involved in jihad activity is Ghassan Elashi, the founder of CAIR's Texas chapter. He was charged with giving Hamas more than $12 million while he was running the Holy Land Foundation for Relief and Development, the charity that has earned CAIR the designation of unindicted co-conspirator. In July 2004 Elashi was convicted of shipping computers illegally to two state-sponsors of terrorism, Libya and Syria. Then in April 2005 he was convicted of knowingly doing business with Mousa Abu Marzook, the senior Hamas leader who founded IAP, some of whose members later created CAIR. He was found guilty of a number of charges, including conspiracy and money laundering.[29]

Regarding Elashi, CAIR points out that it has "hundreds of board members and employees and some 50,000 members. It would be illogical and unfair to hold CAIR responsible for the personal activities of all these people. The fact that Elashi was once associated with one of our more than thirty regional chapters has no legal significance to our corporation given the fact that any actions taken by him were outside the scope and chronology of his association with one of our chapters."[30]

This wording is interesting—Elashi's association with CAIR has no "legal significance" for the organization, "given the fact that any actions taken by him were outside the scope and chronology of his association with one of our chapters." This appears to be claiming that CAIR bears no legal responsibility for Elashi's activities and cannot be included in his prosecution. Fair enough. But conspicuously unstated, in their comments on both Royer and Elashi, is any condemnation of their jihadist actions, or of the philosophy underlying those actions. And since Elashi was doing business with Marzook, who founded IAP, CAIR's predecessor, it is in no sense wild speculation to consider the possibility that Elashi's actions were consistent with, rather than contradictory to, CAIR's actual purposes in the United States. The organization's strangely worded disavowal of Elashi only raises more questions.

The parade of disgraced CAIR officials continues with the March 2003 arrest of Bassem K. Khafagi on charges of bank fraud. News reports identified him as the community affairs director for CAIR's national office in Washington, although CAIR stated that he was "never an employee of CAIR." It acknowledged, however, that he was "an independent contractor for CAIR, effective November 2, 2001."[31] An organization he helped found, the Islamic Assembly of North America (IANA), was suspected of providing websites for two radical Sheikhs with ties to Osama bin Laden.[32] Prosecutors charged that the IANA was dedicated to spreading the "radical Islamic ideology, the purpose of which was indoctrination, recruitment of members, and the instigation of acts of violence and terrorism."[33]

CAIR, however, notes that "on September 10, 2003, EI-Khafagi pleaded guilty to charges of bank and visa fraud. Bank and visa fraud are criminal offenses and not crimes of terrorism. Surely if there had been strong evidence of terrorist activities, the Justice Department would have vigorously pursued those avenues and not allowed him to plead guilty to non-terrorism related charges."[34]

Maybe, maybe not. Given the state of the legal system today, with overloaded dockets and overworked prosecutors and investigators, this assumption is not sound. And here again, CAIR is hewing closely to legal niceties—Khafagi was an independent contractor, not an employee, and pled guilty to bank and visa fraud, not terrorism—while sidestepping the central issues: How did people such as Royer, Elashi, and Khafagi get involved with CAIR in the first place, if the organization is truly moderate and condemns jihad terrorism? How did these men get through the interviewing process? Surely CAIR screens in some way not only prospective employees, but also independent contractors and board members. The Islamic world is engulfed in an immense international upheaval, with millions of jihadists claiming to represent "true Islam" and recruiting among peaceful Muslims on that basis, and somehow that subject never came up when CAIR officials were getting to know Randall Royer, or Bassam Khafagi, or Ghassan Elashi?

CAIR'S "CONDEMNATION" OF TERRORISM

When asked whether they condemn terrorism, CAIR officials frequently point to the organization's endorsement of a fatwa, or

religious ruling, against terrorism issued on July 28, 2005, by the
Fiqh Council of North America, an eighteen-member board of
Islamic scholars and leaders. The declaration received interna-
tional publicity as one of the few instances after the September 11
attacks in which Muslims unequivocally declared that those
attacks were carried out in defiance of the principles of Islam. The
Fiqh Council reissued this fatwa in substantially the same form on
Thanksgiving Day 2007, again to great fanfare.[35]

The original fatwa affirmed "Islam's absolute condemnation of
terrorism and religious extremism." It declared that "Islam strictly
condemns religious extremism and the use of violence against
innocent lives. There is no justification in Islam for extremism or
terrorism." Foreshadowing the State Department's 2008 guidelines directing American officials to refer to jihadists as non-
denominational criminals or evildoers, it declared, "Targeting
civilians' life and property through suicide bombings or any other
method of attack is haram—or forbidden—and those who commit these barbaric acts are criminals, not 'martyrs.' " The statement continued:

> The Qur'an, Islam's revealed text, states: "Whoever kills a
> person [unjustly] ...it is as though he has killed all mankind.
> And whoever saves a life, it is as though he had saved all
> mankind. (Qur'an, 5:32)
>
> Prophet Muhammad said there is no excuse for commit-
> ting unjust acts: "Do not be people without minds of your
> own, saying that if others treat you well you will treat them
> well, and that if they do wrong you will do wrong to them.
> Instead, accustom yourselves to do good if people do good
> and not to do wrong (even) if they do evil." (Al-Tirmidhi)

Extrapolating from such principles, the Fiqh Council declared:

> In the light of the teachings of the Qur'an and Sunnah we
> clearly and strongly state:
>
> 1. All acts of terrorism targeting civilians are haram (forbid-
> den) in Islam.
>
> 2. It is haram for a Muslim to cooperate with any individual
> or group that is involved in any act of terrorism or violence.
>
> 3. It is the civic and religious duty of Muslims to cooperate
> with law enforcement authorities to protect the lives of all
> civilians.[36]

The 2007 version slightly hedges on the third point, rewording it
thusly: "It is the duty of Muslims to report to enforcement authorities any threat which is designed to place a human being in harm's
way, bringing them before a competent court of law and in accordance with due process."[37] The reference to "a competent court
of law and in accordance with due process" may refer to the
ongoing controversy over the jihadists detained at the Guantanamo Bay prison camp, as well as to charges that Muslims in
the U.S. have been unlawfully detained.

In any case, these are not the unequivocal condemnations of
jihad violence that many non-Muslim analysts have taken them to
be. The chief weakness of both declarations is that they don't
define their terms. While non-Muslim Westerners may assume a
particular meaning for "terrorism," "innocent lives," and "civilians," these are in fact hotly debated terms in the Islamic world.

For example, Anjem Choudhury, a spokesman for a leading jihad group in Britain, told an interviewer that the victims of the July 7, 2005 bombings in London were not "innocent," because they were not Muslims: "When we say innocent people, we mean Muslims. As far as non-Muslims are concerned, they have not accepted Islam. As far we are concerned, that is a crime against God....As far as Muslims are concerned, you're innocent if you are a Muslim. Then you are innocent in the eyes of God. If you are non-Muslim, then you are guilty of not believing in God."[38]

This argument is by no means uncommon in the Muslim world. A Palestinian Arab jihadist expressed a similar sentiment in justifying attacks on Israeli civilians. "There are no civilians in Israel. All the Israelis are military, all of them," he insisted. "They are all military and they all have weapons and guns, and the moment they are called up they are going to be using their weapons against me."[39] The Tunisian jihadist Rashid al-Ghannushi has issued a fatwa to the same effect, declaring, "There are no civilians in Israel. The population—males, females, and children—are the army reserve soldiers, and thus can be killed."[40]

What's more, this view—that there are no innocent civilians among Muslims' perceived enemies—is not confined to some extremist Islamic fringe. The internationally influential Sheikh Yusuf al-Qaradawi, who was won praise from Islamic scholar John Esposito for engaging in a "reformist interpretation of Islam and its relationship to democracy, pluralism and human rights," addressed the morality of suicide bombings against Israeli women and civilians thus: "Israeli women are not like women in our society because Israeli women are militarised. Secondly, I consider this type of martyrdom operation as indication of justice of Allah almighty. Allah is just. Through his infinite wisdom he has given the weak what the strong do not possess and that is the ability to turn their bodies into bombs like the Palestinians do."[41]

And this viewpoint is by no means limited to the Israeli-Palestinian conflict. According to the Middle East Media Research Institute, the day after the London bombings, Dr. Hani Al-Siba'i, director of the Al-Maqreze Centre for Historical Studies in London, said on Al-Jazeera, "The term 'civilians' does not exist in Islamic religious law.... I'm familiar with religious law. There is no such term as 'civilians' in the modern Western sense. People are either of Dar Al-Harb [House of War] or not."[42]

The fact that a significant number of Muslims, including such high-profile figures as Qaradawi, hold such views illustrates the inadequacy of the statements issued by the Fiqh Council of North America. Were the issuers of these statements, and its supporters such as CAIR, really trying to convince their fellow Muslims that contemporary jihad terrorism is illegitimate? If so, it was not enough to condemn "terrorism"—not enough, that is, if the council was trying to win over to their point of view people who don't believe that what they are doing constitutes terrorism at all. It is not enough to condemn the killing of "innocent civilians" when the jihadists don't believe their victims are either innocent or civilians.

Moreover, CAIR officials have repeatedly declined to condemn Hamas and Hizballah as terrorist groups. Although they will issue such a condemnation when it's politically necessary—such as Awad's disavowal of Hamas during Keith Ellison's election campaign—CAIR representatives really don't like to speak ill of such organizations. When a reporter from the *Los Angeles Times* asked a CAIR spokeswoman, Munira Syeda, to condemn Hamas or Hizballah as terrorist groups, she responded, "I don't understand what the relevance is."[43] In April 2007 I participated in a heated hour-long radio debate with CAIR's Hussam Ayloush, during which I asked him repeatedly to condemn Hamas and Hizballah as terrorist groups. He refused.

MPAC: GOOD COP TO CAIR'S BAD COP?

Another prominent Muslim organization shares all of CAIR's claims to moderation and on the surface seems to have few, if any, of CAIR's shortcomings: the Muslim Public Affairs Council (MPAC). Immediately after the July 7, 2005 London bombings, MPAC appeared to issue an unequivocal condemnation of the bombers and of terrorism in general. "Any individual or group that claims that these heinous actions serve as a redress for legitimate grievances," MPAC thundered, "is dreadfully mistaken. MPAC condemns the exploitation of people and issues, regardless of the perpetrators and their justifications. This assault is unmistakably an act of terrorism, an attack against humanity."[44]

In a July 12, 2005 statement, the organization went farther: "MPAC has never supported any organizations that support or utilize violence—i.e. terrorism, suicide bombings, beheadings, etc. To do so would be antithetical to the values of sanctity of human life, justice, mercy, and equality for all that make up MPAC's vision statement. In fact, MPAC officials have frequently been on record unequivocally condemning all varieties of violence committed in the name of religion."[45]

As in CAIR's case, such words are welcome but ultimately hollow without deeds to back them up. And far more than CAIR, MPAC can claim that it has done those deeds. For several years after September 11, the group touted its "National Anti-Terrorism Campaign," garnering uncritical publicity in the media and even praise from government officials. The campaign proclaimed,

"It is our duty as American Muslims to protect our country and to contribute to its betterment."[46] MPAC calls for "religious awareness and education to create a strong Islamic environment that does not allow terrorism to be considered as a form of struggle in Islam. The different acceptable forms of struggle in Islam are part of the noble concept of jihad. This doesn't tolerate hurting civilians, suicidal destruction of human life or inflicting harm on non-combatants."[47]

This statement, however, had all the weaknesses of the Fiqh Council's fatwa against terrorism. If MPAC really hopes to have an impact against this kind of thinking among Muslims, it must confront and refute it on Islamic grounds. Its campaign against terrorism did not address that need.

The campaign's inadequacy is evident, among other points, in MPAC's rejection of the "suicidal destruction of human life," a formulation that assumes what it has to establish: that suicide bombing should indeed be classified as suicide and thus considered to be forbidden in Islamic law. This is a much-disputed point; Sheikh Yusuf Al-Qaradawi, for example, argues that such bombers are not, in fact, suicidal: "It's not suicide, it is martyrdom in the name of God, Islamic theologians and jurisprudents have debated this issue. Referring to it as a form of jihad, under the title of jeopardising the life of the mujahideen. It is allowed to jeopardise your soul and cross the path of the enemy and be killed."[48]

How would MPAC propose to disabuse Muslims of such ideas? This should be the only point of Muslim anti-terror campaigns: to convince Muslims that violence and supremacism are not part of their faith. A simple way to do this would be to declare unequivocally two things: that non-Muslim non-combatants always qualify as civilians just like Muslim non-combatants do, and that suicide bombings are, in fact, a form of suicide, and therefore prohibited. But MPAC, like CAIR and the Fiqh Council, made no such statement.

MPAC does, however, convey the *appearance* of working to do just that: it declares that its intention is to "send a clear message to our fellow citizens that terrorism is not a part of our faith, and that we stand shoulder-to-shoulder with them against terrorism and religious extremism."[49] To this end, it calls on mosques to "have a relationship that involves public meetings with the FBI's regional office and local law enforcement" and recommends arrangement of programs "in cooperation with local law enforcement agencies to educate and train the community on how to really detect criminal activities."[50]

Such media-friendly proclamations generate a lot of sympathetic coverage. But in its communications with its own supporters, MPAC appears concerned less with rooting out jihadists from within American Muslim communities than with protecting Muslims from uncomfortable attention from law enforcement. This question appears in a Frequently Asked Questions section of the MPAC anti-terror campaign: "By engaging the FBI and law enforcement, aren't we collaborating with the very agencies trampling our civil rights?" The response: "Actually, it has been MPAC's experience that working with local FBI field offices helps protect our civil liberties . . . . Engagement of local law enforcement and local FBI field offices is absolutely critical in protecting our civil liberties. It counters the basic human weakness to make assumptions about a person/community which they have never been in contact with before."

Answering that question might have been a good opportunity for MPAC to tell American Muslims that the best way they could quell suspicions about their loyalties would be to cooperate fully and openly with anti-terror investigations—that the most effective way to protect their civil liberties would be to demonstrate with decisive action their commitment to protecting and defending the safety of the United States and the stability of its constitutional government. But instead MPAC adopts a defensive tone, portraying its call to cooperate with the police as an attempt to defend Muslims' civil liberties—as opposed to root out terrorists—and later in the website vehemently disavowing any intention to call on American Muslims to "'spy' on each other": "Absolutely not. The thought is anathema to our purpose as an organization."[51]

This amounts to an admission that MPAC is not asking Muslims to report on suspicious activity in U.S. mosques. The statement goes on to assert that "when legitimate differences with our government's policies translate into un-Islamic and illegal behavior the Quran obligates us to speak up and act." MPAC, however, does not define what constitutes "un-Islamic and illegal behavior" with any specificity. With Islamic jihadists portraying their activity as simple loyalty to core Islamic principles—in fact, just the opposite of un-Islamic and illegal behavior—how effective can MPAC's anti-terror campaign be?

The rest of MPAC's recommendations are in the same vein, appearing to be more concerned about misbehavior by non-Muslim law enforcement officials in mosques than the possibility of terrorist activity in those mosques.

Its focus is misplaced in other ways as well. It recommends, for example, that "all activities within the mosque and Islamic centers should be authorized by legitimate, acknowledged leadership."[52] That sounds great until one realizes that if a mosque is involved in or sympathetic to terrorist activity, this is probably not because unauthorized persons have somehow wormed their way in among the moderate community. It is much more likely that the jihadist sentiments will come from the mosque leadership—as per the statement by Naqshbandi Sufi leader Sheikh Muhammad Hisham Kabbani that 80 percent of U.S. mosques are controlled by extremists. MPAC, contrary to its professions of moderation, has not examined Kabbani's charges in any serious way, or developed any programs to counter the jihad ideology and Islamic supremacism within U.S. mosques. Instead, it dismissed Kabbani's statements as "an offhand remark in 1998...in some obscure presentation."[53]

But as we saw in chapter four, Kabbani's charges were not made as an "offhand remark," but as prepared testimony, and not in some "obscure presentation," but before a State Department Open Forum. (MPAC achieved a perfect trifecta by also getting the date wrong—Kabbani made his presentation not in 1998, but on January 7, 1999.)[54] Why would MPAC dismiss Kabbani's statement? What would be the result of dismissing without serious investigation the possibility that Islamic supremacists and jihadists control 80 percent of the mosques in the United States? The only beneficiary would be those Islamic supremacists themselves, who—if they are indeed active in mosques in America— would be able to continue their stealth jihad activities unhindered.

RESISTANCE TO TERRORISM IS TERRORISM!

MPAC has also trafficked in moral equivalence between jihadists and anti-jihadists regarding Israel. It was no surprise when the organization joined CAIR and other groups in 2004 in signing a "Joint Muslims/Arab-American Statement on Israel Violence in Gaza." The organizations echoed some of the most virulent rhetoric that jihadists employ in their offensives against the Jewish state, condemning "Israel's recent indiscriminate killings of innocent Palestinians, including many children," without even mentioning the targeting by Palestinian suicide bombers of Israeli citizens on buses and in restaurants, or the Israeli government's diametrically opposed policy of never targeting civilians.[55]

Such extreme rhetoric was nothing new for MPAC. On the afternoon of September 11, 2001, on a Los Angeles radio show, MPAC's Salam al-Maryati added fuel to the wildest, most paranoid conspiracy theories about the attacks that had just unfolded: "If we're going to look at suspects we should look to the groups that benefit the most from these kinds of incidents, and I think we should put the state of Israel on the suspect list because I think this diverts attention from what's happening in the Palestinian territories so that they can go on with their aggression and occupation and apartheid policies."[56]

This was not al-Maryati's only outburst of anti-Israeli malevolence. Daniel Pipes recounts a "February 1996 incident when a Palestinian named Muhammad Hamida shouted the fundamentalist war cry, *Allahu Akbar* (Allah is Great), as he drove his car intentionally into a crowded bus stop in Jerusalem, killing one Israeli and injuring 23 others. Before he could escape or hurt anyone else, Hamida was shot dead. Commenting on the affair, Mr. Al-Marayati said not a word about Hamida's murderous rampage but instead focused on Hamida's death, which he called 'a provocative act,' and demanded the extradition of his executors to America 'to be tried in a U.S. court' on terrorism charges."[57]

Similarly, Ahmed Younis, who was at that time MPAC's national director, declared in March 2005, according to Pipes, "that Adolf Eichmann was himself a Jew, so in fact Jews killed themselves in the Holocaust."[58]

Like their counterparts at CAIR, MPAC officials are reluctant to condemn specific Islamic terrorist organizations. In fact, they

have publicly expressed a disturbing sympathy for Islamic terrorists. Al-Maryati in 1996 equated violent jihadists with the
Founding Fathers: "Most Islamic movements have been branded
as terrorists as a result of the rising extremism from a handful of
militants. American freedom fighters hundreds of years ago were
also regarded as terrorists by the British."[59] Two years later,
MPAC Senior Advisor Maher Hathout told the National Press
Club that the terrorist group "Hizballah is fighting for freedom.... This is legitimate." That same year, when the U.S.
struck al Qaeda sites in Afghanistan and Sudan, Hathout was
furious: "Our country," he sputtered, "is committing an act of
terrorism. What we did is illegal, immoral, unhuman, unacceptable, stupid and un-American."[60]

MPAC'S JIHAD AGAINST STEVEN EMERSON

If MPAC is indeed committed to rooting out Islamic extremists
and terrorists, then it is strange that it has chosen one of the most
prominent terrorism analysts as the chief target of a media smear
campaign.[61] At a conference on "Countering Religious & Political Extremism" held on December 18, 2004 (and later televised
on C-Span), MPAC distributed a forty-eight-page booklet attacking not Osama bin Laden, or his lieutenant Ayman al-Zawahiri,
or the then-leader of al Qaeda in Iraq, Abu Musab al-Zarqawi,
but Steven Emerson. Entitled "Counterproductive Counterterrorism," the booklet sought to frame opposition to Emerson as a
national security issue, labeling his anti-terror efforts "anti-Muslim" after the manner of CAIR's attacks on others it deemed
"Islamophobes": "In order to enhance the security of our country, it is necessary to expose the vocal minority of Americans who
continue to exploit the tragedy of September 11 to advance their

pre-existing anti-Muslim agenda." MPAC excoriated Emerson for asserting that "political correctness enforced by American Muslim groups has limited the public's knowledge about the spread of radical Islam in the U.S."—yet its report attempted to do just that by discrediting one of the chief investigators of jihadist operations in the United States.[62]

It is revealing that MPAC would think that Emerson is doing so much damage—to the security of our country, no less—as to call for such a response. Emerson's anti-terror work has won accolades from across the political spectrum. Former National Security Council Counterterrorism official Richard Clarke, widely viewed as virtually the sole government analyst to warn of the imminent threat presented by al Qaeda before September 11, said of Emerson, "I think of Steve as the Paul Revere of terrorism," adding that through Emerson's briefings, "We'd always learn things we weren't hearing from the FBI or CIA, things which almost always proved to be true."[63]

MPAC's report cites as one of Emerson's "wild accusations" the "declaration that Muslim terrorist sympathizers were hanging out at the White House." Emerson's "accusation," however, is indisputable: Islamic activist Abdurrahman Alamoudi, now serving a twenty-three-year prison sentence after pleading guilty in a Libyan-related terrorism financing case, was at one time, in the words of Daniel Pipes, "a Washington fixture. He had many meetings with both Clintons in the White House and once joined George W. Bush at a prayer service. He arranged a Ramadan fast-breaking dinner for congressional leaders. He six times lectured abroad for the State Department and founded an organization to provide Muslim chaplains for the Department of Defense."[64] Nor was Alamoudi the only one: Sami Al-Arian, who ultimately pled guilty to a charge of conspiracy to aid Palestinian Islamic Jihad in the United States, attended a White House briefing by a senior Bush administration official in June 2001.[65]

Now, why would MPAC object to light being shed on the activities of the likes of Alamoudi and al-Arian?

MPAC'S MUSLIM BROTHERHOOD CONNECTIONS

The MPAC report charges that "Emerson's lack of precision leads him to conflate legitimate organizations that can help America and secure the homeland with others that are neither genuinely American nor transparent." Here it becomes clear why MPAC is in such a froth about Emerson: because of what he knows about MPAC itself. In *American Jihad*, Emerson notes that when Alamoudi encouraged the crowd at an October 2000 rally cosponsored by MPAC to declare their support of the jihad terror groups Hamas and Hizballah, "MPAC's Political Advisor, Mahdi Bray, stood directly behind Alamoudi and was seen jubilantly exclaiming his support for these two deadly terrorist organizations." This was just three weeks after Bray "coordinated and led a rally where approximately 2,000 people congregated in front of the Israeli Embassy in Washington, D.C." Emerson reports that "at one point during the rally, Mahdi Bray played the tambourine as one of the speakers sang, while the crowd repeated: 'Al-Aqsa [Mosque] is calling us, let's all go into jihad, and throw stones at the face of the Jews.'"[66]

In contrast to the image presented by MPAC's anti-terror campaign, Emerson's Investigative Project has documented the group's indefatigable and consistent opposition to the war on terror; the MPAC-linked magazine *The Minaret* has dismissed key anti-terror operations as part of "[t]he American crusade against Islam and Muslims."[67] Emerson has called attention to the fact that in a book called *In Fraternity: A Message to Muslims in America,* coauthor Hassan Hathout, a former MPAC president, is identified as "a close disciple of the late Hassan al-Banna of Egypt."[68] *The Minaret* spoke of Hassan Hathout's closeness to al-Banna in a 1997 article: "My father would tell me that Hassan Hathout was a companion of Hassan al-Banna....Hassan Hathout would speak of al-Banna with such love and adoration; he would speak of a relationship not guided by politics or law but by a basic sense of human decency."[69]

Al-Banna, of course, founded the Muslim Brotherhood, the foremost stealth jihad organization, in Egypt in 1928.

CATCHING EDINA

On May 23, 2007, Emerson appeared on CNBC's *Kudlow and Company* opposite Edina Lekovic, MPAC's communications director. During a contentious exchange, Emerson brought up "something that Ms. Edina Lekovic should be very familiar with: 'When we hear someone refer to the great Mujahid....Osama bin Laden, as a 'terrorist,' we should defend our brother and refer to him as a freedom fighter; someone who has forsaken wealth and power to fight in Allah's cause and speak out against oppressors.'" Emerson noted that "this statement was made after the '98 bombing [in Kenya and Tanzania], and this was made in *Al-Talib* magazine." *Al-Talib* is the publication of the UCLA chapter of the Muslim Students Association, and Emerson noted that Lekovic was editor of *Al-Talib* when this statement was made.

Lekovic became enraged. "Absolutely no. No, I was not. These are lies," she exclaimed. When Emerson stood by his statement, Lekovic insisted, "No, these are absolute mischaracterizations. Mr.

Emerson, your research is—your research is sloppy." She told Emerson, "For your research—for your research to point out and to conduct this kind of character assassination is quite ridiculous."[70]

Unfortunately for Lekovic and MPAC, however, Emerson later produced a copy of the July 1999 issue of *Al-Talib*, showing that Lekovic was listed as a managing editor of the magazine on the *same page* on which the praise of bin Laden appeared.[71] But this too Lekovic brushed aside in a subsequent statement. She characterized Emerson's charge as the "latest desperate attempt at mudslinging" and herself as a "well-respected mainstream Muslim American leader." Emerson, she said, "maliciously attempted to paint me as a supporter of terrorism based on a student publication I briefly worked with while an undergrad at UCLA."

What about the masthead of July 1999 issue of *Al-Talib*? It was a "printing mistake which I had no part in, but which [Emerson] has exploited to serve his agenda. For reasons unknown to me, given that I had already graduated at that time, my name is listed in the staff box as a managing editor of that issue. I had graduated and had no participation in campus life by that time. I had no role in the publication of that issue of the magazine and I had no part in the writing of the article to which he refers."

A simple mistake, then? Emerson in reply noted that "from October 1997 to May 2002, in addition to the July 1999 'The Spirit of Jihad' issue, there are at least 11 other issues of the newspaper which list Ms. Lekovic as either 'managing editor,' 'copy editor,' 'assistant editor' 'writer,' or give her 'special thanks.'"[72] That's a high number of printing mistakes—and it's especially curious that *Al-Talib* would have continued to list Lekovic on the staff three years after she had graduated, if she indeed had no involvement with the magazine.

MORAL INVERSION

In an appalling but increasingly common display of moral inversion, MPAC implied that Emerson and others were equivalent to Islamic terrorists. In a Frequently Asked Questions section about its anti-terror campaign, MPAC's website posed the question: "Why does this campaign focus just on Muslims? Why not extremists amongst Christians and Jews?" The answer: "Without doubt Christian extremists such as Pat Robertson, Jerry Falwell, and Franklin Graham or Jewish extremists such as Daniel Pipes and Steve Emerson need to be held accountable for their falsehoods and distortions."

If Robertson, Falwell, Graham, Pipes or Emerson were beheading and blowing people up in the name of their religion, this equation of "extremists" might be justified. But in reality it is a ghastly bit of character assassination.

And it gets worse. MPAC continues: "But let's face it, if another terrorist attack occurs Christians and Jews will not be the ones rounded up or have their civil liberties effected [sic]."[73]

Let's face it indeed. No one of any stature in the U.S., not Emerson or anyone else, has ever recommended "rounding up" Muslims. And if Muslims are the focus of any special scrutiny when it comes to security-related issues, it's not because of some irrational prejudice fanned by "Islamophobes," but because it is Muslim groups—not Christian or Jewish ones—that are behind the vast majority of terrorist attacks in the world.

It lies within the power of the Islamic community in the United States, and flagship organizations such as CAIR and MPAC, to head off such suspicions by working forthrightly against the jihad ideology: instituting transparent programs, open for inspection, teaching against the ideology of Islamic supremacism, and against any idea that Muslims should work to impose the societal and political aspects of sharia in the United States.

But neither organization is doing that. Nor is any other major Islamic organization in the country. They have a different agenda altogether, one that finds expression in campaigns such as the Flying Imams lawsuit and MPAC's unhinged assaults on the state of Israel.

With "moderate" organizations like CAIR and MPAC, who needs "extremists"?

CHAPTER SIX

YOUR HOUSE IS OUR HOUSE: ACCOMMODATING ISLAM

THE UGLY MUSLIM?

The Ugly American: ever since 1958, when William Lederer and Eugene Burdick published their political novel by that name, the term has become synonymous with the insensitive boor who refuses to adapt to the norms and customs of the country in which he finds himself, but instead demands that the locals bend to accommodate him. It's the single most prevailing stereotype of Americans abroad.

The Ugly American wasn't malevolent; he was just ignorant and careless, and didn't intend to stay permanently in the country in which he found himself, so perhaps he saw no need to study or respect its customs.

Today the Ugly American has receded from the scene. Much more common is a character one might term the Ugly Muslim: this is not all Muslims by any means, but rather a specific kind of Muslim in America or some other Western country who refuses to adapt to infidel ways, but instead demands that infidels adapt to him, even in their native lands. If they take any notice of his existence at all, analysts might be tempted to excuse the Ugly Muslim along the same lines as the Ugly American: he is not supremacist but merely thoughtless.

However, unlike the Ugly American, the Muslim who demands that American institutions, businesses, and organizations change their practices to accommodate him does indeed intend to stay in his new land. And his contempt for the established mores and practices of that new land doesn't stem from thoughtlessness, but from the conviction that those mores and practices are inferior to the ones he brings with him.

It may seem jarring to charge today's primary recipients of multiculturalist solicitude with cultural insensitivity, but it's true. In Europe, Canada, and the United States, groups of Muslims are increasingly demanding that local custom accommodate to them, rather than the other way around, and are doing so based on the proposition that Islamic culture is superior to Western culture, and that Western culture must ultimately give way to it.

While even American conservatives bemoan the baneful influence of American pop culture in the Islamic world (Dinesh D'Souza goes so far as to claim preposterously that this hegemony led to the September 11 attacks), in reality the cultural imports from the West into Muslim countries are often closely regulated. When Bart Simpson became Badr Shamsoon in an Arabic-language version of The Simpsons late in 2005, Mo's Bar was nowhere in sight, Duff Beer became Arab Soda, and bacon was transformed into beef sausage.[1] Sometimes this can go to absurd extremes: In January 2007 a Qatari man bought a Winnie the Pooh book for his daughter from the Saudi-owned Jarir Bookstore chain. On every page, the character Piglet was blacked out with a heavy magic marker—lest the sight of a cartoon pig offend the sensibilities of Muslims who consider the animal unclean.[2]

When Americans travel to Muslim countries today, both sides frown upon the Ugly American. It is simple good manners for Americans and other foreigners to conform to the mores of Muslim countries when they're visiting them. This has occasionally aroused controversy in the United States: pundits and bloggers criticized House Speaker Nancy Pelosi when she wore a headscarf inside the Umayyad Mosque during her visit to Damascus, Syria, in April 2007, as well as First Lady Laura Bush when she donned an Islamic hijab in Saudi Arabia in October of that year. Some even raised eyebrows when Queen Elizabeth II also put on a headscarf when visiting Turkey's famed Green Mosque in May 2008. But it would have been downright discourteous, as well as culturally insensitive, for any of these women to have done anything else.

But this too can go to absurd—and lethal—extremes. In November 2007, a British elementary school teacher in Sudan, Gillian Gibbons, was jailed, convicted of "insulting religion," and threatened with death after allowing her students to name a teddy bear Muhammad. Sudanese President Omar al-Bashir pardoned Gibbons after an international outcry, but not all observers thought that Sudanese Muslims who were calling for Gibbons' head had gone beyond all bounds of common sense and decent behavior.[3]

And not a few of these were in America. Discussing the Gibbons case and Teddy Bear Rage on ABC's women's show *The View* on November 30, 2007, the co-hosts unanimously sided with the Sudanese who were raging at Gibbons. Co-host Sherri Shepherd, who is apparently not a Muslim, inarticulately blurted out, "I think it's, like, it's sacrilegious to name a stuffed toy Muhammad." She placed all the blame for the incident on Gibbons: "But you know, you would think that with her being in

Sudan, she would know the rules and customs." Shepherd herself, a comedienne, said she had experience with cultural accommodation: "Because I know I performed stand up in Turkey, and they gave me a big thick packet on the customs, and what you could and could not do, and how you would offend people. So I'm surprised that she didn't know it might be offensive."

Her fellow comedienne and co-host, Whoopi Goldberg, agreed: "Yeah, because you'd think if you're going overseas, I mean, we had this discussion yesterday about people coming to America and learning the customs and knowing what is cool, and what isn't cool. But I find that maybe we are not—and I say 'we' just as European and American, we're not as anxious to learn the customs before we go places. It's just one of the reasons we're called the ugly Americans."[4]

They were talking, let us remember, about a fifty-four-year-old English schoolteacher who was in Sudan, a country that has been wracked with violence and has one of the poorest human rights records in the world, to do what she could to help the people of that nation. Gillian Gibbons wasn't an American, of course—but was she in the cultural sense an Ugly American? For naming a teddy bear Muhammad at the suggestion of her Muslim students?[5] That seems to be just the opposite of the culture-blind boorishness that the moniker originally denoted: Gibbons was trying to be accommodating to the children's wishes, and in doing so, found herself on the wrong side of more powerful forces demanding a greater and more comprehensive accommodation to Islamic culture. The Ugly American has given way to the Muslim who demands that his sensibilities be accommodated in all circumstances, in non-Muslim as well as Muslim lands, no matter how outrageous, and no matter how violent the threats and fulminations that accompany the demand for accommodation.

Saudi Arabia, of course, is the most notoriously violent enforcer of the dictum *When in Rome, do as the Romans do*. And the native "Romans" in Saudi Arabia are quite strict. Muslims must abide by Islamic law in all its details, even at the expense of their lives. In Mecca in March 2002, fifteen girls perished in a fire at their school when the Saudi religious police, or *muttawa*, refused to let them out of the building. In the female-only school environment, they had shed the all-concealing outer garments that Saudi women must wear in the presence of men. Preferring that the girls die rather than transgress Islamic law by appearing among men without the proper attire, the *muttawa* actually battled police and firemen who were trying to open the school's doors to free the girls.[6]

Non-Muslims visiting or working in the Kingdom have learned that they enjoy no exemption from Islamic laws—and in those laws few things are frowned upon more than any open display of non-Muslim religiosity, including the most innocuous. Former U.S. Foreign Service Officer Tim Hunter, who served in Saudi Arabia from 1993 to 1995, reported that "on occasion they beat, even tortured, Americans in Jeddah for as little as possessing a photograph with a Star of David in the background or singing Christmas carols.... The Mutawa chained, beat and cast clergy into medieval-style dungeons."[7]

One doesn't have to practice a non-Islamic religion to run afoul of Saudi mores. In February 2008, an American businesswoman was jailed, strip-searched, interrogated by the *muttawa,* and ultimately made to sign a false confession. Her crime? After the power went out in the office where she worked, she went to a Starbuck's coffee shop in Riyadh with a male coworker—a man to whom she was not married. "Some men came up to us," she explained, "with very long beards and white dresses. They asked

'Why are you here together?' I explained about the power being out in our office. They got very angry and told me what I was doing was a great sin." They then seized and jailed her—even though she was wearing an Islamic headscarf and had been careful up to that point not to offend Saudi sensibilities.[8]

Brutal, yes, and matters for human rights organizations to take up—yet nevertheless, until they do, the foreign traveler must resign himself to the status quo. Americans traveling in a Muslim country have learned: they must accommodate their behavior to Muslim sensitivities.

WHEN IN AMERICA, ABIDE BY ISLAMIC CUSTOMS TOO

Yet this doesn't go both ways—at least not today. Muslims don't all come to America resolved to do as the Romans do in their host country. Instead, Muslims in the West are increasingly demanding that, rather than assimilating into Western culture, it is Western culture that must adapt to them.

In May 2008, Belgian police were called out to protect a seventeenth-century pulpit in a Catholic church in the town of Dendermonde. The wooden pulpit was constructed in 1685, two years after Islamic jihad armies besieging Vienna were defeated, marking the beginning of the decline of Islamic power in Eastern Europe and the high-water mark of Islamic expansion into Europe. It depicts a bearded man clutching a book, trodden under the feet of angels who are holding up the pulpit. It isn't certain, but most believe that the bearded man is Muhammad and his book is the Qur'an, and that the pulpit commemorates the victory of Christian forces over Islam at Vienna. The police protection became necessary after the Turkish newspaper *Yeni ag* printed a photo of the pulpit, calling it a "hideous insult" and demanding that it be removed. "We have had the crusades," said *Yeni ag*, "and now they are still trying to humiliate us. This is as bad as the Danish cartoons and Geert Wilders's *Fitna* movie in the Netherlands. Even Pope Benedict does nothing to stop these humiliations."[9]

History? Heritage? Tradition? Forget them all. An insult to Islam—whether real or imaginary—meant that they all had to be swept aside.

The same dynamic is evident in the United States: instead of adapting to American mores, increasing numbers of Muslims are demanding that non-Muslims accommodate to their own sensitivities.

Muslims in America have made such demands of individuals, such as Lina Morales, who for ten months held a job at Rising Star, a telecoms company in Florida. One fateful day in 2004 she was eating a bacon, lettuce, and tomato sandwich at work, and was summarily fired for violating a company rule against eating pork products on company premises. However, Morales said that she had never agreed to comply by any such rule, and indeed, "When I got hired there, they said we don't care what religion you are."

Rising Star's Chief Executive Officer, a Muslim named Kujaatele Kweli, said that he fired Morales as a matter of religious accommodation. "Our point of view," he explained, "is to respect the laws of the land and the laws of the land as I understand it is to accommodate people's right to practice their religions if you can."

But apparently only Muslims have the right to practice their religions—not Morales, who is Catholic. When a reporter asked Kweli, "Shouldn't you be able to accommodate all faiths in the same lunch room?," he replied, "We do, we can." But then why did he fire Morales for eating pork in the company lunch room? Because, Kweli said, "pork is considered unclean."[10]

And the demands for accommodation to Islam didn't stop there: American institutions, not just individuals, have to bend to their will.

GROWING PAINS OF A MULTICULTURAL SOCIETY?

But what might be for some people signs of Islamic supremacism in America are for others simply the growing pains of a multicultural society. In July 2004 the residents of Hamtramck, Michigan voted to approve an amendment to the city's noise ordinance allowing the Islamic call to prayer to be broadcast over loudspeakers. The vote was essentially symbolic, but it was touted by the media as a sign of Americans' openness and generosity— a nation of immigrants welcomes another immigrant group, and is happy to adapt its own laws and customs to make the immigrants' transition easier.

But sounding a sour note amid this multiculturalist generosity was Masud Khan, the secretary of Hamtramck's al-Islah mosque, which began broadcasting the call to prayer in May 2004. After the city voted to approve the broadcasts, Khan declared that the broadcasts would have continued no matter which way city residents had voted.[11] He didn't seem concerned about antagonizing his new neighbors, or making a good impression, or reaching out with a gesture of goodwill. His only concern, evidently, was asserting the will of the mosquegoers, whatever the objections of the community at large.

Khan was not being as multicultural as his hosts, who certainly expected that their gesture of goodwill would be reciprocated.

Instead, he was behaving like an Islamic supremacist, full of contempt for the laws of non-Muslims.

So was Walid Elkhatib, owner of a Dunkin' Donuts franchise in Illinois, when he filed a discrimination lawsuit against Dunkin' Donuts after the corporation declined to renew his contract due to his refusal, for Islamic reasons, to sell the company's ham, bacon, and sausage breakfast sandwiches. In Elkhatib's view, the Dunkin' Donuts product line had to conform to Islamic law, at least in his store, and the company would simply have to acquiesce to the existence of a franchise that didn't sell all the Dunkin' Donuts products.[12]

For it is always the non-Muslim party, never the Muslim one, that must give way.

And there are many such cases—these are simply a few representative ones.

THE SHARIA CAB CONTROVERSY

Late in 2006, the possibility that Islamic supremacists might have taken up residence on U.S. shores began to dawn on some Americans, thanks to an odd story out of Minneapolis: Muslim taxi drivers at Minneapolis-St. Paul International Airport were refusing passengers who carried alcohol or were even *suspected* of carrying alcohol. Justifying their Islamic supremacist behavior, the cab drivers insisted that this was a matter of religious principle, and that they accordingly would not bend. "I am Muslim. I'm not going to carry alcohol," declared cabbie Abdi Mohamed at the height of the controversy. And many cabbies were with him: what started as a discriminatory practice by one driver gradually spread until passengers carrying bottles of spirits were being refused taxi service an average of seventy-seven times a month.[13] By January

2007, Muslim cabbies had denied service to 5,400 passengers because of alcohol.[14]

Airport officials were initially accommodating, drafting a plan to color-code the taxis so that passengers would be able to distinguish an alcohol-carrying cab from a sharia cab.[15] But that didn't satisfy anyone. Airport officials were criticized for kowtowing to the spread of sharia norms in the United States, and non-Muslim cab drivers at the airport complained that the color-coding would confuse passengers and discourage them from using cabs at all. The Metropolitan Airports Commission held a hearing on the matter in February 2007; there, a Muslim activist, Abdifatah Abdi, warned that this was a matter of religious freedom, and as such would not be quickly or easily resolved: "This is a religious freedom issue, and it will not end here. It will go to the courts, even the Supreme Court. The drivers will not relinquish their rights to be protected under American law."

Neither Abdi nor any other defender of the cab drivers, however, explained why the controversy had begun in the first place, since Muhammad's curse on those who transport alcohol had never been an issue in the United States before this incident. So why did the cab drivers start this campaign at all?

The answer lies in a June 6, 2006 religious ruling, or *fatwa*, published by the "fatwa department" of the Minnesota chapter of the Muslim American Society (MAS), which is the Muslim Brotherhood's chief front group in the United States. According to this fatwa, "Islamic jurisprudence" forbids cabbies from picking up passengers who have alcohol with them, because to do so would involve "cooperating in sin according to the Islam." MAS, according to investigative journalist Katherine Kersten, was also playing the role of mediator between the cabbies and the Metropolitan Airports Commission.[16]

One non-Muslim who attended a Metropolitan Airports Commission hearing on the matter in February 2007 put his finger on the stealth jihad aspect of the sharia cab controversy: "I don't have a problem with people practicing their religion," he explained. "I don't even have a problem with people who want everyone to believe what they believe. But I do have a problem when a majority is being forced to observe other religions and customs."[17]

The problem with the sharia cabs was not one of religious freedom at all. No one was preventing the Muslim cab drivers from practicing Islam. But their refusal to carry passengers with alcohol was an assertion of sharia norms over non-Muslims. Had the precedent been established, it would have been entirely conceivable to expect that non-Muslims would then be expected to conform to other sharia norms also. Would cab drivers then refuse to carry passengers with pork products? Would a man with a salami sandwich have to take the bus? Would the cabbies refuse to carry an unmarried man and woman in the same cab? Would a cabbie initially take such a couple, but stop the cab and force them to get out if they held hands or kissed?

There is always more sharia to accommodate.

TARGETING PORK AT TARGET

In light of the involvement of the Minnesota chapter of MAS in the sharia cab controversy, it may come as no surprise that in March 2007 Muslim cashiers at some Target store outlets in Minneapolis began to refuse to ring up pork products, causing delays as they had other cashiers handle the untouchable items or even told customers to ring them up themselves. Target Corporation finally opted for the path of least resistance, offering to allow the

Muslim cashiers to wear gloves while operating the cash register, so as to avoid touching any of the offending pork, or to shift the recalcitrant, pork-hating cashiers to other jobs within the store.

It wasn't just Target, either: a Muslim cashier at Sam's Club in Bloomington, Minnesota, Muse Dahir, quit his job rather than have to ring up pork products. He explained, "They told me, you have to check this. I told them, 'I can't do this.' You want me to do something that's against my religion." Told that it was not a negotiable part of his job, Dahir quit. "I just put down my uniform and I left.... Even if you just sell [pork] to someone, you break a promise to Allah."[18]

Was Dahir's religious freedom violated? Or was this yet another attempt to force Americans to adapt their behavior to Islamic norms—a part of the stealth jihad to Islamize the United States?

WHEN IS A FOOTBATH NOT A FOOTBATH?

One thing is certain: the effort to force Americans to accommodate sharia norms is intensifying. In September 2007, the Indianapolis Airport announced that, as part of a $1.07 billion terminal renovation scheduled to be completed by November 2008, footbaths would be installed in a restroom used by cab drivers—so that the drivers, almost all Muslims, could easily perform the rituals required before Islamic prayers. The floor-level sinks, which cost $400-600 each, would be financed through airport revenue.

An airport spokesman, David Dawson, insisted, "These facilities are for everybody's use."

Really?

It's hard to imagine legions of footsore non-Muslim travelers making their way to this airport restroom in order to wash their feet; in American culture, it should go without saying, foot-washing in public facilities has never been a cultural norm. These footbaths were obviously meant to accommodate Islamic prayer and only Islamic prayer, as no one else would want them. What's more, it's hard to imagine any non-Muslim risking the ire of the Muslim cabbies by using the footbaths for anything other than Islamic rituals.

Supporters of the footbaths, however, said they were simply a public health issue: the cabbies were going to pray in any case, and if they didn't have the footbaths, they'd just wash their feet in the bathroom sinks.[19]

Michael Saahir, an imam at the Nur-Allah Islamic Center of Indianapolis, was pleased by the airport's "accommodations." "Indianapolis," he announced, "is coming of age. They need to have accommodations for all of their citizens."[20]

But is that really true, or was this another sign of steady encroachments, deliberate and systematic, by Muslims attempting to transform the public space?

Would the Indianapolis Airport use airport revenues to install confessional booths for the convenience of Catholic travelers? The very idea is absurd. Yet when it comes to accommodating Islamic religious practice, suddenly the issue is not quite so clear-cut. The footbaths are the consequence of pressure: Muslim groups have successfully portrayed Muslims in the United States as a persecuted minority, requiring special accommodation as redress for claimed discrimination and suspicion.

Indianapolis is not the first airport, and clearly won't be the last, to single out Islam for special accommodation; as far back as 2004, Phoenix's Sky Harbor International Airport installed two footbaths for Muslim cab drivers.[21] As in Indianapolis, the Phoenix airport funded them with airport user fees rather than taxpayer money, but that is still not the equivalent of using private funding.

One may legitimately wonder whether the accommodation would or could end with footbaths, or whether that demand, once satisfied, will only lead to others. A clue comes from Canada: journalist Katherine Kersten of the *Minneapolis Star-Tribune* has noted that "our neighbor to the north" is "farther down the 'accommodations' road," and that the satisfaction of an individual demand is unlikely to "satisfy activists for long."

THE NEEDS OF MUSLIM STUDENTS

If airports find it difficult to defy demands for Islamic accommodation, then universities present an even softer target. Western institutions of higher learning are a natural environment to press forward such demands, since so many administrators are enthralled by an extreme form of multiculturalist dogma that champions "sensitivity" to foreign cultures above all else.

For example, Katherine Kersten reported that a March 2007 report from the Canadian Federation of Students called upon Canadian colleges and universities to eliminate interest-accumulating student loans, since Islam "opposes usury and involvement with interest-bearing loans." It further recommended that schools impose times when only women could use the gym and other athletic facilities, so that Muslim women could exercise comfortably away from men's prying stares—indeed, school officials should make sure to "provide curtains or screens over the observation windows" at the pool. It also called for the construction of facilities for Islamic prayer (includes areas for ritual ablutions) and for the offering of halal food—that is, meat slaughtered according to Islamic ritual specifications.

And what if a college declines to implement all this?

Then, according to Kersten, "it is guilty, says the report, of 'Islamophobia'—an 'emerging form of racism,' according to the Ontario Human Rights Commission.... Everyone on campus should learn to recognize his or her 'collective responsibility to identify and stop Islamophobia.'"

And indeed, this is exactly the response of Muslim activists to anyone who questions their ever-escalating demands for accommodation. For example, regarding the Indianapolis Airport footbaths, the executive director of the Muslim Alliance of Indiana, Shariq A. Siddiqui, vilified opponents of the move, declaring, "We're glad they're dealing with health and safety rather than falling into Islamophobia."[22]

In other words, one must go to extra lengths to accommodate Muslims, making concessions to them and creating facilities for them that have never been granted to any other religious group, or else one will be branded a bigot.

And who was "heavily involved" in the drafting of this Canadian Federation of Students report? Why, none other than that Muslim Brotherhood group, the MSA.[23]

That same organization in August 2007 prevailed upon the University of Michigan at Dearborn to spend $25,000 to install two footbaths on campus for Muslim students—at a time when tuition had increased by almost 8 percent. Around 10 percent of the school's student body is Muslim, which is apparently enough to force religious accommodations on an ostensibly public university. Here again, defenders of the footbaths explained the move as a simple matter of public health and safety, but the accommodationist aspect was glaringly obvious—university officials themselves declared that the footbaths represented their "strong commitment to a pluralistic society," reflecting "our values of respect, tolerance and safe accommodation of student needs."

But not everyone was so sanguine. "Technically," observed Hal Downs of the Michigan chapter of Americans United for Separation of Church and State, "they've got a problem, because it's public money they're using to pay for this."[24] Islamic reformer Zuhdi Jasser of the American Islamic Forum for Democracy said that the footbaths represented the beginning of "a slippery slope of preferential treatment of one religion over another.... These baths exert a monetary cost upon publicly funded institutions which by our Constitution should not appease the financial demands of one faith group over another."[25]

Back in Indianapolis, not everyone was happy with the new multiculturalist paradise, either. Marc Monte, pastor of the Faith Baptist Church in Avon, Indiana, explained, "I continue to oppose (the plan) on the grounds that it shows preferential treatment to that religion. I don't think the Airport Authority is going to let me install a baptismal font to baptize people in." He added trenchantly, "In the name of multiculturalism, people will sell America down the river."[26]

And that is why, at the University of Michigan, the Indianapolis Airport, and elsewhere, a footbath is not just a footbath. These facilities are political and social statements advanced by the Muslim Brotherhood—a group that, by its own admission, is involved in a large-scale effort aimed at "eliminating and destroying the Western civilization from within." It may seem inconceivable that something as insignificant as public footbaths could be part of this effort, but the MSA knows that the footbaths set a precedent: society must meet Muslim demands for special treatment, special facilities, and special consideration. Calls for such accommodation will acclimate American institutions to treating Muslims as a special class. This is an important provision of Islamic sharia law—a practice that, once begun, cannot possibly end well, since sharia is an all-encompassing program for every aspect of life. There is always more sharia to accommodate, once one has started down that road, and eventually—if the accommodation process is not stopped at some point—that will involve accommodating sharia provisions that institutionalize discrimination against women and non-Muslims.

Instead of capitulating to Muslim demands for separate facilities, university administrators and public officials ought to question the overall goals of those making the demands, and consider the incongruity of Muslim claims that the creation of their own enclave is a matter of equal rights for all.

But they won't do this, because they know nothing of the MSA's links with the Brotherhood, or anything about the "grand jihad" memorandum. They have, no doubt, never reflected on the implications of the MSA's separatist agenda.

And so, in the name of diversity, the Islamic supremacist agenda continues to advance. In 2007 another public school, the Minneapolis Community and Technical College, announced plans to construct preparation facilities for Islamic prayer—despite having prohibited a coffee cart from playing Christmas carols on campus the previous year.[27] New York University followed suit in October 2007, as have many other colleges and universities.[28] Seventeen universities have now announced plans to install footbaths, including Boston University, George Washington University, and Temple University. And all of this is going on at the instigation of the MSA—a Muslim Brotherhood organization.[29]

Muslim reformer Zuhdi Jasser recommended that a constitutional issue be made of all this: "Unusual accommodations for one faith at the cost of everybody else doesn't fall on the side of pluralism."[30] Such cases, he says, should go all the way to the top: "Supreme Court cases have been heard on far less-obvious violations of our Establishment Clause." And he pointed out a significant inconsistency in the modus operandi of Muslim activists: "Islamists use the 'free exercise' clause when it suits them and then turn around and use tax monies in the name of Islam when it suits them."[31]

NON-MUSLIMS RUSH TO HELP: PRAYER IN SCHOOL, PORK OUT OF SCHOOL

Meanwhile, efforts to compel Americans to accommodate various aspects of sharia have not been put forward by Muslims alone. Non-Muslims, besotted with multiculturalist fantasies, have been all too happy to help. Ridgeland School District 122—comprising five schools in Oak Lawn, Illinois—blazed a trail when it banned pork from school cafeterias, so as to avoid offending Muslim students. (The possibility that non-Muslim students might be offended by having to conform their eating habits to Islamic dietary regulations was apparently not considered.) The pork ban even included Jell-O, since gelatin is made from pork products.

As if that weren't enough, the district moved in September 2007 to ban Halloween and Christmas celebrations for the same reason, over the vociferous objections of some parents. "It's difficult when you change the school's culture," observed the principal of one of the district schools, with admirable understatement.[32] However, after a contentious school board meeting the following month, the district decided to keep Halloween and Christmas after all, but to add celebrations of Ramadan.[33]

Elsewhere, school districts under pressure from Islamic advocacy groups to add days off for Muslim holidays to already crowded school calendars have opted instead to drop days off for religious observance altogether. In April 2007, the Hillsborough County School District in Florida gave students the day off for Good Friday for the last time. "We, like many districts, have had Christian holidays for years and years," explained District official Steve Hegarty. Students also have had the day off on Yom Kippur. However, in 2006 "a group of Muslims asked for a day off too." The District decided instead, with the Islamic holiday Eid al-Fitr and Yom Kippur both falling on Saturdays during the 2007-2008 school year, simply to drop the day off for Good Friday.[34] But the smart money was on students enjoying a day off for Eid al-Fitr in the 2008-2009 school year, and beyond. This is already the case at Syracuse University, where Eid al-Fitr is an official university holiday. As Muslim writer Naheed Mustafa noted approvingly, "The entire university campus shuts down to mark the end of Ramadan, and the 500 Muslim students and staff now have a chance to celebrate Eid for the entire day instead of just an hour."[35]

In New York City, however, Mayor Michael Bloomberg sounded a sour note amid all the multiculturalist goodwill when he declared in March 2008 that Muslim holidays didn't belong on the New York City public school calendar of days off. Bloomberg framed the issue pragmatically, rather than as a matter of cultural defense: "The truth of the matter is we need more children in school. More, not less."[36] Neither Bloomberg nor any other public figure would go beyond this pragmatic approach to Muslim holidays. No one dared to bring up the fact that American culture has been and largely remains Judeo-Christian, and that to express that character was not "racist" or "exclusionary," but simply a manifestation of who we still overwhelmingly are as a people.

But what one will not defend, one loses, and so school cultures are changing all over the country. Most Americans would have no problem with this: after all, if Muslims now live in the United States, why shouldn't they have their holidays off from school like everyone else? And that does indeed seem reasonable—were it not for the fact that in the case of Islam, there is much more to the story than a group of immigrants trying to find their place in America. The stealth jihad is a program to accustom Americans to accommodating Islamic law, and the push for holidays has been accompanied by an increasing assertiveness and an ever-expanding series of demands that, if all were acceded to, would indeed establish Islam in a privileged position in the United States. A cornerstone of this effort has been a campaign to bring prayer back into public schools, long after the Supreme Court and the ACLU led a successful decades-long war to banish it. But now that public schools have been rendered "safe" from Christian prayer, so far the same anti-prayer zealots have been sanguine about Muslim prayer in public schools. Unlike Christian prayer, it's multicultural! What could be wrong with it?

Thus public schools in the Atlanta area opted in October 2004, after meetings with Islamic leaders (whose efforts were coordinated by none other than the Council on American-Islamic Relations), to allow Muslim students to be excused from class for Islamic Friday prayers.[37] And in San Diego's Carver Elementary School, when over one hundred Somali Muslim students enrolled after a charter school closed in 2006, school officials scheduled breaks so that Muslim students could pray during school time, and even introduced sex-segregated classes to conform to Islamic sensibilities.[38] Pork, of course, vanished from the school cafeteria, and Arabic classes were added to the curriculum. *Investor's Business Daily* went straight to the heart of the problem when it editorialized, "In effect, Carver administrators have carved out a school within a school expressly for Muslims, elevating them above Christian and Jewish students. They've had 15 minutes of instruction time taken away from them, so Muslims can roll out their prayer mats. It amounts to a special privilege afforded a specific religion, which plainly does not have our best interests at heart."[39]

Some of these accommodations were later dropped after a public outcry, but since public awareness of the stealth jihad agenda remain abysmal, these kinds of accommodations will inevitably recur, sometime, at another public school.

DUDE! YOU'RE GETTING A PRAYER ROOM!

While prayer reappears in American public schools, the Council on American-Islamic Relations has been making a concerted effort to force American employers to accommodate Islamic prayer in the workplace. In February 2005, thirty-one Muslims working at the Nashville, Tennessee plant of the computer firm Dell walked off the job after they were denied permission to leave their workstations and pray. Dell fired the Muslim workers, but CAIR took up their cause and began to pressure Dell to change its practices in order to accommodate Islamic prayer during the workday.

It wasn't an isolated incident. Fifty-four employees of the Swift and Company beef processing plant in Cactus, Texas, walked off the job in November 2007 for exactly the same reason.[40] Three months before that, a Swift plant in Grand Island, Nebraska agreed to revise break times in order to allow for Islamic prayer.[41] In Delaware, three Muslim employees at an Exxon Mobil gas station on I-95 filed a $12 million federal civil rights suit for discrimination, harassment, and retaliation against Exxon after a regional manager brusquely rejected their demands for accommodations, saying, "I'm not here to accommodate your religious beliefs. I am running a business, not a religious community."[42]

This lawsuit epitomizes the hardball tactics that CAIR employs in order to compel companies to comply with demands for accommodation. If the targeted company refuses to give in, CAIR operatives will sue it while tarring its management as "racist" and "bigoted," in much the same way that the organization routinely vilifies those who speak out against the Islamic jihad agenda.

The organization has put pressure on businesses that refuse to fall in line. For example, after meetings with CAIR officials, Dell quickly caved. Within a month the corporation had agreed to reinstate the employees who had walked out, give them back pay, and allow them time on the job for Islamic prayer. Dell also agreed to give its managers training in accommodating Muslim demands in the workplace.

A precedent was set in the Dell case, and it was a one-way street. The Muslim employees and their advocates in CAIR were making all the demands, and the employer was making all the concessions; the Dell settlement was entirely in the favor of the Muslim employees. "This settlement," declared CAIR's Legal Director, Arsalan Iftikhar, "can be used as [a] model by other production facilities that employ large numbers of Muslim workers."[43]

Parallel efforts are being undertaken throughout the Western world. In Britain, for example, a company called Kwintessential offers "cross cultural solutions" for the workplace. Muhammad Ridha, Kwintessential's "Middle East and Islam Consultant," offers guidelines for employers in accommodating Islamic prayer during the workday:

> A Muslim, both male and female, is expected to pray five
> times a day. This prayer involves facing Makkah (in Saudi
> Arabia), usually on a prayer mat or clean surface and recit-

ing prayers which follow a procedure of bowing and pros-
trating. This typically takes between 5—15 minutes depending on the individual. Prayer times are calculated according
to the movement of the sun and take place at dawn, midday,
late afternoon, dusk and at night.

Most workplaces, then, should allow Muslim employees
a special five- to fifteen-minute break at midday and late
afternoon which, depending on the size and nature of the
company, could create scheduling havoc, as well as arouse
resentment among non-Muslim personnel who are not
allowed similar breaks.

For Muslims in your company it is a good idea to allocate
a neutral space for them to use for their prayers. This can be
a dedicated prayer room or simply access to a seldom used
office or medical room. Such a space will make your Muslim
staff feel at comfort knowing they have somewhere private
and clean to say their prayers.

Here again this accommodation could easily create immense
inconvenience in the workplace. If there is not enough room for a
place to be set aside for Islamic prayer, the five to fifteen-minute
break could begin to stretch to a half hour of longer, allowing for
time to convert the space into an area suitable for Islamic prayer,
and then back into an office again. But that, once again, is not
considered in these guidelines.

Nor do the accommodations end there:

> If staff are required to be committed to a desk space at cer-
> tain times it may be a good idea to agree on allocated times
> in which they can read their prayers. This may involve the
> use of break times.
>
> Friday Prayers

> Most Muslim men attend the mosque on Friday after-
> noons for obligatory congregational prayers. Let your staff
> know you understand their requirements and agree on an
> extended lunch break and/or allocate their Friday lunch
> breaks to convenient times. Most mosques conduct prayers
> at 1.30 p.m. so try to aim for an hour between 1-2p.m.[44]

Like CAIR in its dustup with Dell, Ridha gives no hint in his recommendations of any possibility that Muslim employees might be
able or willing to adapt their prayer practices to the convenience
of the workplace. And to be sure, Islamic jurists reinforce this
view. *IslamOnline*'s popular online Islamic question and answer
series in March 2004 featured the question, "Is it permissible to
miss prayers because of work and then make them up once I
arrive home?"

The answer? Absolutely not! "It is not permissible for a Muslim to delay his prayers beyond the time when they are due without a legitimate excuse. Legitimate excuses which allow a Muslim
to delay his prayers until the time for them is over include sleep-
ing and forgetting. Doing worldly work is not an excuse for not
praying or for delaying a prayer until its time is over."[45]

That perspective coalesces neatly with the stealth jihad agenda
of compelling Americans to accommodate more and more of
sharia. It places the onus entirely on the employer to change his
business procedures to allow for Islamic practices. It's clear, albeit
unspoken, whom Ridha and CAIR think is boss. Neither one is
mediating between two equals; both are dictating terms to a
defeated supplicant. At the time of the Dell settlement, CAIR's
Rabiah Ahmed asserted that Muslim workplace demands "can be
accommodated if both parties are willing to work at it."[46] But
only one side, apparently, had to do any heavy lifting. The other

side gave nothing, nothing at all, except the assurance that the company, by capitulating, would not be targeted as racist.

And that is why the accommodation of Islamic prayer in the workplace is not simply a matter of cross-cultural generosity, or of adapting to the realities of our new multicultural environment. If the groups making these demands were not connected to an effort to subvert Western civilization, these accommodations might be just that—accommodations. But since the stealth jihad effort has come to light, it would be naïve to consider these efforts in a vacuum. They are a challenge to the West's entire philosophy of government, and an attempt to create a special class—Muslims—that has special privileges recognized in law. And they are part of the Muslim Brotherhood's overall effort to bring Islamic law to the West—piece by piece if necessary, but without ever abandoning the conviction that sharia is a unified whole, and that therefore all of it, not just a few of its elements, must someday be implemented.

THE BROAD MAINSTREAM

In insisting on the accommodation of workplaces to Islam, Ridha and CAIR were not simply manifesting Islamic supremacism; they were delineating the mainstream governmental view. On May 14, 2002, the Equal Employment Opportunity Commission issued a document on the workplace "rights" of Muslims, Arabs, South Asians, and Sikhs. After reporting an increase in charges from these groups of workplace discrimination, the document reproduced a question from a Muslim computer specialist whose work hours prevented him from attending Friday prayers at the local mosque.

The EEOC's reply advised the questioner to "ask your employer for permission to attend services," and informed him that "your employer is required to provide you with such an accommodation unless it would impose an undue hardship on the employer's business."

Of course, what constitutes an "undue hardship" is in the eye of the beholder. Who would be the judge? The EEOC itself, of course. The guidelines go on to advise Muslims to contact the commission if they can't work things out with their employer: "If the accommodation would impose a burden on the employer that cannot be resolved, the employer is not required to allow the accommodation. If your employer is unsure of its obligations to provide you with religious accommodations, feel free to contact EEOC with your questions."[47]

And the EEOC has followed through on this. In October 2007, it filed a suit claiming that Southern Hills Medical Center in Nashville, Tennessee illegally discriminated against a Muslim medical technician, Wali Telwar. Telwar wanted to go on a Hajj, or pilgrimage to Mecca, but alleged in his suit that the hospital told him he would have to resign rather than use his accumulated vacation. He did so, and was not hired back when he returned.

The EEOC suit once again reflected the non-negotiable character of Muslim demands. Senior EEOC trial attorney Sally Ramsey emphasized that the Islamic obligation to go on a Hajj at least once in a lifetime is "a sincerely held religious belief," and thus must be accommodated. To punish the medical center for refusing this accommodation, the suit asked for an injunction banning the center from discriminating on the basis of religion, and for the center to pay back wages and both compensatory and punitive damages to Telwar.[48]

The EEOC's involvement in such suits is puzzling: it's hard to see how giving Muslim employees *special* accommodation for religious observances amounts to *equal* employment opportunity. But it does coincide rather precisely with the stealth jihad agenda of creating a special status for Islamic law in the American public sphere.

The EEOC, of course, knew nothing of the Muslim Brotherhood memorandum, which had not yet been released to the general public, when it formulated its guidelines about accommodating Muslim religious practices. But it would be well-advised to examine them in light of Islam's general political character, as well as the various current initiatives designed to give Muslims rights that the non-Muslim population does not enjoy.

But that, of course, would require a large-scale reexamination of multiculturalist assumptions. Instead, the wind is blowing in the opposite direction.

THE OUTCOME OF
"REASONABLE ACCOMMODATION"

In September 2008, an incident at the Swift Meat Packing Plant in Greeley, Colorado showed the inevitable outcome of the "reasonable" accommodation of Muslim demands in U.S. workplaces.

After the company agreed to demands by Somali Muslim workers to change the work schedule to accommodate their Ramadan fast, around one hundred non-Muslim workers protested at the plant. One Swift employee, Brianna Castillo, declared, "They have no respect for the Spanish or white people. Many times we are forced to pull extra count [i.e., work longer while Muslims go on break]....I don't feel that is right....Somalis are running our plant. They are telling us what to do." [49]

Castillo framed the controversy in racial terms, but it really wasn't about race at all; the core issue was the extent to which U.S. companies and institutions will change their practices and denigrate non-Muslims in order to assuage Muslim demands. The incident shows how measures that seem like "reasonable accommodation" have much larger implications.

Most likely when Muslims at Swift began demanding changes in their break times, many reacted with indifference, thinking, "What's the big deal? So they go on break an hour or two earlier. It doesn't mean we're on the road to becoming an Islamic state." But the Muslims' insistence on accommodation even at the expense of their non-Muslim co-workers reflect the belief among pious Muslims that Islamic religious imperatives take precedence over the needs or wants of unbelievers. In other words, there can be no compromise with sharia provisions: they must be adhered to in full, and once the precedent of accommodation is set, there is no logical end to the demands short of a full sharia regime.

That is why each of the incidents outlined above is important: it may be a small accommodation in itself, but it reinforces the precedent that American norms must give way to Muslim ones whenever they clash. Once that precedent is set, it naturally leads to the steady Islamization of American society, unless at some point non-Muslims draw the line and refuse any further intrusions of Islamic practices. That line will never be drawn, however, as long as Americans continue to fail to see the larger implications and cumulative effect of these individual incidents.

The incident in Greeley was a sign of things to come. We will be seeing much more of this in the near future.

ISLAM IN SCHOOL, AT WORK, AND IN COURT

In 2003, a Muslim woman from Browns Summit, North Carolina, Syidah Mateen, appeared as a witness in a Guilford County, North Carolina, court. Mateen wanted to swear on the Qur'an rather than the Bible, but the courtroom had no Qur'an. When a local Islamic center offered to supply copies, two Guilford County judges turned them down—whereupon the ACLU sued the state.

In May 2007 Wake County Superior Court Judge Paul Ridgeway ruled that "to require pious and faithful practitioners of religions other than Christianity to swear oaths in a form other than the form most meaningful to them would thwart the search for the truth. It would elevate form over substance." He allowed the Qur'an, the Hebrew Bible, and the Bhagavad Gita to be used to swear in witnesses.[50]

That sounds noble and high-minded. Many praised it as both common sense and a manifestation of genuine American pluralism. After all, doesn't it make more sense for someone to swear to tell the truth on a book he values as holy, rather than one he does not?

This question briefly took the national stage when the first Muslim congressman, Keith Ellison (D-MN), was photographed in January 2007 being sworn in by House Speaker Nancy Pelosi on Thomas Jefferson's copy of the Qur'an, borrowed from the National Archives for the occasion. This was just a ceremonial photo op—in fact, representatives are sworn in en masse, without any book at all.[51]

However, the symbolic value was enormous. Talk show host Dennis Prager said that Ellison should not be allowed to be sworn in, even ceremoniously, on the Qur'an—"not because of any American hostility to the Koran, but because the act undermines American civilization."

Why? Because to be sworn in on the Qur'an would be "an act of hubris that perfectly exemplifies multiculturalist activism—my culture trumps America's culture. What Ellison and his Muslim and leftist supporters are saying is that it is of no consequence what America holds as its holiest book; all that matters is what any individual holds to be his holiest book." On the contrary, said Prager, "insofar as a member of Congress taking an oath to serve America and uphold its values is concerned, America is interested in only one book, the Bible."[52]

However, UCLA law professor and popular blogger Eugene Volokh countered that this was precisely American culture: inclusive, and welcoming of diversity. He argued that the Constitution itself made provision for this kind of "multiculturalism." By allowing people the option of affirming, rather than swearing, that they were telling the truth, the Constitution, Volokh asserted, already recognized the religious character of the act of swearing-in, and allowed people to opt out of it. And if people could opt out of swearing at all, why should they be made to swear on a book they didn't recognize as holy? (This would apply, of course, whether it was a courtroom oath to tell the truth or an oath to discharge the duties of one's office faithfully.) "So the Constitution thus already expressly authorizes people not to swear at all, but to affirm, without reference to God or to a sacred work. Atheists and agnostics are thus protected, as well as members of certain Christian groups. Why would Muslims and others not be equally protected from having to perform a religious ritual that expressly invokes a religion in which they do not believe?"[53]

Volokh thus made essentially the same argument as Judge Ridgeway: forcing non-Christians to swear on the Bible would be elevating form over substance. This argument leads to some interesting questions: Can someone, then, choose *any* book he values, and swear on it? Would North Carolina courts allow a witness to swear to tell the truth on the Satanic Bible? Would the House of Representatives countenance a ceremonial swearing-in featuring a new congressman and the Speaker of the House beaming over a copy of *Lady Chatterly's Lover*, or *The Story of O*? Does the content of the book that the person swears on matter at all?

No one ever broached that question, either in North Carolina or in reference to Ellison's swearing-in. No one considered whether or not the Qur'an actually taught the equivalent of the Biblical injunction not to bear false witness, which is one of the main reasons the Bible is used in court. Now, certainly the oath, whether in court or for an oath of office, is largely ceremonial, at least insofar as the content of the Bible is concerned. Those who swear know they are legally bound to tell the truth, but few who swear on the Bible in courtrooms today could explain exactly what the Bible says about telling the truth. That does not, however, render considerations of content entirely irrelevant. The Bible *does* prohibit bearing false witness, whether or not any given witness is aware of that. But does the Qur'an call upon the Muslim to "tell the truth, the whole truth, and nothing but the truth"?

No, it does not. To the contrary, it advises Muslims not to "take disbelievers for their friends in preference to believers." If Muslims do this, they have "no connection with Allah"—unless they are doing it to guard themselves against those unbelievers, as a matter of "security" (Qur'an 3:28).

A mainstream and respected Qur'anic commentator, Ibn Kathir (1301-1372), whose writings are widely read by Muslims today, explained that this verse applied to "believers who in some areas or times fear for their safety from the disbelievers. In this case, such believers are allowed to show friendship to the disbelievers outwardly, but never inwardly." He quoted an early Muslim explaining that "we smile in the face of some people although our hearts curse them," and another saying that religious deception "is allowed until the Day of Resurrection."[54]

Another influential Qur'anic commentary, the *Tafsir al-Jalalayn*, explains the same Qur'an verse as meaning that "as a safeguard," a Muslim "may show patronage" to unbelievers "through words, but not in your hearts."[55]

What all this means is this: now North Carolinians can swear to tell the truth on a book that has been interpreted by its mainstream commentators as allowing for deceptive words to be spoken to non-Muslims.

And there's the real example of form over substance. The high-minded, pluralist visions cherished by Ridgeway, Volokh, and others founder upon the content of the Qur'an itself. American pluralism cannot possibly absorb a supremacist creed that demands the subjugation of others under its rule, and allows for deception even under oath. But so effective has been the stealth jihadist campaign to marginalize and vilify anyone who asks uncomfortable questions about Islam that no one in the public square even dares to raise such questions—if they even know that the Qur'an contains such material.

In any case, the cumulative effect of Ellison's swearing-in and the North Carolina decision is to put the Judeo-Christian and Islamic traditions on an equal footing, as if these historical antagonists were equivalent, interchangeable, and in all senses compatible. And combined with the ongoing official discouragement of any serious investigation of the violent and supremacist elements of Islam, this could only be another victory for the stealth jihad.

So what may have seemed to be a victory for multiculturalism in the North Carolina court may help to hasten the end of multiculturalism itself, for it has helped to legitimize a creed that brooks no competitors, instead relegating them to a chastened and controlled second-class status. It's not beyond the realm of possibility that one day, in a North Carolina in which Muslims have gained considerably more power, a court will decide to cut its losses and end the absurd proliferation of books required to be on hand for the odd swearing-in. But by then, America will be that much farther removed from the Judeo-Christian values upon which, as Prager pointed out, it was indeed built.

CHAPTER SEVEN

SEPARATE AND UNEQUAL: ISLAMIC SEPARATISM

During the heyday of the civil rights movement, black Americans battled Southern segregation laws and asked for "a place at the table." They worked for full inclusion in the larger secular democratic culture, as opposed to carving out their own enclave within it. In fact, they had their own enclaves already, and that was precisely the problem: they had separate schools, separate neighborhoods, separate stores, separate hotels, even separate sports leagues. The Supreme Court concluded in *Brown* v. *the Board of Education of Topeka* that "in the field of public education, the doctrine of separate but equal has no place," because "separate educational facilities are inherently unequal."

Lately, however, there has been a new push for separate educational facilities and separate facilities of other kinds—not from white racists but from Muslims. Segregation is back in American public schools, aided and abetted by multiculturalist ideologues, thanks to the ideology of Islamic supremacism that holds unbelievers to be unworthy of casual contact with Muslims.

LET'S SHARE: ALL FOR ME,
NONE FOR YOU

In many public colleges and universities, pressure from the Muslim Brotherhood's Muslim Students Association (MSA) has led to the establishment of separate "Muslims-only" prayer rooms—often, again, at public expense. Nine universities now have Muslim-only prayer rooms, including Stanford, Emory, and the University of Virginia.[1] Meanwhile, where facilities have been established for use by both Muslims and non-Muslims, Muslims have, in several notable cases, taken them over. This is a variant on the "your house is our house" demand for segregation: in accord with the classic Islamic supremacist mindset, requests for separate Islamic spaces are not accompanied by any consideration at all for non-Muslims. Supremacist assumptions emanating from the proposition that the Muslims are the "best of people" (Qur'an 3:110) and the unbelievers are the "vilest of created beings" (Qur'an 98:6) often lead to a separatism that proceeds by frankly and unapologetically excluding non-Muslims from ostensibly shared premises.

At George Mason University in Fairfax, Virginia, after the university made available a "meditation space" for all students, Muslim students swiftly transformed the room into a mosque, and soon made it clear that non-Muslim students were unwelcome to use it on an equal footing with Muslims. They laid out Islamic prayer rugs and separated the sexes—which is their prerogative for Islamic prayer, to be sure. But then they began asking non-Muslim students to observe Islamic regulations by removing their shoes and maintaining sex segregation even during their own prayers.

After all this was written up in the school paper, administrators asked the Muslims to take up their prayer rugs and remove the dividers separating the sexes when they had finished their prayers.

This example illustrates in microcosm that the separatist and non-multicultural tendencies of Islam are alive and well among Muslims in the United States—and all too often, they're aided and abetted by ignorant non-Muslim multiculturalists. A similar incident to the one at George Mason occurred at Normandale Community College in Bloomington, Minnesota. Not long after school officials converted the college's racquetball court into an interfaith space for "meditation," Muslim students began telling non-Muslims to leave the room. The college even built a barrier to separate the sexes, and posted a sign asking students to remove their shoes. The dean of student affairs, Ralph Anderson, explained that this was "basically a courtesy to Muslim students," who "prefer that areas be divided into male and female.... Other students don't care." In defiance of reality, Anderson insisted that the "meditation room" was still "open to everyone."

Reporter Katherine Kersten also noted that a schedule for Islam's five daily prayers was posted at the entrance to the room, an arrow pointed the way to Mecca, and literature in the room said that Jews and Christians were "the enemies of Allah's religion" and that people should "enter into Islam completely and accept all the rulings of Islam." There were no Jewish or Christian tracts or religious articles in the room.[2]

Another incident of Islamic separatism occurred at Illinois' Ridgeland School District 122—the same district that banned pork from lunchroom menus and added Ramadan to school celebrations, as discussed in the previous chapter. This was also the site of an attempt to advance the idea that Muslims require not only special accommodations, but separate facilities, when Elizabeth Zahdan, a Muslim mother of three, asked school officials to allow her children to sit apart from non-Muslims at lunchtime during Ramadan.

The request incensed some non-Muslim parents. "I don't ever remember one of us asking for our child to be separated from classmates during Ash Wednesday when they were fasting, or on every Friday of Lent when our children are not allowed to eat meat," said one parent. Another attacked the accommodationist agenda itself: "If Muslims want the school holidays, menus and school traditions to become tailored to their needs or beliefs, then they should go to private school next to their mosque." An area woman summed up the issue succinctly: "We're letting you come here, we're honoring you, don't dishonor us."[3]

But honoring their hosts is not what significant numbers of Muslims in the West have in mind. Rather, they are intent on carving out their own Islamic enclaves in Western countries and securing separate facilities and the segregation of Muslims from non-Muslims in accordance with Islamic laws and practices.

And it isn't only in the schools. At Salt Lake City International Airport, Muslim cab drivers transformed what had been a "quiet room" in a building set aside for drivers to rest into an Islamic prayer room—essentially, a mosque, cleared of tables and chairs, furnished with prayer rugs and Qur'ans, and requiring removal of shoes for entry. A non-Muslim cab driver complained, "We cannot have breakfast, we cannot go to [the] restroom, we cannot play chess."[4] In October 2007, an airport shuttle driver, Jeff Brueningsen, filed a complaint over the room, saying, "I almost quit last summer because I didn't want to live and work under sharia [Islamic] law...sponsored by the airport." In his complaint he commented, "Islamists are required to wage cultural jihad and they seem to be engaging in 'sharia [sic] by the inch' here."

In January 2008 Brueningsen was charged with assaulting a Muslim cab driver, although he says it was the Muslim cabbies who assaulted and threatened him. Details of his interaction with the cabbies over the room are disputed. But his allegations about how the room was used are not in doubt. *Salt Lake Tribune* columnist Rebecca Walsh called it a "government-sanctioned Islamic center." Airport spokeswoman Barbara Gann acknowledged, "We never intended this to be a prayer room, nor did we create it as that. But, in fact, that's what it became."

The airport closed the building permanently in January 2008.[5] This may have been a setback for Islamic separatism, but it was also a defeat for the non-Muslim cabbies who lost their place to relax. The airport, it seems, didn't feel comfortable simply telling the Muslims cabbies not to use their relaxation area as a mosque. Fearing accusations of intolerance, no doubt, airport officials preferred to inconvenience all their cab drivers rather than draw some redlines for Islamic religious practices.

YOU CAN SWIM—IF YOU'RE MUSLIM

More often, such efforts proceed by means of very small steps—so small that few people even realize what is happening. This is occurring not just in America, but in places throughout the Western world where large Muslim communities have grown increasingly assertive. In London in 2006, for example, a public "leisure centre" established a Sunday-afternoon session for Muslim swimmers. The men-only swim time lasted two hours, and non-Muslims were banned from the pool during that time unless they complied with Islamic sharia rules dictating that bathing suits cover their navels and knees.

"I turned up," said a local man, "and saw a sign saying it was closing early for Muslim afternoon—I couldn't believe it." What one might have expected in a healthy society—that newcomers would as a matter of course comply with the customs and mores of the society to which they had immigrated—had been completely turned on its head. Another local resident, Alex Craig, commented, "It seems the issue here is over modesty. Surely if Muslims want to swim then they should just turn up with their modest swimwear at the same time as everyone else. To make a special provision for them is just ridiculous and strikes me as imposing an 'Us and them' mentality which is wrong."

A mosque official, however, was adamant: "Muslims are not allowed to show intimate parts of their body. This is non-negotiable. Muslims have as much right to go swimming as anyone else."

And so the British, in publicly funded facilities, would have to be the ones to bend.

Craig remarked, "I think it is preposterous that a council should be encouraging this type of segregation over municipal facilities."[6]

Indeed it is, but British officials show no signs of stopping. In April 2008 a non-Muslim, David Toube, and his five-year-old son were denied entry into another public swimming pool in Britain after arriving during Muslim men-only swim time. Toube described the incident: "I asked whether my son and I could go as we were both male. I was told that the session was for Muslims only and that we could not be admitted. I asked what would happen if I turned up and insisted I was Muslim. The manager suggested that they might ask the Muslims swimming if they minded my son and I swimming with them. If they didn't object, we might be allowed in."

However, another official told him at another time that "it was a requirement of the Muslim religion that Muslims could not swim with non-Muslims"—and turned him away again. In fact, there is nothing in Islamic law that forbids Muslims from swim-

ming with non-Muslims—the official's reply, in which he probably repeated something he was told by the Muslim swimmers, was
a straightforward expression of the Islamic separatist and
supremacist agenda.[7]

Despite attempts to hide this agenda in the guise of multicultural tolerance, it was also evident at Harvard University, when in
February 2008 university administrators instituted six women-
only hours at the university gym, so as to make Muslim women
feel more comfortable while working out. Supporters presented
the initiative as a simple matter of fairness. Ola Aljawhary, a Harvard undergraduate and officer of the Harvard Islamic Society's
Islamic Knowledge Committee, explained: "These hours are necessary because there is a segment of the Harvard female population that is not found in gyms not because they don't want to
work out, but because for them working out in a co-ed gym is
uncomfortable, awkward or problematic in some way."

Aljawhary declared that in a multicultural environment, everyone had to give a little: "We live together in one community, it
only makes sense for everyone to compromise slightly in order for
everyone to live happily. This matter is simple: Can't we just display basic decency and show tolerance and inclusion for people
not a part of the mainstream majority?"[8] Certainly, but here
again, she did not explain how the Harvard Islamic community
was compromising at all in its insistence on segregation. The only
conceivable compromise Harvard Muslims were making was not
insisting that the gym be segregated at all times and that gym
clothing be brought into full compliance with Islamic law.

Meanwhile, even though protests at Harvard were decidedly
muted, as might be expected in such a multiculturalist haven, a
spokesman for the British Equality and Human Rights Commission pinpointed the problem with all this separatism: "Segregating

services may amount to unlawful discrimination and could create a sense of unfairness, inadvertently increasing community
tension."[9]

And "community tension" is exactly what Islamic separatism
has created everywhere from England to Massachusetts. In any
country, when a significant part of one community views other
groups as so objectionable that it wishes to separate itself from
them, it's rare that the result will be multicultural harmony. This
was the case with apartheid and Jim Crow separatism, and there's
no reason to believe that the consequences of Islamic separatism
will be any more positive.

SEPARATE BUT UNEQUAL

In February 2008, Muslim students at Australian universities
demanded that class schedules be changed to work around their
prayer times, and that male and female students be provided with
separate cafeterias and recreational areas.[10]

This is in line with similar initiatives in the United States, where
the Muslim Brotherhood-affiliated Muslim Students Association
displays, on the "Muslim Accommodations Task Force" page of
its website, pamphlets entitled "How to Achieve Islamic Holidays
on Campus," "How to Establish a Prayer Room on Campus,"
and "How to Achieve Halal Food on Campus."[11] Another guide,
now no longer available at the site, tells MSA members that "as
Muslims, we are a nation elected by God to lead humanity."[12]

The means that the MSA is using to bring Muslims into leadership in the U.S. are stealthy rather than violent, and they make
canny use of mainstream liberal cant and national traumas over
race. When Muslim students present these demands to school
administrators, they do so in language that those administrators

find difficult to refuse. The MSA directs Muslim students to present its demands in the context of multiculturalism and civil rights. "Most campuses," explains the publication on getting recognition of Islamic holy days, "include respecting diversity as a part of their mission statement. They consider enrollment of diverse students an asset to the community, as they enhance the classroom learning experience and enrich student life. Try to find these statements specific to your campus, and explain that recognition of Islamic holidays would serve as a practical example of upholding these ideals."

Such recognition would also serve to right wrongs done to Muslims on campus: "If any cases of bias against Muslims took place on campus in the recent past, present the proposal as an opportunity to foster cooperation and increase understanding." It would be a simple matter of civil rights: "Additionally, if special holiday recognition is being offered to other faith communities (Jewish, Catholic, Protestant), Muslims have strong grounds to make a petition for equal consideration of their holiday requirements."

Who could possibly object? On the face of it, all this sounds reasonable. In a pluralistic, multicultural society that celebrates diversity, only bigots and xenophobes could object to the accommodation of cultural practices, right?

Maybe not. Those who understand the actual goals of the civil rights movement in American history should immediately recognize the difference between that movement and the MSA initiatives on campuses today. The calls for separate eating and exercise facilities are a strange, discordant note for a movement that claims for itself the mantle of the American civil rights movement. It's ironic that the civil rights movement's calls for *equal* consideration for black Americans are now invoked in support of an agenda that is not interested in equal consideration, but in being *separate*. By the MSA's lights, the Muslim Rosa Parks would insist on sitting in a separate place on the bus, and Muslim students would demand the right *not* to have to eat at infidel lunch counters.

This is one of the primary reasons, but by no means the only one, why the increasingly shrill demands in Western countries for accommodation of Islamic separatist practices are not, contrary to the claims of those who are making them, the latest manifestation of the push for equal rights for minorities. Demanding a place at the table is not the same thing as demanding a separate table of one's own. And just as segregation was deemed unequal in 1954 because it abetted cultural attitudes that exalted one group as superior to the other, so it is today: the demands of Muslim groups for separate facilities are in the service of a supremacist ideology that emanates from the Qur'anic assertions that Muslims are innately superior to unbelievers, which leads to the conclusion, reasonable to the pious, that Muslims should be wary of contact with them. Every Western capitulation made to demands for separate accommodations for Muslims only feeds these supremacist notions, and works directly against the actual goals of the civil rights movement in America, which was, at least originally, working for equal justice and equal rights for all.

This just postpones the inevitable conflict over the stealth jihad to impose sharia in America. Will Muslims receive special permission in American society to discriminate against certain people? Or will there be a searching reevaluation of what we stand for as a society, and a concomitant reevaluation of immigration policies and much more? This debate is going to have to take place sooner or later.

A TOUCH OF MECCA IN THE CATSKILLS

In some cases, the West's Islamic enclaves are exactly that: communities in which the population is secretive, separatist, and entirely Muslim. Authorities estimate that there are at least eleven such communities in rural America, but given the secrecy with which they operate, there could be more. One is "Islamberg," a remote seventy-acre compound in the Catskill mountain foothills near Hancock, New York. Hundreds of Muslims, all apparently black American converts to Islam, live there.

But beyond that, little is known about the place. Terror researcher Paul Williams tried to visit Islamberg in 2007, but a sentry at the compound entrance turned him away, saying only, "Our community is not open to visitors." The secrecy of the place unsettles its neighbors; one said, "The place is dangerous. You can hear gunfire up there. I can't understand why the FBI won't shut it down." Another told Williams that the camp maintains armed guards.

The intelligence service Stratfor reported some disturbing revelations about the camp. For example, members of an Islamic group linked to Islamberg "own several security companies, which provide a source of income and security for the group and its compounds, but also offer a plausible explanation for the presence of firing ranges on the properties—a cover for the paramilitary training that allegedly is conducted at the compounds."[13]

That Islamic group is Jamaat al-Fuqra. According to Stratfor, the organization was "founded in the 1980s by Sheikh Mubarak Ali Gilani, a religious figure from Pakistan who incorporated the group as a tax- exempt organization under the name Muslims of the Americas. Its educational arm, the Quranic Open University, takes American Muslims to Pakistan for training, expecting them to return and instruct others."[14]

According to Stratfor, "Many of the original al-Fuqra members were converts to Islam, and most were African Americans"—like the population of Islamberg. During the 1980s and 1990s, al-Fuqra members were responsible for at least thirteen bombings and arson attacks, as well as seventeen murders—including some of Muslims who belonged to groups considered heretical by orthodox Sunnis. "In 1991," Stratfor reports, "five al-Fuqra members were arrested at a border crossing in Niagara Falls, N.Y., after authorities found their plans to attack an Indian cinema and a Hindu temple in Toronto, Canada. Three of the five later were convicted on charges stemming from the plot." Al-Fuqra members were also involved in the assassination of Rabbi Meir Kahane in 1990 and the first World Trade Center bombing in 1993. Beltway sniper John Muhammad and shoe bomber Richard Reid have also been linked to al-Fuqra.[15]

Williams says that Jamaat al-Fuqra has established compounds like the one in Islamberg in "Hyattsville, Maryland; Red House, Virginia; Falls Church, Virginia; Macon, Georgia; York, South Carolina; Dover, Tennessee; Buena Vista, Colorado; Talihina, Oklahoma; Tulare Country, California; Commerce, California; and Onalaska, Washington. Others are being built, including an expansive facility in Sherman, Pennsylvania."[16]

Jamaat al-Fuqra is not the only Muslim group establishing enclaves in the United States. In 2004, The Islamic Center for Human Excellence in Little Rock, Arkansas, received official approval for its plan for an Islamic enclave that would be, according to its leader, Imam Aquil Hamidullah, "a clean community, free of alcohol, drugs, and free of gangs." In Baltimore, the Gwynnoaks Muslim Residential Development group was established, in the words of John Yahya Cason of the Islamic Education and Community Development Initiative, because "there was no community in the U.S. that showed the totality of the essential components of Muslim social, economic, and political structure."[17]

What Cason and Hamidullah had in mind was not entirely clear. Would Cason's group be enforcing sharia law? If Hamidullah's community would be "free of alcohol," would it punish in some way those who had it? What would be the relationship in such communities between American law and Islamic law?

Unfortunately, American officials seemed disinclined to ask such questions. But they must eventually be addressed. Attorney David Houck observes that the ways in which "Muslims reconcile Islamic polity within the confines of Western liberal democracy is an unresolved issue"—and that makes it all the more urgent, especially given the supremacist and all-encompassing aspects of Islamic law. "The local planning commission in Little Rock, Arkansas," says Houck, "might proceed with the proposed Muslim enclave, but the Arkansas courts and its legislature should not abdicate its responsibilities to ensure that Western liberal rights and protections remain supreme. The government should monitor both the rhetoric and behavior of these communities."[18]

Indeed it should. But as troubling as these compounds may be, they are not the principal front of the stealth jihad in the United States. For the most part, Muslims are not establishing separatist enclaves, but are working to change American society to bring it in line with Islamic law.

DISREGARDING WESTERN LAW

Sometimes the Islamic separatist impulse manifests itself in a simple disregard for the laws and customs of non-Islamic societies. A house fire in March 2007 that killed a woman and nine children in a Bronx row house brought to light what had been up to that time a seldom-noted phenomenon: Islamic polygamy in the United States. Moussa Magassa, the owner of the house and father of five of the children who were killed, had two wives (both of whom survived the fire). The *New York Times* reported that "immigration to New York and other American cities has soared from places where polygamy is lawful and widespread, especially from West African countries like Mali, where demographic surveys show that 43 percent of women are in polygamous marriages."[19]

A senior London imam, Mufti Barkatullah, estimated in 2004 that there were as many as 4,000 polygamous families in Great Britain.[20] By late 2004 the British government was even considering legalizing polygamy for tax purposes, and in early 2007 it was revealed that Muslim immigrants who arrived in Britain with multiple wives were being allowed to claim extra welfare benefits, even though polygamy remained illegal.[21]

And if it was illegal, then why was it practiced at all? An answer came in August 2007, when a Muslim woman in Philadelphia murdered her husband on the day he was set to fly to Morocco in order to marry another wife. Asked for comment, Ibrahim Hooper of CAIR replied, according to the Associated Press, that a "minority" of Muslims in America practiced polygamy, and explained that "Islamic scholars would differ on whether one could do so while living in the United States."[22]

The idea that any Islamic scholar would say that Muslims could lawfully practice polygamy in the United States could only have come from the assumption that Muslims were free to disregard American law when it conflicts with Islam. This is another manifestation of Islamic supremacism: the only laws that matter are the laws of Allah, and the laws of infidel polities are to be respected insofar as it's necessary, and ignored or discarded when possible. Aly Hindy, a prominent imam in Toronto, was explicit and unapologetic about this regarding Canadian law and any non-Muslim law. "This is in our religion and nobody can force us to do anything against our religion," he declared. "If the laws of the country conflict with Islamic law, if one goes against the other, then I am going to follow Islamic law, simple as that."[23]

Apparently many Muslims in America agree with Hindy. In May 2008 researchers estimated that between 50,000 and 100,000 Muslims were living in polygamous arrangements in the United States.[24]

SHARIA FINANCE

Instead of forthrightly discussing Islamic separatism as a social problem, American and European elites are busy debating how they can further expand and institutionalize accommodation to Islam, including its separatist tendencies. The most notorious example of this is the popularity of sharia finance, which Western banking institutions are rushing to offer to Muslims in the West. Timur Kuran, a professor of economics and law at the University of Southern California, has explained that while sharia finance arrangements have "promoted Islamic norms of economic behavior and founded redistribution systems modeled after early Islamic fiscal practices," in fact "the doctrine of Islamic economics is simplistic, incoherent and largely irrelevant to present economic challenges." Kuran adds, "Few Muslims take it seriously, and its practical applications have had no discernible effects on efficiency, growth or poverty reduction."

Why, then, are Muslim states and organizations pushing it so aggressively? "The real purpose of Islamic economics," Kuran explains, "has not been economic improvement but cultivation of a distinct Islamic identity to resist cultural globalization. It has served the cause of global Islamism, known also as 'Islamic fundamentalism,' by fueling the illusion that Muslim societies have lived, or can live, by distinct economic rules."[25]

That makes sharia finance the most serious—and most notorious—example of Islamic separatism. But who cares about that, when there is so much money to be made? Najib Fayyad of Unicorn Capital Turkey explained, "Islamic finance has rapidly emerged as one of the most dynamic segments of the global financial services industry and is today a global phenomenon. There are Islamic finance institutions operating in over 75 countries and with assets estimated at around US$700 billion, a figure which is growing at a rate of about 15% a year."[26] With a May 2008 report declaring that approximately $4 trillion was available for investment in the Middle East, Islamic separatism in the form of sharia finance has become a big business—with Western financial institutions hurrying to get in on it by accommodating Muslims in setting up parallel financial structures in the West.[27]

To take just one of many examples, in May 2008, Allianz Global Investors, one of the world's top active asset managers, opened an office in Bahrain in order to expand its operations in the Middle East, and launched two sharia-compliant equity funds, the Allianz RCM Islamic Global Emerging Markets Equity Fund and the Allianz RCM Islamic Global Equity Opportunities Fund. These steps, the company explained, were "part of its long term strategy and commitment to Middle Eastern clients."

Nick Smith, head of Fund Distribution at Allianz Global Investors in Britain, noted that "there is growing demand over the long term for sharia-compliant funds."[28] And that demand is quickly being met: some of the West's leading financial institutions, including Barclays, Citibank, Credit Suisse, Deutsche Bank, Dow Jones, Goldman Sachs, HSBC Bank, Lloyd's, Merrill Lynch,

Morgan Stanley, and Standard & Poors, have created "sharia Advisory Boards" staffed with Islamic clerics and scholars. This effort aims to help clients bring their financial practices in line with Islamic norms—so as to attract Muslim investors and help Muslims in the West find ways to avoid breaking Islamic law in their financial transactions.[29]

These initiatives have support at the highest levels of Western governments. In 2006, when current British prime minister Gordon Brown was Chancellor of the Exchequer, he told business leaders that it is the "entrepreneurial vibrancy and dynamism of Britain's Muslims, combined with Britain's openness to the world and the historic ties with Muslim countries, that makes the ambition to make Britain the gateway to Islamic finance and trade a realistic and realisable ambition." In order to realize this ambition, he announced that the Labour government of then-prime minister Tony Blair would pursue "tax and regulatory reform to support the development of Shari'a-compliant finance."[30]

Yet the financial rewards may not end up being so great. A journalist who has exhaustively documented sharia finance initiatives, Alyssa A. Lappen, reported that "among the perils of shari'a finance, according to a January [2008] analysis by Moody's Investors Service are: A central role in investment decisions for shari'a scholars who are actually Islamic clerics; investors being forced to accept weak positions; short track records of major investors; multiple complex asset types; risky interest rates and new ventures; plus a lack of transparency combined with corporate management and risk control in the hosting Third World countries."[31]

All this can add up to financial ruin. "Islamic banking defies the separation between economics and religion," says USC Islamic scholar Timur Kuran—and that's why it can cause serious trouble for non-Muslims.[32] Noting that "shari'a regulations override commercial decisions," Lappen relates a disturbing example: "Citibank...launched Saudi American Bank (SAB) in Jeddah and its Riyadh branch in 1955 and 1966 respectively, apparently without considering business risks under shari'a. The Saudis abruptly seized SAB in 1980, denied Citi all future profits, and ordered the bank to train Saudi staffers. Why? Because under shari'a, the bank was judged insufficiently Muslim."[33]

But of course, businesses may be willing to take such risks in the interests of a greater good. Politicians and bankers want to make Muslim immigrants feel at home in Western countries, and encourage Muslim investment in the West, which can only make for peace, no? If Muslims have a significant enough financial stake in America and Europe, they will likely stop their coreligionists from waging violent jihad against them, won't they?

Maybe they will—or maybe bombs and guns will become unnecessary, because the objective will already have been attained. Michael Nazir-Ali, the Anglican Bishop of Rochester, England, noted in January 2008 that "there is pressure already to relate aspects of the sharia to civil law in Britain. To some extent this is already true of arrangements for sharia-compliant banking but have the far-reaching implications of this been fully considered?"[34]

Indeed they haven't. Christopher Holton, vice president of the Center for Security Policy, says flatly, "America is losing the financial war on terror because Wall Street is embracing a subversive enemy ideology on one hand and providing corporate life support to state sponsors of terrorism on the other hand." He illustrates the absurdity of this with a trenchant analogy: "Imagine that it is 1943 and titans of Wall Street are promoting something called 'Shinto Finance,' based on the Japanese theopolitical doctrine, while at the same time, they invest American dollars in foreign companies with active business ties to Imperial Japan."

What's more, sharia finance is another tool of Islamic separatism: instead of assimilating into American society, Muslims are demanding, and receiving, parallel financial institutions that reinforce the idea that they are unique, not subject to the laws and norms to which the rest of us are subject—a privileged class. At the same time, sharia finance initiatives are giving Islamic interests increasing control over Western economic life. In April 2008, journalists Lappen and Rachel Ehrenfeld warned that "the growing U.S. and European financial crisis gives Islamic banking and shari'a finance proponents increasing leverage over Western markets and economics. In reality, their acquisitions of ever-larger stakes in U.S. and Western strategic financial and other assets, amounts to economic warfare against the West."[35]

The multiculturalist anxiety to accommodate non-Muslim principles and practices only makes Westerners even more vulnerable. In an essay on how Muslims can avoid dealing with interest in the American economy, the Chicago imam and Muslim activist Abdul Malik Mujahid claimed that in several incidents, non-Muslims—as soon as they discovered the Islamic prohibition on interest—told Muslims they didn't have to pay their debts. One of these non-Muslims was, according to Mujahid, none other than the Internal Revenue Service:

> One Muslim was asked to pay interest by the IRS because of some problems on his tax return. His secretary told the auditing agent that her boss neither paid nor took any interest since he was a Muslim. The secretary was a non-Muslim who knew the Islamic position. When the secretary remained undeterred on the issue of interest, the IRS agent asked if she could give any references. She showed him the book which contained the Quranic verse prohibiting interest.

The IRS agent had to consult his supervisor—Guess what? He won. Well, the secretary won since the boss didn't know yet what a fight she—a non-Muslim secretary—was putting up with the IRS, knowing the belief and character of her boss. He did not have to pay interest to the IRS on religious grounds.

Mujahid also tells the story of a Muslim physician who was "charged interest on a construction job because he inadvertently delayed payment of the bill for one month. He wrote to apologize for the delay and informed the authorities that Islam did not allow him to pay or receive interest on any transaction. Not only were the interest charges removed, but an opportunity for Dawa came up"—that is, Islamic proselytizing.

Muslims who own credit cards, says Mujahid, should cut them in half and return them to the credit card company, explaining that Islam forbids Muslims to pay interest. Mujahid says that when some Muslims did this, the credit card companies were happy to oblige them. One Muslim who "forgot to pay his bill on time" asked that the resulting finance charges be deleted, explaining that "his position on interest was not to be compromised" and enclosing "his Mastercard in two pieces." Not only did Master-Card delete the finance charges, according to Mujahid, but "they sent him a new card with the same credit line as before."[36]

The ways that sharia finance furthers this Islamization of the West are in line with traditional Islamic law. Sharia finance forbids interest, in line with Qur'anic prohibitions on usury. Sharia-minded Western firms have also devised ways for Muslim homebuyers and small businessmen to work around the prohibition on interest. Sharia finance further prohibits investment in companies that have anything to do with pornography or gambling—prohibitions that may appeal to conservative Americans—

but also with alcohol and even pork. And companies with ties to or investments in Israel are, of course, anathema.

THE WIDER AGENDA

These examples demonstrate an aspiration among some Muslims in America that non-Muslims ignore at their own risk. For what will be the outcome of this kind of thing? Holton predicts that "at best, the result could be Muslim enclaves in Western communities in which sharia supercedes native law." Or "at worst, sharia could start to creep into our lives and laws, changing our way of life little by little over time." That would be entirely in line with the stealth jihad goal of Islamizing American society.

The agents of this societal change are, all too often, Islamic scholars who have made no secret of their support for Islamic supremacism, whether advanced by violent or non-violent means. Holton notes that Mufti Muhammad Taqi Usmani, who has served on the Board of the Dow Jones Islamic Index (IMANX) and still holds a place on the sharia Advisory Boards of several international financial institutions, explains that "the purpose of Jihad aims at breaking the grandeur of unbelievers and establish[ing] that of Muslims." He further insists that Muslims in Western countries "must live in peace until strong enough to wage Jihad"—and once they are strong enough, they will "establish the supremacy of Islam."[37]

Is it farfetched to imagine that Usmani is advancing "the supremacy of Islam" by means of sharia finance, as part of a larger stealth jihad?

And not necessarily always stealthy, either. Alex Alexiev of the Center for Security Policy, which has led the fight against sharia finance initiatives, explains that "far from being a legitimate investment vehicle, sharia finance facilitates religiously sanctioned support for terrorist organizations—as well as providing radical Islamists with highly paid sinecures as sharia-finance board advisors in the sanctum sanctorum of capitalism, all the while that they are pursuing a subversive campaign to destroy it."[38]

As one might expect, the Muslim Brotherhood's hand is evident in all this. Another influential figure in the world of sharia finance is none other than the Brotherhood's Sheikh Yusuf al-Qaradawi, the U.S.-designated supporter of terrorism who has justified suicide attacks against Israeli civilians—and who has also advised the policymakers who early in 2008 declared the word "jihad" off-limits to American officials.[39] Qaradawi, says Holton, has advocated "Jihad with money," saying that "Allah has ordered us to fight enemies with our lives and with our money."

What's more, one of the Brotherhood organizations listed in the 1991 "grand jihad" memorandum, the North American Islamic Trust (NAIT), was named an unindicted co-conspirator in the Holy Land Foundation jihad terror funding—and is also a key player in the sharia finance initiative. It is, according to Holton, "listed as an adviser to the Dow Jones fund."

The ultimate goal? The International Islamic Finance Market is forthright, including among its objectives the aim of "wider sharia acceptance."[40] And it is working: the Kuwait News Agency reported in May 2008 that "it seems as if the future is heading towards a rise in the number of these Islamic institutions," and indeed that "many traditional investment companies" have transformed themselves into "Islamic firms."[41]

Wider acceptance of sharia, of course, leads to wider acceptance of sharia supremacy.

CHAPTER EIGHT

READIN', WRITIN', AND SUBJUGATIN' THE INFIDEL: THE STEALTH JIHAD IN AMERICAN SCHOOLS

O f all the arenas in which the stealth jihad is advancing, one of the most crucial is in our schools, where stealth jihadists have found a welcoming environment among teachers deeply steeped in the credo of multiculturalism. With the mandate of "tolerance" robbing many educators of their ability to evaluate non-Western cultures critically, teachers are highly susceptible to an organized campaign by U.S.-based Islamic organizations and their primary benefactor, Saudi Arabia, to present a view of Islam that whitewashes its violent history and intolerant religious imperatives.

Meanwhile, in America's Islamic academies, teaching materials, some direct from Saudi Arabia, instill unequivocal hatred toward non-Muslims and a deep suspicion of Western culture. But one would never know that such attitudes even exist among Muslims from reading the lessons placed in mainstream public schools by U.S.-based Islamic groups. In contrast to the antagonistic teachings found at Islamic academies, these groups ensure that the

Islamic instruction in public schools presents a picture of Islam that is so pristine and peaceful that it sometimes crosses the boundary from mere pro-Muslim bias into outright Islamic proselytizing.

THE ISLAMIZATION OF THE TEXTBOOKS

While Muslims in the West grow increasingly more assertive in demanding that Western institutions accommodate sharia provisions, American schoolchildren are learning a partial and rosy view of Islam in American public schools—using books that have been vetted by organizations linked to the stealth jihad.

In a study released in June 2008, the American Textbook Council, an independent national research organization that evaluates the quality of textbooks, issued a report finding that ten of the most widely used middle school and high school social studies textbooks "present an incomplete and confected view of Islam that misrepresents its foundations and challenges to international security." The report found that the books present highly tendentious constructions as undisputed truth, making common cause with West-hating multiculturalists to bowdlerize the presentation of Islam, denigrate or downplay Christianity and Western civilization, and transform many public school textbooks into proselytizing tracts.

And this tendency has only intensified since September 11.

California seventh graders, for example, use a text called *History Alive! The Medieval World and Beyond,* produced by the Teachers' Curriculum Institute. Defining jihad, the book tells students that "Muslims should fulfill jihad with the heart, tongue, and hand. Muslims use the heart in their struggle to resist evil. The tongue may convince others to take up worthy causes, such as funding medical research. Hands may perform good works and correct wrongs." It gives no idea that Muslims have ever viewed jihad as involving, in whole or part, warfare against unbelievers, or have ever waged war on that basis. Muhammad, meanwhile, far from exhorting his followers to subjugate unbelievers, "taught equality" and was a prototypical compassionate liberal who instructed Muslims "to share their wealth and to care for the less fortunate in society."[1]

There are a few notable exceptions to the textbooks' tendency to ignore or downplay violent jihad. For example, Holt's *Medieval to Early Modern Times* approaches an honest account in defining jihad as referring not only to "the inner struggle people go through in their effort to obey God and behave according to Islamic ways," but also to "the struggle to defend the Muslim community, or, historically, to convert people to Islam. The word has also been translated as holy war."[2] Similarly, Prentice Hall's *Medieval and Early Modern Times* at least admits that, besides spiritual struggle, jihad "can also mean waging war to spread the Islamic faith," before it assures students that "another factor helping the Arabs" in the early Islamic conquests "was their tolerance for other religions."[3]

But the textbook explanations of jihad usually lack any reference at all to its violent component or even deny outright that such a component exists. A typical example is Houghton Mifflin's middle school world history book, *Across the Centuries,* which was at the center of a failed attempt by non-Muslim parents in 2003 to stop Islamic indoctrination in California public school classrooms.[4] It defines jihad as a struggle "to do one's best to resist temptation and overcome evil."[5] Prentice Hall's high school world history text *Connections to Today* offers a similar take, defining jihad as "effort in God's service," and

explaining that "jihad has often been mistakenly translated simply as 'holy war.' In fact, it may include acts of charity or an
inner struggle to achieve spiritual peace, as well as any battle in
defense of Islam."[6] Most egregious is *History Alive!*, which says
that jihad "represents the human struggle to overcome difficulties and do things that are pleasing to God." Might this struggle
ever involve the force of arms? Why, yes: sometimes jihad can
become a "physical struggle." Muslims must "fight to protect
themselves from those who would do them harm or to right a
terrible wrong."[7]

Who could object to that?

Very few people. But one of them is former congressman Tom
Tancredo (R-CO), who on the floor of the House of Representatives in 2004 starkly described the result of all this whitewashing:

> In a textbook called Across the Centuries, which is used for
> seventh grade history...the book defines the word jihad as,
> "To do one's best to resist temptation and overcome evil." So
> now this is what children are taught the word jihad means.
> When this child watches a program on television and this
> word [jihad] is used, and it is a word used in conjunction
> with someone who has just blown himself or herself up, and
> a lot of other innocent human beings around them, this kid
> is supposed to think that that is what somebody is doing in
> order to resist temptation and overcome evil. And if we con-
> demn jihad against the United States, then we are condemn-
> ing someone who is just simply trying to overcome evil. This
> is what we tell our children?[8]

Yes, it is. And it gets worse.

NO JIHAD, NO DHIMMITUDE

In light of the attempt of many textbooks to whitewash violence from Islam, it's no surprise that the early spread of Islam is generally presented in benign or even positive terms. The *History Alive!* text is typical when it reports that Islam "spread" but does not explain how, implying that it all took place through peaceful missionary activity and voluntary conversion: "Although the first Muslims lived in Arabia, Islam spread through the Middle East." Similarly, McDougal Littell's *World History: Medieval and Early Modern Times* asserts that "there was much blending of cultures under Muslim rule. Over time, many peoples in Muslim-ruled territories converted to Islam. They were attracted by Islam's message of equality and hope for salvation." The American Textbook Council report notes that "McDougal Littell's Teacher's Annotated Edition reiterates this theme, telling instructors to stress that 'many conquered people became Muslims [because] they found Islam's message of equality and hope attractive.'"[9]

The experience of non-Muslims who were conquered and subjugated by the early jihad warriors, however, tells a very different story. The early Muslim conquests saw the warriors of jihad sweep out of Arabia and become the masters of a vast empire stretching from Spain to India within a century of Muhammad's death. Islam "spread" through the Middle East when the indigenous populations in the conquered areas were subjugated as dhimmis: all they had to do to be free of the onerous tax burden and the other discriminatory hallmarks of dhimmitude was convert to Islam. And over time, they did so, in large numbers. One would think that the coercive nature of Islam's dhimmi system would warrant a mention in these textbooks—particularly since it remains part of the system of Islamic law that jihadists are fighting, in various ways, to impose upon the West.

But no such luck. Another text, Prentice Hall's *Medieval and Early Modern Times* even goes so far as to call medieval Muslim Spain a "multicultural society." *History Alive!* says that in medieval Spain "a unique culture flourished in cities like Cordoba and Toledo, where Muslims, Jews, and Christians lived together in peace."[10] Of course, this is a common historical myth today: even the conservative flagship *National Review* gushed in 2002 about medieval Spain as a multicultural paradise featuring "a vibrant economy and an adventurous intellectual community, ruled by a benign Islamic monarch whose Jewish right-hand man helps bring about a mutually beneficial relationship with Orthodox Christians."[11]

But *pace* Dr. Goebbels, constant repetition does not make this sort of thing true, and it has no business being in a school textbook where it can mislead students about exactly what kind of society jihadists wish to establish by imposing sharia. Even historian Maria Rosa Menocal, who has with her book, *The Ornament of the World*, popularized the notion of a tolerant, pluralistic Islamic al-Andalus, acknowledged in that book that Christians and Jews living in Muslim Spain had to abide by the laws of dhimmitude that enforced their second-class status. In return for relative religious freedom, she writes, Jews and Christians "were required to pay a special tax—no Muslims paid taxes—and to observe a number of restrictive regulations: Christians and Jews were prohibited from attempting to proselytize Muslims, from building new places of worship, from displaying crosses or ringing bells. In sum, they were forbidden most public displays of their religious rituals."[12]

Historian Kenneth Baxter Wolf observes that, once they conquered Spain, the new Muslim rulers enacted a series of laws largely "aimed at limiting those aspects of the Christian cult which seemed to compromise the dominant position of Islam." After enumerating a list of such laws, he adds, "Aside from such cultic restrictions most of the laws were simply designed to underscore the position of the dimmis as second-class citizens."[13]

A "multicultural society"? Not in the way that the students who use the Prentice Hall textbook will understand the term.

Sharia in general gets short shrift in these texts. Students learn that it "makes no distinction between religious beliefs and daily life" (*Medieval to Early Modern Times*), and that it "helps Muslims live by the teachings of the Qur'an" (*History Alive!*), but they hear nothing about stonings or amputation or the subjugation of women and dhimmis. Sharia "is an Arabic word meaning 'the way that leads to God,'" explains Prentice Hall, but says nothing about the fate that awaits those who, in this life, falter on that way.[14]

ISLAM GOOD, CHRISTIANITY BAD

The most glaring example of anti-Western cultural bias and complicity (whether witting or unwitting) with the stealth jihad is the contrast between the textbooks' treatment of Islam and the way they deal with Christianity. The Textbook Council notes, "While seventh-grade textbooks describe Islam in glowing language, they portray Christianity in harsh light. Students encounter a startling contrast. Islam is featured as a model of interfaith tolerance; Christians wage wars of aggression and kill Jews. Islam provides models of harmony and civilization. Anti-Semitism, the Inquisition, and wars of religion bespot the Christian record." The Crusades, which began as a response to a call for help from the Byzantine Emperor in Constantinople, and were a tardy and small-scale response to 450 years of jihadist aggression that had overwhelmed the formerly Christian lands of the Middle East and North Africa, are uniformly presented as an act of unprovoked aggression by Christian Europe against a pacifistic Islamic Middle East. Overlooking the fact that Islamic forces ultimately prevailed in the Crusades, *History Alive!* presents Muslims as victims—a fashionable and politically useful appellation these days. The Crusades were, according to the book, "religious wars launched against Muslims by European Christians," and were "a terrible ordeal for many Muslims. An unknown number of Muslims lost their lives in battles and massacres. Crusaders also destroyed Muslim property."

The Textbook Council report observes that "when Muslim groups attack Christian peoples, kill them, and take their lands, the process is referred to as 'building' an empire. Christian attempts to restore those lands are labeled as 'violent attacks' or 'massacres.' A passage about the Second Crusade characterizes Christians as 'invaders'—something they would have denied— while the Seljuks are simply 'migrating' into Christian territories."[15]

SERVING THE STEALTH JIHAD AGENDA

This whitewashing of history serves modern political agendas. UCLA academic Gary B. Nash, one of the authors of the *Across the Centuries* textbook, observes forthrightly that there is today a battle to change history textbooks—to "redistribute historical capital"—in order to serve contemporary political programs.[16] If students learn that medieval Muslims were tolerant, magnanimous, and peaceful, while Christians were bigoted, rapacious, and brutal, they internalize paradigms that they'll use in evaluating current events—and all too many teachers are no doubt very happy to help them with this exercise. If sharia is a benevolent system of law under which diverse peoples prosper, who could possibly object to the accommodation of various elements of it by Western institutions in order to make Muslim immigrants feel welcome? No hint is given in any of this material, of course, of the supremacist imperatives within sharia to subjugate non-Muslims, or to deny them (and women) equality of rights before the law. No hint is given of the violence that lies at the heart of the Islamic doctrine of jihad.

These political agendas become clearer in what the textbooks say about modern Islamic terrorism. Glencoe's high school text *World History: Modern Times*, for example, explains that some modern terrorists are "militant nationalists who want to create their own state or expand national territory." The book offers one example of this: the Irish Republican Army. "Other terrorists," the book says, "work for one nation to undermine the government of another. This kind of terrorism is called *state-sponsored terrorism*. Militant governments in Iraq, Iran, Syria, Libya, and North Korea have sponsored terrorist acts. There are also states that secretly finance, train, or hide terrorists."[17] *World History: Modern Times* also takes students on a lightning tour of common explanations for Islamic jihad terrorism:

> Some analysts say this terrorism is rooted in the clash of modern and Islamic cultures. They argue that because many states in the former Ottoman Empire did not modernize along Western lines, Muslims have not accommodated their religious beliefs to the modern world. Other analysts note that the Christians and Muslims have viewed each other with hostility since at least the time of the Crusades. Others suggest that

poverty and ignorance lie at the root of the problem—extremists find it easy to stir up resentment against wealthy Western
societies. Finally, some say terrorism would be rare if the
Israeli-Palestinian conflict could be solved.[18]

Nowhere does the book offer the possibility that Islamic terrorists
are committing violence against unbelievers and pursuing a
supremacist agenda for reasons arising from imperatives of the
Islamic religion. But they can perhaps be forgiven for this since,
as we have seen, so few analysts anywhere along the political spectrum are prepared to consider this possibility.

The Prentice Hall high school text *World History: The Modern
World* is even worse, echoing the jihad terrorists themselves (as
well as many mainstream liberal analysts) by blaming Islamic terrorism on the West and Israel: "Increasingly, the Middle East has
become a training ground and source for terrorism. One historical
reason for this has been Western colonial domination in the region.
The establishment of the state of Israel in 1948 helped focus anti-
Western resentment among many Arabs."[19] How Western "domination" or the establishment of the state of Israel gave rise to
Islamic jihad terrorism in Indonesia, the Philippines, Thailand,
Kashmir, Chechnya, Nigeria, and elsewhere is not explained. The
book informs students with reasonable accuracy that "Islamic fundamentalism refers to the religious belief that society should be
governed by Islamic law," but never explains how deeply rooted
that belief is within traditional Islam, and once again attributes its
rise to causes outside Islam altogether: "Islamic fundamentalism
was encouraged by a lack of basic resources in many Arab nations.
Islamic fundamentalists found it easy to make Israel or Western
nations scapegoats for their problems. In the past few decades, terrorist attacks have increased against these scapegoats."[20]

Why? Glencoe's high school American history book, *American Vision*, says flatly—and inaccurately—that "the reason Middle Eastern terrorists have targeted Americans can be traced back to events early in the twentieth century."[21] What they mean by this is left vague, but it becomes clearer in *World History: Modern Times*, also from Glencoe, which suggests that it's because of the West's dependence on oil:

> Many terrorist attacks since World War II have been carried out by Middle Eastern groups against Western countries. One reason Middle Eastern terrorists have targeted Americans can be traced to developments in the 1900s. As oil became important to the American economy in the 1920s, the United States invested heavily in the Middle East oil industry. This industry brought great wealth to the ruling families in some Middle Eastern kingdoms, but most ordinary citizens remained poor. Some became angry at the United States for supporting the wealthy kingdoms and families.[22]

Like the academic Marxists who probably taught them in college, the textbook's authors wave away the possibility of an ideologically driven Islamic jihad movement and attribute it all to anger over domestic economic inequalities.

American Vision does acknowledge the existence of "new movements" in Muslim countries

> calling for a strict interpretation of the Quran—the Muslim holy book—and a return to traditional Muslim religious laws. These Muslim movements wanted to overthrow pro-Western governments in the Middle East and create a pure Islamic society. Muslims who support these movements are

referred to as fundamentalist militants. Although the vast majority of Muslims believe terrorism is *contrary* to their faith, militants began using terrorism to achieve their goals.[23]

Unfortunately, however, the notion that "the vast majority of Muslims" view terrorism as un-Islamic, no matter how often repeated, remains unproven. Nor is it certain, as we saw in chapter five, that those who ostensibly reject "terrorism" define the word in the same way as Westerners do.

THE COUNCIL ON ISLAMIC EDUCATION'S "BLOODLESS REVOLUTION"

How did all this political and religious propaganda get into public school textbooks? The smoking gun is not hard to find. The American Textbook Council report notes that "Islamic organizations, willing to sow misinformation, are active in curriculum politics. These activists are eager to expunge any critical thought about Islam from textbooks and all public discourse. They are succeeding, assisted by partisan scholars and associations."[24]

Specifically, "from 2001 on, *Connections to Today,* Prentice Hall's market-dominant high school world history then and now, and several spin-off versions customized for California and other states, listed Shabbir Mansuri and Susan Douglass of the Council on Islamic Education (CIE) as academic reviewers." One enthusiastic article describes CIE as "the only national faith-based organization in the United States that is directly involved in the process of reviewing public school textbooks from a multicultural perspective."[25] Houghton Mifflin editor Abigail Jungreis, who has praised Douglass's breadth of knowledge, remarked about CIE, "We've had a really good relationship with them over the years.

Their reviewers are knowledgeable."[26] According to one estimate, CIE and Douglass have trained over 8,000 public school teachers.[27]

The effects of this are manifest. The American Textbook Council report notes that

> as early as 2002 another high-profile textbook, *Patterns of Interaction,* a high school world history textbook published by Houghton Mifflin under the McDougal Littell imprint, did not mention jihad. Houghton Mifflin's multigrade series then dropped jihad from textbooks; by 2005 Houghton Mifflin had apparently removed jihad from its entire series of social studies textbooks. The advisory role of the Council on Islamic Education in making these editorial decisions remains unclear.[28]

Yet it is an active role:

> In 2008, the Council on Islamic Education, trading on its influence with textbook publishers, opened a website for the entirely spectral Institute for Religion and Civic Values. It offered "consulting, training and resources pertaining to issues of religion, identity, freedom, and pluralism to policymakers, educators, the media, organizations and communities, in order to strengthen civil society." In the case of Islamic activism, theological aims are often concealed in familiar, appealing civic language.[29]

What is behind this civic language, however, is neither familiar nor appealing. CIE founder and director Shabbir Mansuri has waged, according to a 2001 interview, "what he calls a 'bloodless' revolution: promoting an increased emphasis on world cultures and faiths—including Islam—inside American junior high and high school classrooms."[30] Mansuri has written a six-step guide on "how to get religious accommodation in the public school system," specifically directed toward getting public schools to provide prayer rooms for Muslim students, time out of classes for Islamic prayer, and days off for Islamic holidays. In it, he advises parents to "understand what is defined as a 'reasonable limit' on religious freedom." He explains, "In the United States, one of the strongest arguments in favor of seeking religious accommodation for your child is former president Bill Clinton's 1995 statement of principles addressing the extent to which religious expression and activity are permitted in public school. This was given to every school district in the U.S."

That statement, however, while defending students' rights to pray privately and in informal groups on school grounds, says nothing about school administrators providing special accommodation for religious practices.[31] Mansuri says, however, that Muslim accommodation is simply a matter of "my exercising my constitutional rights," and advises Muslim parents to kill their opponents with kindness, inviting recalcitrant school administrators over to dinner to convince them to grant the accommodation. If administrators remain reluctant, Muslim parents should begin to write letters to the school and ultimately take their complaint to the school district, but always in a polite and non-confrontational way.[32]

At the same time, however, CIE is endeavoring to inculcate into American students a healthy dose of self-hatred. "American children need to know that genocide was part of the birth of this nation.... The Holocaust began at home," declared CIE board member Ali A. Mazrui of the State University of New York at Binghamton in the early 1990s. A 2003 *Middle East Quarterly* report observes that "since its creation in 1989, the Council has repeatedly allied itself with academics and journalists who take an antagonistic view of the U.S. and Western civilization."

ISLAMIC CURRICULA COURTESY OF OUR FRIENDS, THE SAUDIS

This antagonism toward Western culture is glaringly displayed at the 900-student Islamic Saudi Academy in Alexandria, Virginia, a Saudi-funded school that teaches Islamic supremacism and hatred of Jews and Christians. An eleventh-grade text used in the school contains a notorious Islamic tradition in which Muhammad says that a sign of the Day of Judgment will be Muslims killing Jews, who will hide behind stones and trees, and the stones and trees will cry out: "Oh Muslim, oh servant of God, here is a Jew hiding behind me. Come here and kill him." Other passages that the school used during the 2007-2008 academic year, even after the congressionally appointed U.S. Commission on International Religious Freedom recommended that the school be closed due to the Islamic supremacism and hatred of non-Muslims taught there, declared that "the Jews conspired against Islam and its people," and that Muslims could lawfully kill and seize the property of polytheists. A twelfth-grade text teaches that adulterers and apostates from Islam should be put to death.

The AP reported in June 2008 that "the academy has come under scrutiny from critics who allege that it fosters an intolerant brand of Islam similar to that taught in the conservative Saudi kingdom. In the review, [the U.S. Commission on International Religious Freedom] recommended that the school make all of its textbooks available to the State Department so changes can be made before the next school year."

Fairfax County Supervisor Gerald Hyland attributed the problem to misunderstandings of the Qur'an. "I would be less than frank," he told reporters, "if I didn't tell you that the curriculum does contain references to the Qur'an, which, if taken out of context and read literally, would cause some concern."[33]

Ah yes, those Qur'an quotes are only incendiary when "taken out of context and read literally." When one reads them figuratively and puts them in context—a context, by the way, that is never supplied, but only alluded to by Islamic spokesmen in the West—they're no longer deeply worrisome; they're transformed into declarations of peace and love. Of course.

One would think Hyland would hesitate to claim that an Islamic school, staffed by people who know the Qur'an far better than he does, was misreading the Qur'an, but he feels compelled to jump into the PC lockstep, no matter how absurd it makes him look. Unfortunately for Hyland, the incendiary passages in textbooks at the Islamic Saudi Academy reflect traditional and mainstream Islamic teaching. In one Islamic tradition recorded in *Sahih Bukhari*, (the collection of hadith, the words and deeds of Muhammad, that Muslims consider most reliable) Jews conspire to murder Muhammad.[34] In another hadith from *Bukhari*, Muhammad says that the lives and property of unbelievers are safe from him as long as they convert to Islam—implying that if they don't, their lives and property are fair game.[35] And in a third, Muhammad instructs, "If somebody [a Muslim] discards his religion, kill him."[36]

American officials were thus in the peculiar position of pretending that the Islamic Saudi Academy was twisting the true teachings of Islam, and asking it to stop teaching what were actually traditional and deeply rooted Islamic tenets. But the need for this was urgent, as the Commission on International

Religious Freedom has also found that "some Saudi government-funded textbooks used in North American Islamic schools have been found to encourage incitement to violence against non-Muslims."[37]

Does that incitement translate into action? It certainly has. In 1999 the Islamic Saudi Academy's valedictorian was a young man named Ahmed Omar Abu Ali, who spent his extracurricular hours teaching Islamic studies at the Dar Al Hijrah Islamic Center in Falls Church, Virginia, which is closely tied to the Muslim Brotherhood.[38] Abu Ali's classmates at the Academy voted him "most likely to become a martyr." He got his chance in 2002 while studying Islam in Saudi Arabia, when he joined a plot by al Qaeda to kill President George W. Bush. In 2006 Abu Ali was sentenced to thirty years in prison for this conspiracy.[39]

Did Ahmed Omar Abu Ali learn any of his hatred of America at the Islamic Saudi Academy or the Brotherhood-affiliated Dar Al Hijrah Islamic Center? Or if he picked up this hatred elsewhere, did he learn anything at either place that might have given him a different perspective? In light of Abu Ali's recruitment into al Qaeda, these are questions with implications for America's national security. But once again, we find that multiculturalism dictates that such vital questions not even be asked—to do so would be "Islamophobic."

Not coincidentally, CIE was one of the earliest proponents of the policy now adopted by the State Department and the Department of Homeland Security, to refer to jihad activity not as jihad but as "hirabah," the Arabic word for unlawful warfare. CIE researcher Susan Douglass coauthored a guide for teachers in 2003 entitled "Hirabah, Not Jihad," which "discusses the distinction between jihad as a principle of social justice, and as a military institution entrusted to authorities in society. Students learn about the categories of illegitimate violence in society, namely rebellion and terrorism, brigandage and other forms of mayhem against the public."[40] As we saw in chapter three, this initiative actually impedes analysts' ability to understand the motives and goals of the jihadists, and hence imperils all the potential victims of that jihad. The only beneficiaries of this policy are the stealth jihadists.

The American Textbook Council concludes that CIE now enjoys "virtually unchecked power over publishers" and is an "agent of contemporary censorship," exercising its authority haughtily, informing publishers that it may "decline requests for reviewing published materials, unless a substantial and substantive revision is planned by the publisher." Yet despite this high-handedness, "for more than a decade, history textbook editors have done the Council's bidding, and as a result, history textbooks accommodate Islam on terms that Islamists demand."[41]

And those terms coincide perfectly with the aims and goals of the stealth jihad.

Nor is the Council on Islamic Education the sole Islamic organization involved in vetting textbooks. *National Review*'s Stanley Kurtz reports that the Saudis have bought their way into the process: "The system of federal subsidies to university programs of Middle East Studies (under Title VI of the Higher Education Act) has been serving as a kind of Trojan horse for Saudi influence over American K-12 education." These university programs design "lesson plans and seminars on the Middle East for America's K-12 teachers," which are then adopted "without being subject to the normal public vetting processes."

Since education authorities at the federal level have "effectively abandoned oversight" of these programs, the Saudis have stepped in to fill the gap, "lavishly funding several organizations that design Saudi-friendly English-language K-12 curricula," and then working to "convince the 'outreach coordinators' at prestigious, federally subsidized universities to purvey these materials to America's teachers. And wouldn't you know it, outreach coordinators or teacher-trainers at a number of university Middle East Studies centers have themselves been trained by the very same Saudi-funded foundations that design K-12 course materials. These Saudi-friendly folks are happy to build their outreach efforts around Saudi-financed K-12 curricula."

The result is that the "government-approved K-12 Middle East studies curriculum" has actually "been bought and paid for by the Saudis"—and "the American government is asleep at the wheel."[42]

What's more, this Saudi influence continues to spread. Journalist Cinnamon Stillwell reported in June 2008 that "the Saudi funded Prince Alwaleed Bin Talal Center for Muslim-Christian Understanding at Georgetown University now offers professional development workshops for K-12 teachers. The workshops take place at the hosting institution and provide teachers with classroom material. They are free of charge and ACMCU throws in lunch to boot." One "education consultant" for the Center was none other than Susan Douglass.[43]

Thus, through a mix of petrodollars and U.S.-based Islamic pressure groups, Saudi values have connived their way into the U.S. education system.

NOT JUST THE BOOKS

Resourceful and well-informed teachers may be able to work around the textbooks' biased presentations, but such teachers are rather thin on the ground these days. More common, in public education and in other fields, are teachers and administrators who are all too happy, in the name of multiculturalism and tolerance, to go along with and actively further the textbooks' unabashedly pro-Islamic teachings.

In doing so, the taboo about teaching religion in the public schools, so zealously established and guarded against Christian prayer by the ACLU and the Supreme Court over the last few decades, is frequently set aside. In Amherst, New Hampshire, in May 2007, seventh graders at Amherst Middle School set up what a local newspaper called a "Saudi Arabian Bedouin tent community" that was open to the town. Visitors were given Arabic names and asked to fill out a genuine Saudi customs form, complete with the legend across the top of the form, "Death for Drug Trafficking." Student exhibits were sex-segregated, girls modeled hijabs and veils, and "an Islamic religion station included a Muslim prayer rug with a compass imbedded in it to locate Mecca, readings on the Islamic faith, call to prayer items and prayer beads."[44]

An Islamic religion station offering "readings on the Islamic faith" and "prayer beads" in a public school's social studies exhibit? Sex segregation among American seventh graders? Perhaps it was all in good fun—but it wasn't the first time that it was hard to distinguish between role-playing and proselytizing for Islam in an American public school.

One notorious example of this came in 2003, when several parents filed suit against the Byron Union School District in Byron, California, charging that several exercises that students were required to complete during their study of Islam amounted to proselytizing for the religion. The controversial exercises came in part from Houghton Mifflin's *Across the Centuries* text, along with a role-playing handbook that the CIE helped develop that told students, "From the beginning, you and your classmates will become Muslims."[45] Students were directed to memorize portions of the Fatiha, the first chapter of the Qur'an and most important prayer in Islam, to adopt Muslim names and to shout "Allahu akbar" (Allah is greatest), the cry made famous by jihadists worldwide. Students were even encouraged to skip lunch in order to simulate the Ramadan fast. By way of contrast, a companion unit on Christianity did not require students to pretend they were any kind of Christian, recite any Scripture, or memorize any Christian prayer.[46]

The workbook on Islam, however, required students to make statements of Islamic faith in order to answer them correctly— affirming, for example, that "Muhammad is the prophet of Allah," rather than that "Muslims believe that Muhammad is the prophet of Allah." Yet despite all this, a judge ruled that this program did not contain "any devotional or religious intent."

Richard Thompson, chief counsel for the Thomas More Law Center, which pursued the case on the parents' behalf, noted the double standard: "While public schools prohibit Christian students from reading the Bible, praying, displaying the Ten Commandments, and even mentioning the word 'God,' students in California are being indoctrinated into the religion of Islam. Public schools would never tolerate teaching Christianity in this way. Just imagine the ACLU's outcry if students were told that they had to pray the Lord's Prayer, memorize the Ten Commandments, use such phrases as 'Jesus is the Messiah,' and fast during Lent."[47]

This kind of school-sponsored Islamic proselytizing has become increasingly common in recent years. In October 2004, public elementary schoolchildren in Herndon, Virginia, were also given instruction in Islam and made to participate in Muslim role-playing games. "Multicultural trainer" Afeefa Syeed also helped them understand the Ramadan fast, freely admitting that her instruction was meant to serve a larger agenda: "For teachers and administrators, as well as fellow students, explaining Ramadan helps the school accommodate the religious requirements of the holiday."[48]

Similarly, in May 2008 at Friendswood Junior High in Friendswood, Texas, near Houston, principal Robin Lowe, without giving parents any notice, canceled a physical education class and required students to attend a presentation on Islam given by two women from the Houston office of the Council on American-Islamic Relations. According to students who attended, the session was essentially an exercise in proselytizing; students were taught that there is one God, Allah, that Jesus is one of his prophets, that one should pray five times daily, and other basic tenets of Islam.[49] Lowe was apparently so intent on exposing students to this material that she even defied the district superintendent, who had told her not to allow the presentation to go on.[50] After an outcry from parents, the school district moved Lowe to another job.[51]

If you can't imagine a public school principal defying orders and sacrificing her job in order to make sure students attended a presentation on the basics of Christianity, it's only because you know which way the wind is blowing. None of the encroachments of Islam in public schools should come as any real surprise. Multiculturalism, after all, amounts to respect for every culture except one's own. The Western embarrassment, regret, and even self-hatred that has been inculcated in American public school students for decades now has created a vacuum that the stealth jihadists have shown themselves to be all too eager to fill. Certainly the lawyers or others involved in defending the Byron Union School District from the parents who sued, or the judges who ruled against the parents, would disavow that they would like to see Islamic law implemented in the United States, and would indignantly deny that their efforts were furthering that end in any way. They just did it all for tolerance, pluralism, and multiculturalism.

Unfortunately, in the end it amounts to the same thing.

A MADRASSA GROWS IN BROOKLYN

The Khalil Gibran International Academy in Brooklyn, a public secondary school focusing on Middle Eastern culture and Arabic language instruction, was supposed to be a crown jewel of multiculturalism when it opened in September 2007. Yet, although a Department of Education spokesman, David Cantor, insisted before the school opened that it would "not be a vehicle for political ideology," it has been and remains engulfed in controversy.[52]

The school's first principal was Dhabah ("Debbie") Almontaser who, in a telling indication of where her own sympathies lay, had accepted an award from the stealth jihadist extraordinaire, the Council on American-Islamic Relations. When asked about CAIR, Almontaser defended the organization as a victimized "civil rights" group, neglecting to mention any of its officials' ties to terrorism or their statements of Islamic supremacism:

> CAIR-New York is one of the most prominent civil rights organizations in New York City, as well as across the country. The president of CAIR sits on the Human Rights Commission of New York City. He was appointed by Mayor Bloomberg. So if Mayor Bloomberg has no issues with working closely with CAIR, I don't see why anyone should have any issues. CAIR, unfortunately, has been targeted, because it is fighting

for the civil rights of Arabs and Muslims. And, you know, this organization, as well as other organizations fighting for civil rights of Arabs and Muslims, is very much needed.[53]

The *New York Sun* noted in May 2007 that "when one of our reporters asked Ms. Almontaser whether she considers Hamas and Hizballah to be terrorist organizations and who she thinks was behind the terrorist attacks of September 11, 2001, she declined to answer, suggesting she shouldn't be singled out for such questions."[54]

None of that caused Almontaser any serious trouble; however, on August 6, 2007, she ignited a firestorm when she downplayed the significance of T-shirts that were being sold by a group sharing office space with the Saba Association of American Yemenis, for whom Almontaser is a spokeswoman. The shirts bore the legend *Intifada NYC;* "intifada," of course, is the term Palestinian jihad terrorists use for their violent campaign against Israel, which has seen the murder of scores of Israeli civilians in suicide bombings. Nonsensically, Almontaser justified the T-shirts as an indication of the wearers' integration into New York society:

> The word [intifada] basically means 'shaking off.' That is the root word if you look it up in Arabic. I understand it is developing a negative connotation due to the uprising in the Palestinian-Israeli areas. I don't believe the intention is to have any of that kind of [violence] in New York City. I think it's pretty much an opportunity for girls to express that they are part of New York City society...and shaking off oppression.[55]

Facing vociferous criticism the next day, Almontaser backtracked: "The word 'intifada' is completely inappropriate as a T-shirt slogan. I regret suggesting otherwise. By minimizing the word's historical associations, I implied that I condone violence and threats of violence. That view is anathema to me."[56] However, many politicians and public officials began calling for her resignation. A *New York Post* editorial went to the heart of the problem:

> But if [*intifada*'s] generally accepted meaning were as benign as she insists, you can bet no one would be wearing it on a T-shirt. You can further bet that she knows it. Now, if Dhabah Almontaser is going to be as disingenuous about something like this, why should New Yorkers believe her claim that "you won't find religious or political indoctrination or anti-Americanism" at her Khalil Gibran school?[57]

On August 10, 2007, Almontaser resigned, blaming "a small group of highly misguided individuals" who had "launched a relentless attack on me because of my religion." She charged that they "used my religion as the pretext to undermine the Academy and have taken my words out of context to distort my record and portray me as something that I am not."[58] Today, she is trying to regain her job as principal, while continuing to tar her opponents as bigots and racists.

Despite Almontaser's removal, however, questions remain about the Khalil Gibran International Academy. A member of the academy's board, Imam Khalid Latif, New York University's Muslim chaplain, in March 2006 wrote to John Sexton, president of New York University, protesting a planned exhibition of the cartoons of the Muslim prophet Muhammad that had first appeared in a Danish newspaper. Latif's letter contained an unmistakable threat: after explaining to Sexton why he objected to the cartoons, Latif warned that "if ideas like that are not enough to keep these images from being displayed, the potential of what might happen after they are shown is something else that should be considered and not taken lightly."[59]

Meanwhile, the source of the academy's original curriculum should raise some eyebrows; it came courtesy of the American Arab Anti-Discrimination Committee which, according to Militant Islam Monitor, has filed numerous "discrimination lawsuits and legal challenges aimed at obstructing the FBI, JTTF and Homeland Security from investigating Arab[s] and Muslims who pose potential terrorism threats."[60] This, combined with Almontaser's defense of CAIR and her disingenuous reaction to the "intifada" controversy, lead to reasonable suspicion as to whether the school will become a hotbed of anti-Americanism and Islamic supremacism—another outpost of the stealth jihad.

MULTICULTURALISM, ARABIC INSTRUCTION, AND THE STEALTH JIHAD

Yet most observers will never acknowledge that possibility— to do so would violate the dogma of multiculturalism.

Tolerance and pluralism are all that education officials see when they look at schools such as Amana Academy, a public charter school in Fulton County, Georgia. The school boasts of its "partnership" with the Arabic Language Institute Foundation (ALIF), which the Amana Academy website describes as "a comprehensive education, cultural, arts and enrichment center with a focus on the Arab culture and Arab Americans."[61]

Certainly in the post-September 11 world there is a great need for Americans who understand Arabic and Arab culture, but that is not the ALIF's only goal. As Islam analyst Daniel Pipes has pointed out, Akhtar H. Emon, ALIF's president, has spoken of the need to remake America according to the dictates of Islam, and about Arabic language instruction as a springboard to Islamization:

> Arabic is the language of the Qur'an. In order to convey the message of Qur'an in North America and Europe, we have to first deliver its language. Knowledge of Arabic can then help the Western countries recover from the present moral decay. Shootings of the likes in Columbine High School, and San Diego schools are the symptoms and the signs (Ayah) from Allah. High School students in North America deserve better than the metal detectors to protect them. The whole system of education needs a moral shake-up. The Arabic Language Institute Foundation (ALIF), a Los Angeles-based organization is committed to this goal.[62]

One would think that an institute with such a goal partnering with a public school would draw some attention, but no one seems particularly concerned; as we've seen, multiculturalism trumps everything, including religion/state concerns.

Arabic language instruction is closely linked to the promotion of Islam in other public schools as well. Arabic classes were introduced as an elective at Manhattan's prestigious Stuyvesant High School in September 2005, after the school's chapter of the Muslim Brotherhood-linked Muslim Student Association carried out an extensive fundraising effort to finance the program.

The MSA's motives were explicitly religious, as reporter Sara G. Levin revealed in a glowing report about the new program:

> Growing up in a religious family, Batool Ali, co-leader of the Stuyvesant M.S.A., had learned to read Arabic from the time she could interpret the prayers, but she has never spoken the

language. When she left Al-Iman, a Muslim school in Queens, to attend prestigious Stuyvesant in Lower Manhattan three years ago, she carried Islam with her. Ali joined M.S.A., where other students, some with religious upbringings and some without, met to discuss interpretations of the Koran. But like her, few of the students, many of whom were from the Asian subcontinent, could speak Arabic and even fewer could read it.

Levin quotes Ali explaining the Islamic importance of Arabic: "For Muslims, you have to read the Koran and knowing Arabic adds a more personal aspect." Another student, Shams Billah, explained that most of the funding came from local mosques and individual Muslims: "We started writing foundations like the Rockefeller Foundation. We got lots of letters back but no money. What we finally ended up doing was starting private fundraisers. We went to our families' friends, relatives for donations. We went to mosques and after a prayer we'd stand up and speak, ask for donations."[63]

These students' resourcefulness is admirable. If they had worked this hard and raised money to fund an athletic program, or a course of another kind, there would be no cause for concern. But recall that an Islamic leader—Akhtar Emon—is on record saying that "in order to convey the message of Qur'an in North America and Europe, we have to first deliver its language." When one considers this alongside the facts that at least some of the students who are responsible for bringing the Arabic course to Stuyvesant have explicitly Islamic motives, and that they themselves are part of a student association that is part of a larger Islamic supremacist endeavor in the United States, it's not unreasonable to ask some hard questions about the goals Stuyvesant's Arabic program.

Stuyvesant, however, has nothing on two public charter schools in Columbus, Ohio: the International Academy of Columbus and Westside Academy. Both, according to Patrick Poole, a writer on jihad and member of Central Ohioans Against Terror, are "operated by a politically-connected group of Islamic extremists associated with both the national and Ohio chapters of the Council on American-Islamic Relations (CAIR). At least one of the taxpayer-financed schools has been used during the last school year to play host to an anti-Israel CAIR-OH 'teach-in.'"

The schools focus on Arabic rather than English instruction, with the predictable result that "standardized test scores for the schools are well below state standards." But befuddled Ohio multiculturalist educators insist on "pumping millions of taxpayer dollars into each school every year to keep the schools open and renewing their contracts." In line with the general policy of trying to intimidate non-Muslims into granting accommodations for Islamic practices, "one board member for both schools has even co-authored an article advocating an educational policy of 'accommodation without assimilation'"[64]

This, of course, is a near-perfect encapsulation of one of the primary goals of the stealth jihad. Westernized Muslims with strong American identities are of little use in achieving the ultimate goal of instituting sharia in the United States. But a large pool of Muslims raised on a pedagogy that resists assimilation and instead emphasizes the need for societal "accommodation" to Islam—now that's a promising group of future activists for the cause of Islamic supremacy.

MINNESOTA'S PUBLICLY FUNDED MADRASSA

As appalling as it may be that taxpayer money is funding these schools, even that is not the worst of it. Non-Muslim officials

have aided, once again, no doubt, in the interests of multiculturalism, in the funneling of public education money to at least one
school that appears to be, for all intents and purposes, an Islamic
madrassa. *Madrassa* in Arabic means simply "school," but in
English the word has become associated with schools that teach
Islam as truth—something that belongs in private schools, not
public ones.

Can you imagine a public school founded by two Christian
ministers, and housed in the same building as a church? Add to
that—in the same building—a prominent chapel. And let's say the
students are required to fast during Lent, and attend Bible studies
right after school. All with your tax dollars.

Inconceivable? Sure. If such a place existed, ACLU lawyers
would descend on it like locusts. It would be shut down before
you could say "separation of church and state," to the accompa-
niment of *New York Times* and *Washington Post* editorials warning darkly about the growing influence of the Religious Right in
America.

But such a school does exist in Minnesota, in a different religious context. And while the ACLU in early 2008 launched a
desultory investigation, they pursued it with none of the energy
and righteous indignation they routinely muster for their never-
ending sallies against Christian activities in public schools.

Although the school did ultimately receive a weak reprimand
from the Minnesota Department of Education, as of this writing
tax money continues to flow to the Tarek ibn Ziyad Academy, a
popular, rapidly growing K-8 charter school with campuses in
Inver Grove Heights and Blaine, Minnesota. According to the
Minnesota Department of Education, as a Minnesota charter
school implementing a statewide "performance and professional
pay program" known as Q-Comp, Tarek ibn Ziyad Academy

pocketed $65,260 in state money for the 2006–07 school year,[65] and was slated to receive $3.8 million for the 2007–08 school year.[66] The school's website, meanwhile, boasted that it offers a "rigorous Arabic language program" and an "environment that fosters your cultural values and heritage."[67]

Whose cultural values and heritage? According to the indefatigable investigative reporter Katherine Kersten, there were "strong indications" in early 2008 "that religion plays a central role" at the school.[68] The "central issue," she explained, was "whether this publicly financed school is skirting or breaking the law that all others must observe when it comes to religious endorsement. If this were a bunch of Baptists or Catholics with the kids being led to the rosary on Mondays through Thursday and led to Mass on Fridays there wouldn't be any question that this is crossing the line."[69]

But when it comes to the Tarek ibn Ziyad Academy, since Islam is involved, the issues are not nearly so clear-cut.

Islamic religious practice is clearly of paramount importance to the academy: it was co-founded by two imams; it is housed in the same building as a mosque; it features a carpeted space for prayer; it serves halal food in the school cafeteria; all students fast during Ramadan; and the students attend classes—after school, but on the same grounds—on the Qur'an and Sunnah, or Islamic tradition and law. What's more, the school is closely tied to the Minnesota chapter of the Muslim American Society (MAS), which also shares the same building. Kersten observes that "at MAS-MN's 2007 convention, for example, the program featured an advertisement for the 'Muslim American Society of Minnesota,' superimposed on a picture of a mosque. Under the motto 'Establishing Islam in Minnesota,' it asked: 'Did you know that MAS-MN...houses a full-time elementary school'?

On the adjacent page was an application for TIZA"—the Tarek ibn Ziyad Academy.

The existence of the Tarek ibn Ziyad Academy is, of course, yet another manifestation of the witless multiculturalism that grants protected victim status to Muslim groups in view of the "racism" and "Islamophobia" from which they supposedly suffer. Latitude that would never be granted to other faith groups, particularly but not only Christians, is readily given here.

But it's even worse than that. According to a 2004 *Chicago Tribune* exposé, the Muslim American Society is the name under which the Muslim Brotherhood operates in the United States.[70] Is the Tarek ibn Ziyad Academy also then part of the Brotherhood's stealth jihad in the United States?

A clue comes from the name of the school itself. Kersten notes that it was named after the eighth-century Muslim conqueror of Spain. *Islam Online* praised Tarek ibn Ziyad in a 2004 article as a "man of valor, a man of extraordinary courage and a true leader." He is chiefly remembered for one incident in particular. A military commander who sailed with his army to Spain in the eighth century, he ordered the Muslim forces' boats to be burned, telling his soldiers, "Brothers in Islam! We now have the enemy in front of us and the deep sea behind us. We cannot return to our homes, because we have burnt our boats. We shall now either defeat the enemy and win or die a coward's death by drowning in the sea. Who will follow me?" The soldiers, crying "Allahu akbar," rushed ahead and defeated a vastly superior Spanish force.[71] This commenced a seven hundred-year-long period in which the Iberian Peninsula or parts of it remained under Muslim occupation.

Does the Tarek ibn Ziyad Academy's name symbolize the same idea—the arrival of Muslims in a foreign land as a prelude to its conquest? In light of the Brotherhood memorandum and other evidence about the jihadist allegiances of the Muslim American

Society, this is a perfectly reasonable question. If a Christian group opened a Christian school in an Islamic country that were named after an eleventh-century crusader, you can bet the local authorities would ask some tough questions about the school's source of inspiration.

But what public official, in Minnesota or elsewhere, had the courage to ask such questions of an Islamic institution? No one would have dared at all had there not been a public outcry, owing largely to Kersten's untiring efforts to bring the truth to light. Finally, in May 2008, the Minnesota Department of Education asked the school to change some of its practices regarding Islamic prayer and its after-school Qur'an study classes. This amounted to an official acknowledgment that the concerns Kersten and others had raised about the school were legitimate—and those concerns were reinforced when school officials had a physical confrontation with a news photographer who had gone with reporters to the school to ask for school administrators' reaction to the Department of Education requests. The photographer suffered minor injuries.[72]

Suffering worse injuries in that assault was the tradition of civil discourse and debate in the American public square. Muslims, on American soil, had challenged non-Muslims' right to question the practices of Muslims, in effect asserting the sharia provision that dhimmis must know their place and not speak ill of Islam or Muslims.

Given the near-unanimous official and media indifference to the stealth jihad, it was a harbinger of things to come.

INSIDE ISLAMIC SCHOOLS IN THE UNITED STATES

Private Islamic schools, as one might expect, are often even worse. Take, for example, the "Islamic Pledge of Allegiance" devised by the Bureau of Islamic and Arabic Education, a Southern California organization dedicated to developing material for the study of the Qur'an, Islam, and Arabic in Islamic schools:

> As an American Muslim,
>
> I pledge allegiance to ALLAH and His Prophet,
>
> I respect and love my family and my community,
>
> and I dedicate my life to serving the cause of truth and justice.
>
> As an American citizen, with rights and responsibilities,
>
> I pledge allegiance to the flag of the United States
>
> of America
>
> And to the republic for which it stands,
>
> one nation,
>
> Under God,
>
> indivisible,
>
> with liberty and justice for all.[73]

Some may find it gratifying that the Bureau has seen fit to include the entirety of the standard Pledge of Allegiance within its own pledge. One may reasonably wonder, however, what the significance may be of the allegiance given *first* to "Allah and His Prophet."

Allegiance to "Allah and His Prophet" involves, among many other things, affirming that Jews will be the "strongest among men in enmity to the believers" (Qur'an 5:82). At the Abraar Islamic School in Ottawa, Canada, in March 2005, one student dramatized that enmity in an essay that glorified a fictitious Palestinian who killed Jews: "Without thinking, Ahmed took his M16 machine gun and threw the bombs, and he showered the Jews; this resulted in the killing of the soldiers. Salah said: 'You killed them all.' Ahmed answered: 'Praise be to God.'" The story's heroes vow, "We promise God and the heroes of Al-Aqsa that we will continue the path, we will continue in spite of the difficulties and the hardships until the victory of the martyrdom, we will not surrender; we will fight for the sake of God until the end." The student who wrote this illustrated his story by drawing a flaming Star of David and a machine gun.

A teacher thought this little paean to homicide was just dandy, and wrote in the margins, "God bless you, your efforts are good. The story of the hero Ahmed and the hero Salah is still alive. The end will be soon when God unites us all in Jerusalem to pray there."

The school's headmistress, Aisha Sherazi, said she was "extremely shocked, disturbed and concerned" about the story—but there was no sign that she had expressed her shock in any way before the essay came to media attention.[74] Her shock seemed even less credible in light of a 2005 study by the Center for Religious Freedom, which found that "Saudi textbooks and documents spread throughout American mosques preach a Nazi-like hatred for Jews, treat the forged *Protocols of the Elders of Zion* as historical fact, and avow that the Muslim's duty is to eliminate the state of Israel."[75] Would Canadian mosques and schools be all that different?

The Center for Religious Freedom report confirmed the findings of a 2003 survey of textbooks used in Islamic schools in New York City. The *New York Daily News* survey found that the New York Islamic school texts "are rife with inaccuracies, sweeping condemnations of Jews and Christians, and triumphalist declarations of Islam's supremacy." They contained "passages that are blatantly anti-Semitic, condemning Jews as a people, repeating old canards about the Jews wanting to kill Christ and faking their Holy Scriptures to mock God." One textbook, *Mercy to Mankind,* said that "Allah revealed to Muhammed that the Jews had changed their Book, the Torah, killed their own prophets and disobeyed Allah. And the Jews did not want the Arabs to know about these shameful things."

The *Daily News* shouldn't have been shocked: this was simply a straightforward teaching of the Qur'an. According to the Muslim holy book, the Jews claimed, "We killed Christ Jesus the son of Mary, the Messenger of Allah," although in reality—goes the Qur'anic claim—"they killed him not, nor crucified him, but so it was made to appear to them" (Qur'an 4:157). And as for faking the Holy Scriptures, the Qur'an says this in a passage commonly understood in Islamic tradition to refer to the Jews: "Then woe to those who write the Book with their own hands, and then say: 'This is from Allah,' to traffic with it for miserable price! Woe to them for what their hands do write, and for the gain they make thereby" (2:79). Having dared corrupt their own Scriptures, "their forgeries deceive them as to their own religion" (3:24). The Qur'an asks the Jews, "Why then have ye slain the prophets of Allah in times gone by, if ye did indeed believe?" (2:91).

As such it is even less likely that in Ottawa, Aisha Sherazi would have been genuinely shocked by an essay reflecting such perspectives. But that wasn't all. One of the New York Islamic school textbooks, entitled *What Islam Is all About*, claimed that Jews subscribed "to a belief in racial superiority" and that they "call down curses upon the worship places of non-Jews whenever they pass by them!" Christians get off relatively lightly: they simply "worship statues." However, "many" Jews and Christians "lead such decadent and immoral lives that lying, alcohol, nudity, pornography, racism, foul language, premarital sex, homosexuality and everything else are accepted in their society, churches and synagogues."

Confronted with this material, Yahiya Emerick of the Islamic Foundation of North America was unapologetic: "Islam, like any belief system, believes its program is better than others. I don't feel embarrassed to say that." But triumphalism was one thing, and political supremacism quite another; Emerick, however, took no notice of the latter, or of the potential of such textbooks to inculcate in Muslim students the idea that they must labor to bring Islamic law to America, "cleansing" American society by means of the Qur'an the way the Alif Institute's Akhtar Emon dreamed of doing.

Washington Post reporter Marc Fisher encountered similar triumphalist and supremacist attitudes among students at the Muslim Community School in Potomac, Maryland, not long after the September 11 attacks. He met "six young people, all born in this country, all American citizens," who "told me that no, they did not believe that Osama bin Laden was necessarily the bad guy the president says he is, and no, they did not think the United States should be attacking Afghanistan, and, no, they might not be able to serve their country if it meant taking up arms against fellow Muslims." An eighth grader said, "If I had to choose sides, I'd stay with being Muslim. Being an American means nothing to me. I'm not even proud of telling my cousins in Pakistan that I'm American." The school principal added, "Allegiance to national authority is one thing, but the one who gives us life is more entitled to that authority. This is the story of religion through all time. When national laws and values go counter to what the Creator believes, we are 100 percent against it."[76]

Certainly that was a belief Christians had held ever since Peter and the apostles said, "We must obey God rather than men" (Acts 5:29). But coming from an adherent of a religion containing a comprehensive system of laws believed to be the immutable law of the supreme deity, the affirmation that divine laws superseded national laws took on a very different quality.

Was the Muslim Community School teaching its students that Islamic law must one day replace U.S. constitutional law? If it adhered to Islamic orthodoxy, that was much more likely than the notion that it was teaching Muslim students to accept American pluralism and republican rule.

Can our schools (particularly those that are publicly funded) be allowed to teach doctrines that flatly contradict the spirit and letter of the Constitution, as sharia does? Should publicly funded schools inculcate notions such as the idea that students must work to remove all obstacles to the spread and dominance of Islam and sharia?

Such questions cannot continue to be ignored or treated cavalierly. They should be discussed, rationally, by an informed citizenry that has already sufficiently familiarized themselves with the actual texts and tenets of Islam, not the soothing distortions of the stealth jihadists. Mere guesswork, and the comforting idea that "all religions are good and want the same thing," are simply no longer adequate, if they ever were.

CHAPTER NINE

EDUCATION OR INDOCTRINATION? THE ISLAMIC IDEOLOGICAL STRAITJACKET IN AMERICAN UNIVERSITIES

The function of the university is to seek and to transmit knowledge and to train students in the processes whereby truth is to be made known. To convert, or to make converts, is alien and hostile to this dispassionate duty. Where it becomes necessary in performing this function of a university, to consider political, social, or sectarian movements, they are dissected and examined, not taught, and the conclusion left, with no tipping of the scales, to the logic of the facts.

So stated the University of California at Berkeley's Academic Personnel Manual, in a section inserted by University of California President Robert Gordon Sproul in 1934. It is a ringing affirmation of the commitment of the university to education, not propaganda.

Alas, this is no longer the ideal throughout vast swaths of our higher education system. In college after college, the acolytes of multiculturalism have gained control of the faculty and administration. From these positions of power, they have systematically undermined the historic educational ideal of free inquiry in favor of a relentlessly partisan agenda. Instead of teaching the dispassionate pursuit of knowledge, university students nationwide are now indoctrinated into a post-American ideology that denounces as "racist" the criticism of any culture other than our own. In a depressing sign of the times, Berkeley removed its endorsement of dispassionate inquiry from its academic manual in 2003.[1]

The ascendency of multiculturalism has made academia into a welcoming environment for the stealth jihad. Anti-Western professors, often backed up by Saudi money, have turned Middle Eastern Studies departments into propaganda mills for the view that Westerners themselves, and Americans in particular, are ultimately to blame for the actions of Islamic terrorists. Meanwhile, extremist Islamic student groups are not only tolerated on campuses, but are financially supported by guilt-ridden university officials.

Lacking any confidence in their own civilization and culture, university administrators and professors are unwilling and unable to halt the spread of Islamic supremacism in their own backyards.

OMID SAFI:
THE PROFESSOR AS PROPAGANDIST

In Spring 2004, Professor Omid Safi of Colgate University in Hamilton, New York, offered a class called "Islam and modernity," during which he gave this assignment (spelling and grammar as in the original):

> Critical reports on Islamophobes, Neo-cons, Western tri-
> umphalists, etc.: 3 pages each on. Include: a brief biography,
> intellectual history, and comments on Islam (and/or Middle
> East where relevant)
>
> -1) Bernard Lewis, 2)Samuel Huntington, 3)Fareed
> Zakaria, 4)David Frum, 5)Paul Wolfowitz, 6) Leo Strauss, 7)
> William Kristol, 8) William Bennett, 9) Daniel Pipes, 10)
> Charles Krauthammer, 11) Alan Bloom, 12) Robert Spencer,
> 13) David Pryce-Jones, 14) Stephen Schwartz, 15) Bat
> Yeor,16) Jerry Falwell, 17Pat Robertson, 18 Francis Fukuya-
> man, 19Patricia Crone 20 Niall Ferguson 21 Robert Kagan
> 22 Dore Gold 23 Ibn Warraq

Over several years of teaching this course, Safi never bothered to correct the misspelled names and tortured syntax, although after I criticized him for the one-size-fits-all quality of his enemies' list, he added this explanatory note: "This group is a broad coalition that includes folks from diverse backgrounds, such as unrepentant Orientalists, outright Islamophobes, Neo-conservatives, Western Triumphalists, right-wing Christian Evangelicals, etc."[2]

This explanation, however, did not adequately account for the oddness of his list. I was honored to be included with ground-breaking scholars like Bat Ye'or, Ibn Warraq, Patricia Crone, and Samuel Huntington, even though by grouping us together Safi only meant to cast aspersions on all our work. Furthermore, by lumping us together with activists like the late Jerry Falwell and Pat Robertson, Safi's list suggested that all were motivated not by a scholarly interest in truth, but only by religious bigotry or prejudice. I intend in that no insult to Falwell or Robertson, although Safi obviously intended one; I only mean that their statements and writings about Islam are not scholarly, but religious and political.

To include scholars on the list with political advocates as if they were all examples of the same phenomenon—so-called Islamophobia—slyly demeaned the scholars' objectivity and the value of their work. Which was, I expect, exactly what Safi meant to do.

Indeed, the propagandistic nature of this list and the course in general had no business in a university classroom. Labeling a group of people "Islamophobes" in a course about Islam is hardly conducive to freedom of thought. (It was especially silly in light of the fact that one person on Safi's enemies list, Stephen Schwartz, is himself a Muslim—a fact that Safi duly noted in later editions of the list.) By classifying this truly diverse group of people as "unrepentant Orientalists, outright Islamophobes, Neo-conservatives, Western Triumphalists, right-wing Christian Evangelicals, etc.," Safi was not teaching his students to think for themselves; he was propagandizing, carefully molding their reactions in advance, and making it difficult for them to come to their own judgments as to whether or not those on his list did or did not fit his pre-fabricated categories. He wasn't allowing his students to evaluate on its own merits the monumental work of Bat Ye'or, or Ibn Warraq, or that of Samuel Huntington, or Patricia Crone. No, Professor Safi kindly did their thinking for them; the students were already instructed that the scholarly achievements of the people on Safi's list had no merit, for they were all merely a product of "unrepentant" Orientalism.

Safi, in presenting his enemies' list to his students, abandoned the traditional professorial ideal of the disinterested pursuit of knowledge, and instead simply tried to purvey propaganda. He should have been laughed out of his profession for this, but in fact his course is not at all unusual today in Middle East Studies departments at universities all over the country. Universities, especially when it comes to Islam, now place little value on objective inquiry and freedom of thought. Not only did Safi suffer no loss of academic reputation, but he soon obtained a position at the University of North Carolina at Chapel Hill, a much larger and more prestigious school than Colgate.

Is Safi a stealth jihadist? There is no evidence that he is. But professors who prevent their students from learning about Islam in an objective manner, and those like Safi who place an ideological straitjacket on their students, are performing a valuable service for the stealth jihad. For in this manner Safi signaled to students that any investigation of Islamic supremacism, violent or non-violent, would be classed as "Islamophobia," "unrepentant Orientalism," "Western triumphalism," and even "neo-conservatism"— all the worst epithets in today's academy.

Safi's course was just one example among many of how Middle East Studies in American universities has been taken over by propagandist-professors and political agitators who are working, wittingly or unwittingly, for goals that overlap or coincide with those of the stealth jihadists. Students, untutored in these matters, and often trusting in the "scholarly" nature of the undertaking (and the personal charm that can be turned on by those intent on winning over students for various purposes), are frequently defensive about these professors. Only later, when some of them study the same subject in relative freedom, do they come to realize what a shoddy bill of goods they have been sold. But for many, the views that are inculcated when they are young take a long time to undo—if they're ever undone at all.

IN MY MIND I'M WAGIN' JIHAD AT CAROLINA

Omid Safi's new home, the University of North Carolina at Chapel Hill, gained nationwide attention in 2002, when all incoming freshmen were assigned to read an annotated rendition of parts of the Qur'an. The book was *Approaching the Qur'an: The Early Revelations*, translated and annotated by Michael Sells. The Qur'an's "early revelations" of the subtitle generally preach a relative tolerance and mutual coexistence between Muslims and nonbelievers; the doctrines of jihad and dhimmitude that—according to mainstream Islamic theologians—actually supersede the more tolerant verses, and that have proven so oppressive to Jews, Christians, and other non-Muslims throughout history, unfold in later Qur'anic revelations. Thus they are not included in the book.

One may wonder what such a misleading presentation was designed to accomplish. Sells defended his decision to translate only the more moderate Meccan Suras on the grounds that they are the most accessible introduction to the Qur'an and Islamic study as a whole. While that may be true, taken in isolation *Approaching the Qur'an* is severely misleading about the nature of the religion as a whole and about the intentions and motives of Islamic jihadists, the very people who have made Islam such a hot topic for students.

On the Carolina faculty Safi joined Carl Ernst, another academic propagandist. In his highly apologetic 2003 work *Following Muhammad*, Ernst marvels that "in all the images of Islam that are commonly circulated in European and American culture, little can be found that is positive." He concludes, "Although I am not a psychologist, I cannot help but feel that there is a mechanism of projection operating here, along the lines spoken of by Jungians, in which one's negative characteristics are projected onto others."[3]

Projection? So we are to believe that the September 11 attacks in New York and Washington, the 2005 attacks in London, the

Madrid subway bombing, the attacks on a school in Beslan and a theatre in Moscow, the 2002 and 2005 Bali bombings, the murder of Theo van Gogh in the streets of Amsterdam, the beheadings of Nicholas Berg and Daniel Pearl, the murder of scores of Buddhists in southern Thailand, and over ten thousand other jihadist terror attacks around the world since September 11—all committed by Muslims and in the name of Islam—have nothing to do with Islam's negative image in the West?[4] No, it is all projection, and the entire Western world of accusing infidels must sit on the couch and endure years of therapy with Herr Doktor Jung in order to get to the psychic origins of the particular projection in question.

This is the state of the academy in the early twenty-first century, precisely when our nation needs people who have academic training in the ideology of those who would destroy us. But such politically incorrect training is not to be had—and its absence serves the purposes of the stealth jihadists.

After I spoke at the University of North Carolina in 2004, Professor Ernst wrote a piece about me. Declining to provide any evidence to challenge my analysis of Islam and Islamic jihad, he simply warned that my books were non-scholarly and were published by presses that he believed reflected a conservative political agenda.[5] In this display Ernst epitomized the decline of the academy into a propaganda mill; it's a sad spectacle to see a university professor criticize a book not because of any faulty arguments, but because it was published by people on the wrong side of the political fence. This demonstrated yet again how far American universities have fallen away from Berkeley's former assertion that the university exists to train students to find the truth. The idea of pursuing and uncovering the truth did not seem even to occur to Professor Ernst, who was clearly more concerned with gaining recruits for his particular point of view.

Aside from the degradation of academic culture, the white-washing of Islam presents a more immediate danger. This was horrifically brought home at UNC itself on March 3, 2006, when a twenty-two-year-old Iranian student named Mohammed Reza Taheri-azar drove an SUV onto the Carolina campus, deliberately trying to kill people and succeeding in injuring nine. After the incident he seemed singularly pleased with himself, smiling and waving to crowds after a court appearance at which he explained he was "thankful for the opportunity to spread the will of Allah."[6]

Taheri-azar left a letter in his apartment explaining his rampage. It is chillingly detached, almost clinical: "In the name of Allah, the merciful, the compassionate. To whom it may concern: I am writing this letter to inform you of my reasons for premeditating and attempting to murder citizens and residents of the United States of America on Friday, March 3, 2006 in the city of Chapel Hill, North Carolina by running them over with my automobile and stabbing them with a knife if the opportunities are presented to me by Allah."

In the letter, Taheri-azar identifies himself simply as "a servant of Allah." He declares that "in the Qur'an, Allah states that the believing men and women have permission to murder anyone responsible for the killing of other believing men and women.... After extensive contemplation and reflection, I have made the decision to exercise the right of violent retaliation that Allah has given me to the fullest extent to which I am capable at present." And further, "Allah's commandments are never to be questioned and all of Allah's commandments must be obeyed. Those who violate Allah's commandments and purposefully follow human fabrication and falsehood as their religion will burn in fire for eternity in accordance with Allah's will."

In a letter written a week later, Taheri-azar asserted, "I live with the holy Koran as my constitution for right and wrong and definition of justice....Allah gives permission in the Koran for the followers of Allah to attack those who have raged [sic] war against them, with the expectation of eternal paradise in case of martyrdom and/or living one's life in obedience of all of Allah's commandments found throughout the Koran's 114 chapters. I've read all 114 chapters approximately 15 times since June of 2003 when I started reading the Koran." And he did not try to murder UNC students "out of hatred for Americans, but out of love for Allah instead. I live only to serve Allah, by obeying all of Allah's commandments of which I am aware by reading and learning the contents of the Koran."[7] Later he expanded on this by sending a detailed exposition of the Qur'an's teachings on warfare to the Carolina campus newspaper, *The Daily Tar Heel*.[8]

Thus nine University of North Carolina students fell victim to a Muslim motivated by a violent Islamic ideology that UNC professors had taken great pains to downplay or to deny existed at all. If they had instead acknowledged the existence of the jihadist ideology after September 11 and, in its program for freshmen the next year, called upon local Muslim groups—including the local chapter of the Muslim Students Association—to develop comprehensive programs teaching against the jihad ideology and Islamic supremacism, Mohammed Reza Taheri-azar might never have rented an SUV with an intent to kill on that day in March.

To be sure, the MSA dissociated itself from Taheri-azar's actions, but it could do nothing else, and no one in the area was knowledgeable or courageous enough to ask them hard questions about what they intended to do to prevent the spread of Taheri-azar's ideology among UNC's Muslim students in the future.

The writings of Carl Ernst and Michael Sells made sure of that. And Omid Safi is now at UNC to pitch in as well.

THE SAIDIST STRAITJACKET OF INTELLECTUAL CONFORMITY

The likes of Safi and Ernst are the rule, not the exception, on American campuses today, and this has come at the detriment of our national security. It's difficult to anticipate the attacks of our enemies, and to devise a comprehensive strategy to defeat them, when so many of the nation's top experts in Islam and the Middle East are beholden to a rigid, politically correct ideology that ignores or denies the theological roots of Islamic terrorism and supremacism.

This became evident immediately after September 11. With so many academics invested in the interpretation of Islam as a religion of peace, the attacks came as a complete surprise to nearly the entire profession. Thomas Hegghammer, a postdoctoral research fellow at Princeton University and a research fellow at the Norwegian Defence Research Establishment in Oslo, has noted that academics as well as defense and security officials were caught off guard by September 11, since "Middle East scholars on both sides of the Atlantic had long shunned the study of Islamist militancy for fear of promoting Islamophobia and of being associated with a pro-Israeli political agenda. In these communities, there was a tendency to rely on simple grievance-based explanations of terrorism and to ignore the role of entrepreneurial individuals and organizations in the generation of violence. This is part of the reason why the main contributions to the literature on al Qaeda in the first few years after 9/11 came from investigative journalists, not academics."[9]

Boston University professor Richard Landes observes that "the problem with Middle Eastern Studies in the USA (*a fortiori* in Europe) is that it's been colonized by Muslim and Arab scholars who have politicized the field and intimidated Western scholars....Today's Middle Eastern Studies more closely resembles the kind of atmosphere that dominated the late medieval university (inquisitorial) than a free and meritocratic culture committed to honesty."[10]

Historian Bernard Lewis, the first name on Professor Safi's enemies list, warned in April 2008 of the dangers of the prevailing ideological straitjacket, pointing out that Middle East Studies departments in universities all over the country now manifest "a degree of thought control and limitations of freedom of expression without parallel in the Western world since the 18th century, and in some areas longer than that....It seems to me it's a very dangerous situation, because it makes any kind of scholarly discussion of Islam, to say the least, dangerous. Islam and Islamic values now have a level of immunity from comment and criticism in the Western world that Christianity has lost and Judaism has never had."[11]

The intellectual godfather of this brand of stifling conformism on American campuses today was Professor Edward Said (1935-2003), whose 1978 book *Orientalism* has become the philosophical foundation for the anti-Americanism and benign view of jihadist activity and Islamic supremacism that now prevail almost everywhere. Not that Said is responsible for the decline of the academy all by himself. The cult of the Third World, multiculturalism, the expansion of universities and of their faculties, and the rampant careerism in today's academy have all played a role, as has the exaggerated attention now paid to the racial, sexual, and ethnic identity of writers.

Nevertheless, while the Left has been blazing an anti-American course in academia since the 1960s, Said's work provided an intellectual framework for it in Middle East Studies, making possible a wholesale purge from academia of the Western, non-Muslim "Orientalists" who had previously pursued the study of Islam and the Muslim world as an academic discipline.

The former Muslim and scholar of early Islam, Ibn Warraq, penned a blistering critique of *Orientalism* entitled "Edward Said and the Saidists, Or, Third World Intellectual Terrorism." As noted by Ibn Warraq, "Said attacks not only the entire discipline of Orientalism, which is devoted to the academic study of the Orient but which Said accuses of perpetuating negative racial stereotypes, anti-Arab and anti-Islamic prejudice," but he also "accuses Orientalists as a group of complicity with imperial power, and holds them responsible for creating the distinction between Western superiority and Oriental inferiority." In short, Ibn Warraq charges, Said contends that up until 1978, "much of what was written about the Orient in general, and Islam and Islamic civilisation in particular, was false."[12]

Predictably, Said became a kind of academic rock star, as professors became enthralled by his denunciation of nearly the entire canon of scholarship that preceded him. The result has been insidious. "The most pernicious legacy of Said's *Orientalism*," states Ibn Warraq, "is its support for religious fundamentalism, and on its insistence that 'all the ills [of the Arab world] emanate from Orientalism and have nothing to do with the socioeconomic, political and ideological makeup of the Arab lands or with the cultural historical backwardness which stands behind it.'" *Orientalism*, Ibn Warraq concludes, is "worthless as intellectual history" and "has left Western scholars in fear of asking questions—in other words, has inhibited their research. Said's work, with its strident anti-Westernism, has made the goal of modernization of the Middle Eastern societies that much more difficult. His work, wherein all the ills of Middle Eastern societies is blamed on the wicked West, has made much-needed self-criticism nearly impossible. His work has encouraged Islamic fundamentalists whose impact on world affairs needs no underlining."[13]

Said's anti-Western "scholarship" has certainly undermined those who seek to resist the jihadists' agenda. What's even worse is that much of the Said-style pedagogy in academia is funded by foreign Islamic fundamentalists who hardly have America's best interests at heart.

FOLLOW THE MONEY

Those who propagate the anti-Western agenda are rewarded handsomely. Safi's propagandizing earned him a position at a major university. And Ernst, for his apologetic *Following Muhammad*, which displaced responsibility for the ills of the Islamic world onto the West, was awarded the Distinguished Prize in the Humanities by the board of trustees of the Cairo-based Shaykh Muhammad Salih Bashrahil Prize for Outstanding Cultural Creativity. The award comes with a $30,000 cash prize.[14]

Most important, an influx of huge amounts of money from Islamic donors has made it clear to scholars, academic departments, and entire universities that an outwardly pro-Islamic orientation will pay off in spades. The source of much of this largess is the plutocrat Prince Alwaleed bin Talal, a member of the Saudi royal family.

Alwaleed's own political views became clear when he achieved worldwide notoriety in October 2001 after presenting New York mayor Rudolph Giuliani with a check for $10 million for the

Twin Towers Fund, a charity devoted to aiding relatives of police and firefighters killed on September 11. Along with the check, Alwaleed released a statement about the terrorist attacks, declaring, "At times like this one, we must address some of the issues that led to such a criminal attack. I believe that the government of the United States of America should re-examine its policies in the Middle East and adopt a more balanced stance towards the Palestinian cause." In response, Giuliani rejected the check and denounced Alwaleed's display of moral equivalence.[15] "There is no moral equivalent for this act," Giuliani proclaimed. "There is no justification for it. The people who did it lost any right to ask for it when they slaughtered 4,000 or 5,000 innocent people. And to suggest that there's a justification for it only invites this happening in the future. It is highly irresponsible and very, very dangerous."[16]

While Giuliani had the moral fortitude to sacrifice millions of dollars to take a moral stand against Alwaleed, the same cannot be said of the administrators at Harvard and Georgetown universities, both of which accepted $20 million donations from Alwaleed in December 2005 to finance Islamic studies departments. Harvard's provost, Steven E. Hyman, gushed about its new program, "For a university with global aspirations, it is critical that Harvard have a strong program on Islam that is worldwide and interdisciplinary in scope." Georgetown, meanwhile, renamed its Center for Muslim-Christian Understanding after its new benefactor—the center is now the "H.R.H. Prince Alwaleed bin Talal Center for Muslim-Christian Understanding."

Alwaleed was well aware of what he was buying. Martin Kramer, author of the superb expose of academic bias in Middle East Studies in American universities, *Ivory Towers on Sand: The Failure of Middle Eastern Studies in America*, remarked, "Prince

Alwaleed knows that if you want to have an impact, places like Harvard or Georgetown, which is inside the Beltway, will make a difference."[17]

And Harvard and Georgetown have by no means been the only recipient of the Prince's largesse: in May 2008 he announced a sixteen-million-pound (or $29 million) gift to Cambridge and Edinburgh Universities—again for Islamic study centers ostensibly devoted to building bridges of understanding between the Western and Islamic worlds.[18] This came as part of an even larger initiative by wealthy Muslims to influence university life in Britain: in April 2008, Jonathan Evans, the director-general of MI5, the British intelligence and security service, declared that after British universities had received donations amounting to nearly 500 million pounds (or $915 million) from Muslim donors from Saudi Arabia, Pakistan, and elsewhere, there had been a "dangerous increase in the spread of extremism in leading university campuses." He said that many of the donations came from Muslim organizations "which are known to have ties to extremist groups, [and] some have links to terrorist organizations."[19]

These donations are not intended to fund objective scholarship on Islam; they're meant to forward a very specific agenda. Even the Muslim American Society imam W. Deen Mohammed, the son of Nation of Islam leader Elijah Mohammed, has acknowledged that Saudi money comes with strings. He told the *Los Angeles Times* that "in Saudi Arabia it's the Wahabi school of thought ... and they say, 'We're gonna give you our money, then we want you to ... prefer our school of thought.' That's in there whether they say it or not. So there is a problem receiving gifts that seem to have no attachment, no strings attached." Mohamed said of his own dealings with the Saudis, "I suspected some strings were attached. I said I can't accept this kind of relationship. They were choosing my friends for me, too. The enemy of the friends who were giving me money was supposed to be my enemy, too."[20]

Who are the enemies of Alwaleed? Are they now the enemies of Harvard and Georgetown also? What is his money paying for?

Clues to these questions can be found in the work of one of Alwaleed's primary beneficiaries.

JOHN ESPOSITO AND THE FACTS

Georgetown Islamic Studies professor John Esposito has for many years proffered Alwaleed's brand of moral equivalence. At the Conference for Civilisational Dialogue in Malaysia in 1997, Esposito, according to a report on the conference, "explained that one man's terrorist is another man's freedom fighter; and that terrorism, as seen in the case of Israel's or the Tel Aviv regime's treatment of Palestinians, can and has been used to legitimate wanton violence and continued acts of oppression."[21]

It should come as no surprise, then, that Esposito became director of Georgetown's Prince Alwaleed bin Talal Center for Muslim-Christian Understanding. Years prior to that, Esposito was the Clinton administration's Islamic expert and a media favorite. Kramer offers a blistering analysis of Esposito's thought in *Ivory Towers on Sand:* in the 1990s Esposito's peculiar genius, says Kramer, was in convincing people that "Islamist movements were nothing other than movements of democratic reform."[22] Esposito has also actively discouraged academic investigations of the jihad ideology and Islamic supremacism; Kramer notes that in the 1992 edition of Esposito's since-revised book, *The Islamic Threat: Myth or Reality?*, Esposito deems "Islamist violence" to be "beyond the bounds of approved research. Dwelling upon it would only reinforce stereotypes. After all, announced Esposito, 'most' Islamic movements had reached the conclusion that violence was 'counterproductive.' 'They speak of the need to prepare people for an Islamic order rather than to impose it.'"[23]

It's clear why Esposito saw a need for post-September 11 revisions to this book, but it's also noteworthy that he implicitly acknowledges that the Islamic supremacist agenda is proceeding not just by violence, but also by more stealthy means: violence, notes Esposito, could be "counterproductive" to the overall goal of instituting an "Islamic order" in the West. He did not say that the Islamic groups set aside the goal of establishing an Islamic order; he simply noted that they were going about it by different means.

Also in *The Islamic Threat,* Esposito defines jihad as "the effort to lead a good life, to make society more moral and just, and to spread Islam through preaching, teaching, or armed struggle."[24] Yet as we saw in chapter two, this definition bears little resemblance to the statements on jihad by classic Islamic jurists. And Rice University professor David Cook, author of *Understanding Jihad* and one of the few academics who retains a spirit of independent inquiry into Islam, observes that Esposito's definition of jihad "has virtually no validity in Islam and is derived almost entirely from the apologetic work of nineteenth- and twentieth-century Muslim modernists. To maintain that *jihad* means 'the effort to lead a good life' is pathetic and laughable in any case."[25]

Esposito was even more disingenuous in his 2008 book *Who Speaks for Islam?: What a Billion Muslims Really Think,* cowritten with Dalia Mogahed, the executive director of the Gallup Center for Muslim Studies. In this purportedly comprehensive Gallup World Poll of global Muslim attitudes toward terrorism and other issues, Esposito and Mogahed quote Albert Einstein: "A man should look for what is, and not what he thinks should be." And they state grandly that "the data should lead the discourse."[26]

But that is just what *Who Speaks for Islam?* does not do. Robert Satloff, executive director of the Washington Institute for Near East Policy, in a devastating review of the book in *The Weekly Standard,* pointed out that Esposito and Mogahed had played games with the survey data in order to present the Islamic world as more moderate and pro-democracy than it really is. "Mogahed," said Satloff, "publicly admitted they knew certain people weren't moderates but they still termed them so. She and Esposito cooked the books and dumbed down the text." Esposito and Mogahed report that 13.5 percent of Muslims believe that the September 11 attacks were fully justified, but Satloff reveals that "the full data from the 9/11 question show that, in addition to the 13.5 percent, there is another 23.1 percent of respondents—300 million Muslims—who told pollsters the attacks were in some way justified. Esposito and Mogahed don't utter a word about the vast sea of intolerance in which the radicals operate."

"Amazing as it sounds," Satloff notes, "according to Esposito and Mogahed, the proper term for a Muslim who hates America, wants to impose sharia law, supports suicide bombing, and opposes equal rights for women but does not 'completely' justify 9/11 is ... 'moderates.'"[27]

Hillel Fradkin, director of the Center for Islam, Democracy and the Future of the Muslim World and senior fellow of the Hudson Institute in Washington, also denounced the book for distorting the results of the poll on which it's based. He concludes that "the book is a confidence game or fraud, of which Esposito should be ashamed. So too should the Gallup Organization, its publisher."

Most disturbing of all may be the authors' refusal to consider the real implications of their own finding that "Muslims—women as well as men—want to ground their 'democracy' partly or entirely in sharia or Islamic law." Unlike Esposito and Mogahed, the Muslims who answered the survey most likely thoroughly understand what sharia really means. And to the extent that they support the onset of sharia, they support the goals of both the violent and stealth jihadists.[28]

Esposito, then, has essentially made a career (both before and after receiving Alwaleed's millions) out of denying or minimizing the jihadist threat, while arguing that the problem within Islam is restricted to a tiny minority who misunderstand the teachings of their own religion, and who are too powerless to undertake any stealth jihad in the United States. It is a soothing picture, and one that many Americans want to hear. But insofar as Esposito's picture of jihad and Islamic supremacism is (at best) misleading, and the stealth jihad really exists, this popular analyst's findings only leave us unprepared in the face of an actual threat.

Esposito is only the most prominent of a legion of tenured Islamic "experts" who have convinced innumerable officials and a large segment of the American public that the solution to the conflict between the West and the Islamic world lies in economic and social solutions, as well as in political accommodation to the perceived slights decried by the Islamic world.

The problem with all this is that while there are politicians on both sides of the aisle who are all too willing to make these accommodations and implement these economic and political solutions, they have no apparent fallback position if they find that after the Islamic grievances have all been met, the Islamic supremacist agenda remains.

SAUDI MONEY AND WHAT IT BUYS

Esposito is hardly the only academic who has benefited, in terms of both financial support and career advancement, from the inflow of Islamic money into American universities. Another is Columbia professor Rashid Khalidi, who taught a fifteen-week teacher training course on Middle Eastern politics offered by Columbia's Middle East Institute. The institute was yet another academic institution bankrolled by the Saudis who, the *New York Sun* reported in March 2005, "funneled tens of thousands of dollars" into the institute's teacher outreach programs.[29]

However, New York City's schools chancellor, Joel Klein, removed Khalidi from the program, and Columbia president Lee Bollinger withdrew the university's support for the course, after radical statements by Khalidi surfaced in the media, such as his sly justification for jihad terror attacks against Israeli civilians: "Killing civilians is a war crime, whoever does it. But resistance to occupation is legitimate in international law."[30]

Nevertheless, at Columbia Khalidi continues to hold the Edward Said Chair in Arab Studies, which is endowed to the tune of $2.1 million. After coming under criticism for failing to report foreign donors for this chair, Columbia revealed its contributors, which included the United Arab Emirates (which donated $200,000) and the Olayan Charitable Trust, a Saudi-based charity. Commented Martin Kramer, "If you're a Saudi, it's very convenient for Rashid Khalidi to claim that the source of America's problems in the region is not their special relationship with Saudi Arabia, but their special relationship with Israel. All he has to do is say it's Palestine, stupid."[31]

For propagating the Saudi line, Khalidi has not only received a chair at Columbia University; he has also made friends in the highest places. In 2001 and 2002, the virulently anti-Israeli Arab American Action Network (AAAN), which was headed by Khalidi's wife Mona, received $75,000 in grants from the Woods Fund, a Chicago-based nonprofit organization. One of the members of the Woods Fund board of directors at that time was 2008 Democratic presidential candidate Barack Obama, Khalidi's former colleague back in the 1990s, when they both taught at the University of Chicago. In 2000, Khalidi held a fundraiser for Obama's unsuccessful run for a seat in the House of Representatives.[32] Obama's meteoric rise to the top of national politics only places Khalidi, the point of view he represents, and the moneyed forces behind him, even closer to the centers of power than they were already.

MEANWHILE, IN THE ACADEMIC DESERT

While conformity to Edward Said's anti-Western agenda is driven from the top down by administrators and professors at our nation's universities, often with massive amounts of money from the Islamic world as an incentive, the Muslim Students Association of the United States and Canada (MSA) fights for the Islamization of America among college students.

We have already discussed numerous examples of the role in the stealth jihad played by the MSA, which the Muslim Brotherhood memorandum lists as a principal actor in its "grand jihad" in the United States. However, like other stealth jihadist organizations, the MSA seeks to portray itself as a moderate, mainstream Islamic group. A loose association of Muslim student groups located on more than seven hundred American and Canadian campuses, the MSA lists a set of "Guiding Principles" on its website that paint a picture of an earnest and high-minded religious organization:

- Sincerity is the foundation of our existence.
- Knowledge precedes our actions.

- Humility guides our conduct.
- Truthfulness is the mark of our speech.
- Moderation is the compass of our journey.
- Tolerance is the banner of our outreach.
- Forgiveness precedes our reconciliatory efforts.
- Patience is the hallmark of our planning.
- Gratitude binds our hearts together.[33]

The "Constitution of The Muslim Student's Association of the United States and Canada" states that "the aims and purposes of MSA shall be to serve the best interest of Islam and Muslims in the United States and Canada so as to enable them to practice Islam as a complete way of life. Towards this end, it shall, in cooperation with the Islamic Society of North America:

1. help Muslim student organisations carry out Islamic programs and projects;
2. assist Muslim students organising themselves for Islamic activities;
3. mobilise and coordinate the human and material resources of Muslim student organisations."[34]

And who could object to any of that? Most university administrators today assume that the MSA is an innocuous religious organization, and at some schools they donate considerable sums to MSA chapters in an effort to offset what they see as the "Islamophobia" of the Bush administration. According to conservative activist David Horowitz, MSA chapters are "all funded by student activities fees and by outside sources that are not disclosed. At the University of Pennsylvania, the Muslim Students' Association boasts a $50,000 annual budget. Of this total $20,000 comes from student fees. By contrast, College Democrats and College Republicans at the University of Pennsylvania receive no student funding."[35]

Yet, if the MSA is indeed the moderate organization that university administrators believe it is, then why do we find MSA chapters at schools such as New York City's Queensborough Community College sponsoring incendiary speakers proclaiming that "eventually there will be a Muslim in the White House dictating the laws of sharia"?[36]

That the MSA is not the moderate group it claims to be is evident from the close ties the organization maintains to a number of radical Islamic organizations. Besides the Brotherhood connection, the MSA has links to the Wahhabis, the Islamic supremacist sect that controls Saudi Arabia. Hamid Algar, a professor at the University of California at Berkeley, in his *Wahhabism: A Critical Essay* observes that "some Muslim student organizations have . . . functioned at times as Saudi-supported channels for the propagation of Wahhabism abroad, especially in the United States." He notes that over time the MSA gradually "diversified its connections with Arab states"—that is, it no longer depended solely upon Saudi Arabia, but "official approval of Wahhabism remained strong."[37]

The MSA has also been linked to the Muslim World League, a group that has financed the jihad terror group Hamas. Furthermore, it sought donations for the Holy Land Foundation, whose assets were seized by the U.S. government in December 2001 to prevent it from funding Hamas.[38] In many ways the MSA serves as a reminder of the close connection and overlap between the agents of the stealth jihad and the soldiers of the violent jihad. Both are working for the same goals, and they find their paths crossing quite often.

Moreover, MSA chapters have fostered anti-American paranoia with actions such as the endorsement of a 2002 document devised by the Revolutionary Communist Party that claimed the U.S. government was "coming for the Arab, Muslim and South Asian immigrants.... The recent 'disappearances,' indefinite detention, the round-ups, the secret military tribunals, the denial of legal representation, evidence kept a secret from the accused, the denial of any due process for Arab, Muslim, South Asians and others, have chilling similarities to a police state."[39]

Despite the MSA's pretense at moderation, the jihadist sentiments of many MSA members have been known for many years. On October 22, 2000, Arif Shaikh and Ahmed Shama of the MSA chapter at UCLA led a demonstration at the Israeli Consulate in Los Angeles. Shama shouted, "Victory to Islam! Death to the Jews!" and told the crowd: "Our solution is simple.... Our solution is the establishment of justice by Islamic means. That is the only solution to this Israeli apartheid." As we saw in chapter two, "justice by Islamic means" refers to warfare against unbelievers and their subjugation under Islamic law. Even worse, as Shama burned the Israeli flag, the crowd chanted, "Khaibar, Khaibar, O Jews, the army of Mohammed is coming for you," and "Death to Israel, victory to Islam."[40]

When MSA members at another campus, the University of Michigan, hosted speaker Sami al-Arian (who later pled guilty to aiding a terrorist group, Palestinian Islamic Jihad) in October 2002, the crowd also chanted "Death to Israel."[41] But the Khaibar reference at UCLA was even more pointed for those who knew Islamic history, as it refers to a Jewish Arabian oasis conquered by a Muslim expedition led by Muhammad. After conquering Khaibar, Muhammad banished most of the Jews into exile, commanding them to leave behind all their gold and silver.[42] Some

Jews remained at Khaibar, but later, during the caliphate of Umar (634-644), the rest of the Khaibar Jews were banished to Syria and their remaining land was seized.[43]

These were the glories that the MSA commemorated during their demonstration in front of the Israeli Consulate. In chanting "Khaibar, Khaibar, O Jews, the army of Mohammed is coming for you," the crowd was expressing its desire for the eradication of Israel. And Israel isn't the only country that MSA-sponsored agitators want to see wiped out: in January 2001, Abdul-Alim Musa, Imam of Masjid al-Islam in Washington, D.C., spoke at an event hosted by the MSA at UCLA. He declared, "If you were to say that the Soviet Union was wiped off the face of the earth . . . people would have thought you were crazy, right? . . . We saw the fall of one so-called superpower, Old Uncle Sam is next."[44]

Do such views reflect the MSA's own perspective? If they don't, one might legitimately wonder why such sentiments are expressed over and over again at MSA-sponsored speeches, activities, and publications. For example, the UCLA MSA chapter publishes a news magazine, *Al-Talib*, which for a time, as we have seen, boasted MPAC's Edina Lekovic as its editor. This is no small-time campus paper: the MSA prints 20,000 copies of each issue, and *Al-Talib* has 56,000 readers in thirty-seven states. In July 1999 *Al-Talib* featured Osama bin Laden on its cover. The story on him declared, "When we hear someone refer to the great Mujahid . . . Osama bin Laden, as a 'terrorist,' we should defend our brother and refer to him as a freedom fighter."[45] In November 2000, *Al-Talib* said this of Abdullah Azzam, who cofounded al Qaeda with Osama bin Laden: "We pray that Sheik Azzam's dream of a true Islamic state comes true." After September 11, *Al-Talib* carried advertisements for three Islamic charities that were later shut down for funneling money to jihad terror groups: the Holy Land

Foundation for Relief and Development, the Global Relief Foundation, and the Benevolence International Foundation.[46]

The UCLA chapter of the MSA is no anomaly. The Muslim Student Union (MSU) at the University of California at Irvine—that is, the local MSA chapter—has sponsored several talks by Imam Abdel Malik-Ali, a fiery American convert to Islam. At an MSU event on October 5, 2006, as students cheered he shouted, "They [sic] Jews think they are superman, but we, the Muslims, are kryptonite. They [sic] Jews know that their days are numbered."[47] Ominous in a different way was the February 2006 declaration of the MSA at Columbia University denouncing the Danish Muhammad cartoons. "We are protesting the newspapers' insult to Islam.... Freedom of expression is not absolute."[48]

Perhaps not, but the problem with restricting free speech is that insults and "hate speech" are in the eye of the beholder. Such restrictions become weapons in the hands of those who wield political power, or who are jockeying for that power—weapons to silence their opponents. Today's worldwide effort by Islamic jihadists and their allies and dupes to classify all critical examination of Islamic supremacism as "hate speech" only benefits Islamic supremacists: if this effort succeeds, we Americans will be mute and hence defenseless in the face of the jihadist onslaught.

MSA chapters have worked for restrictions on free speech. In April 2006, MSA members at Michigan State University staged a protest against the Danish Muhammad cartoons, which they declared to be "hate speech." This incensed Indrek Wichman, a professor of mechanical engineering at the university, who fired off an email to the school's MSA chapter in which he declared:

> I intend to protest your protest. I am offended not by cartoons, but by more mundane things like beheadings of civil-

ians, cowardly attacks on public buildings, suicide murders, murders of Catholic priests (the latest in Turkey!), burnings of Christian churches, the continued persecution of Coptic Christians in Egypt, the imposition of sharia law on non-Muslims, the rapes of Scandinavian girls and women (called 'whores' in your culture), the murder of film directors in Holland, and the rioting and looting in Paris France .... If you do not like the values of the West—see the 1st Amendment— you are free to leave. I hope for God's sake that most of you choose that option. Please return to your ancestral homelands and build them up yourselves instead of troubling Americans.

For this the MSA demanded that Professor Wichman be reprimanded and that faculty members and freshman students be forced to undergo mandatory "diversity training." After extensive negotiations with the MSA and CAIR, the university instituted university-funded—though non-mandatory—diversity training for faculty and students, including an MSA-led workshop.[49]

Meanwhile, the MSA chapter at Penn State has hosted Sheikh Khalid Yasin, an American convert to Islam who has shown his support for Islamic supremacism by declaring, "If you don't have a people that is governed by sharia, then you have a lawless people."[50] Similarly, the MSA chapters at Temple University and George Washington University have hosted Imam Zaid Shakir, who has stated that "every Muslim who is honest . . . would like to see America become a Muslim country," and that American Constitutional government is "against the orders and ordainments of Allah."[51] The MSA at Virginia Commonwealth University has hosted Imam Siraj Wahhaj, who, as we have seen, has declared, "If only Muslims were clever politically, they could take over the

United States and replace its constitutional government with a caliphate."[52]

Unfortunately, such statements hardly raise eyebrows among the professors who make up the Middle East Studies establishment. American universities have become propaganda centers not only for the anti-American Left, but for stealth jihadists and their allies—the apologists who are dedicated to lulling Americans into believing there is no jihadist threat.

If we are to win the war against the jihadists, we need to have a thorough understanding of their doctrine, history, and sources of inspiration. Sadly, the segment of America most suited to investigating these questions—academic experts in Middle Eastern Studies—has rejected this responsibility. Instead, it has adopted a politically correct orthodoxy that values "tolerance" of non-Western cultures above any objective search for truth. The mere suggestion that the jihadists' hatred for us is rooted in the Qur'an and other fundamental Islamic texts is simply not tolerated in academia. As a result, many American citizens as well as policy makers continue to cast about in vain for a way to satisfy our enemies' grievances.

CHAPTER TEN

COMPROMISED

Many influential officials in America's security services are standing by passively as the stealth jihad advances. This is largely because they're ignorant of what is happening, and because those who understand don't tell them. In sum, willfully blind officials, dedicated to "multiculturalism" and "diversity" no matter what the cost, are hindering the investigation of and resistance to the stealth jihad.

It is difficult to gauge the extent of stealth jihadist infiltration of U.S. intelligence and law enforcement agencies. But there is no question that the chief enabler of that infiltration has been political correctness among U.S. officials. In this great war against the global jihad network, no one wants to appear anti-Arab or anti-Muslim—and this has led to serious lapses in national security.

ARABIC TRANSLATOR FOLLIES

This problem is particularly evident in the U.S. government's hiring of Arabic translators. Despite the immense need for Arabic translators, numerous Arabic-speaking Jews and Christians have been turned away by government agencies. Late in 2001 over ninety Arabic-speaking Jews, some of whom had worked translating Arabic for the Israeli military and news media, applied to the New York office of the FBI. All were rejected. Doug Balin of the Sephardic Bikur Holim, a Jewish social-services agency in Brooklyn, remarked, "We sent them a lot of people, and nobody made it to the finish line. Not one person was found eligible for these jobs, which is outrageous.... Maybe the FBI is not hiring Jewish people that often, I don't know."[1]

The FBI denies this, but it's certainly true that religious Muslims dislike Jews or Christians being in positions of authority over them, for it violates the Islamic principle that "Islam must dominate, and not be dominated." It would thus smooth matters, as well as coalesce nicely with the agenda of political correctness, if as many Arabic translators as possible were Muslim.

And the government is making a concerted effort to recruit them. For example, an Arabic-language billboard appeared in Detroit in March 2008. Designed to appeal to the city's sizable Muslim community to become, among other things, U.S. Army translators, the sign read, "In the land of different opportunities, this is one you might not have heard before: job opportunities with the U.S. Army." The initial reaction to the sign was hostile, to the point that those Muslims who took the job felt compelled to conceal their employment from their community. Hassan Jaber of Dearborn's Arab Community Center for Economic and Social Services reported that "to my knowledge, people who are volunteering and taking these jobs are doing it in secret. It might be a factor of shame, and that they go in there . . . because of the money offered, not necessarily because they feel the war is justified."

A Lebanese U.S. Army sergeant recruiter based in Detroit further observed, "I had the idea in my mind that I can go talk to this community and probably get at least two or three people a day to join the army. This is not the case. The idea that people have here, as soon as they see me in uniform is: 'Oh, you're in the U.S. Army? You're in Iraq killing your own people?'" Still, the army pressed on in Detroit, recruiting 277 Arabic translators in 2006 and 250 in 2007.[2]

The need for Arabic translators is obvious, but the potential for infiltration is immense when recruitment focuses on members of Islamic communities that deeply distrust the U.S. military. And it's compounded by the fact that political correctness renders officials unwilling to probe the backgrounds or sentiments of their Muslim recruits—and most officials don't know enough about the nature of the jihadist threat to do so effectively anyway.

And just how extensive is the jihadist infiltration of the military and our security agencies? The government is reluctant to discuss this issue due to politically correct sensitivities. And of course, an organization that can't even discuss a problem is unlikely to adopt effective measures to combat it. But there are disturbing reports that jihadist infiltrators are already compromising our national security.

Journalist Paul Sperry is the author of the eye-opening book *Infiltration*, which traces jihadist influence in government agencies. Jihadists, he says, have "infiltrated every security agency from the FBI to the Pentagon to the prison system, which is the top recruiting ground for al-Qaida right now." According to Sperry, some of the Arabic translators the FBI hired after September 11 have:

...sold us out. Case agents I talked to say they can't trust
these guys. They say some have tipped off targets of terror
investigations, while others are holding back key information
from case agents they're working with—who are completely
at their mercy because they don't speak Arabic and these
other tongues. The Muslim translators are claiming the information is "NOT PERTINENT" to their investigations when
in fact it is. They've also had a problem with laptops with
classified al-Qaida information disappearing from that translation unit at [the] FBI's Washington field office. It's a mess
there, a veritable Muslim "mole house," as one bureau source
put it. Some devout Muslims in the unit have gotten so cocky
they're actually demanding separate potties from the "infidel"
agents so they won't get dirty sitting on the same toilets. Others go around the language squad saying America had 9/11
coming to it because of our pro-Israel policies. It's outrageous,
it's flat-out betrayal, and these are the people who are supposed to be protecting us from another 9/11.

And what are FBI officials doing about this? Sperry reports that
they're "putting the infidel agents through Muslim sensitivity
training while promoting the Muslims who threaten to sue for discrimination."[3]

One of the foremost people to have exposed this sorry situation
was Sibel Edmonds, a former FBI translator who was fired in
2002, according to the *Times* of London, after accusing an FBI
colleague of covering up illegal activity involving Turkish agents.[4]
Edmonds argued that "the issues and problems within the FBI's
translation units range from security failures to questions of loyalty to competence of translation personnel to systemic problems
within their low-to-mid-level management practices."

In a 2003 letter to the National Commission on Terrorist Attacks upon the United States, she explained, "During my work with the bureau, I was seriously taken aback by what I heard and witnessed within the translation department. There were those who openly divided the fronts as 'Us'—the Middle-Easterners who shared certain views—and 'Them'—the Americans who were the outsiders [whose] arrogance was now 'leading to their own destruction.'" One translator, according to Edmonds, declared openly about the September 11 attacks, "It is about time that they get a taste of what they have been giving to the rest of the Middle East."[5]

Edmonds says that she found evidence that a high-placed State Department official was selling information to Turkish agents, who were then passing on the information to high-level contacts in Pakistan. According to Edmonds, "He was aiding foreign operatives against US interests by passing them highly classified information, not only from the State Department but also from the Pentagon, in exchange for money, position and political objectives." Pentagon officials, she says, were also aiding foreign entities. According to the *Times*, "Edmonds says packages containing nuclear secrets were delivered by Turkish operatives, using their cover as members of the diplomatic and military community, to contacts at the Pakistani embassy in Washington." The Office of the Inspector General found in 2005 that Edmonds had been dismissed for, among other reasons, making valid complaints that made her superiors uncomfortable. [6]

The State Department official accused by Edmonds denies all her charges. However, as we shall see, Edmonds' case fits an unsettling larger picture within the government and military of political correctness trumping security concerns, whistleblowers being summarily dismissed from their positions, and proven infiltrators receiving startlingly light punishments.

"THERE IS A CERTAIN AMOUNT OF BIZARRENESS ABOUT THIS CASE"

One would think that the U.S. Army would maintain constant vigilance against jihadist infiltrators. But a number of cases in the last few years signify, at a minimum, that even while fighting an array of jihadist enemies in foreign lands, the army has paid insufficient attention to the damage that could be inflicted by jihadists operating inside the U.S. armed forces.

For example, Noureddine Malki is a Moroccan Muslim who immigrated to the United States in the late 1980s, worked for L-3 Titan Group as a translator for the U.S. Army in Iraq in 2003 and 2004, and returned to his Brooklyn apartment in 2005. When he left Iraq, he took with him battle maps that indicated the routes to be taken by American troops, lists of terrorists the army was hunting, and lists of sites that U.S. authorities suspected of being hiding places for Saddam's weapons of mass destruction. Malki was arrested and jailed shortly after his return, and the documents were found in his apartment.

Did Malki pass on this information to Iraqi jihadists? No one knows for sure, but phone records revealed that he had repeatedly called numbers linked to jihadists in Iraq, and had accepted bribes totaling at least $11,500 from Iraqi insurgents. Prosecutors declared they were able to "establish that the defendant had an opportunity to provide stolen classified information to anti-coalition forces." Lieutenant Colonel Michele Bredenkamp explained that the documents would have been of immense interest to Iraqi jihadist forces: "The information is so critical that you do not want the information to get into the hands of anyone without the need to know." When a prosecutor asked if these documents might be "the type of thing for a soldier to take for a keepsake," Bredenkamp replied, "That's absurd."

Malki pleaded guilty to possessing national defense information without authorization, but insisted, "I never had bad intentions whatsoever." His sister, Sonia Malki, declared, "This is not a terrorism case. This could happen to any immigrant." She didn't explain, however, how any immigrant could end up with classified documents hidden in his apartment.[7]

Judge Edward Korman sentenced Malki to eleven years in prison, a much lighter sentence than Malki could have received. Korman explained that "there is a certain amount of bizarreness about this case," as the judge was "not 100 percent sure if we are dealing with a spy or someone who has other problems. It causes me to have some hesitation about the sentence. It could be he's something more than someone who is acting bizarrely. But there just isn't that degree of certainty."[8]

Maybe not. Unfortunately, however, Malki is by no means the only Muslim in the U.S. military who has been "acting bizarrely" in this way. Most notorious was Ali Mohamed, a U.S. Army sergeant who trained as a Green Beret—and operated in the inner sanctum of al Qaeda. Mohamed played a key role in the 1998 bombings of the U.S. embassies in Tanzania and Kenya. According to Larry Johnson, the State Deparment's director of counterterrorism in the early 1990s, "He was an active source for the FBI, a double agent."

Mohamed was a major in the Egyptian special forces who joined a jihadist group after Egyptian president Anwar Sadat signed a peace accord with Israel in 1978. In 1984, he left the Egyptian Army and contacted the CIA. A U.S. official explains, "This individual approached the CIA to offer information. Some time later, we found out he was talking to known terrorists and had identified himself as a CIA agent. We felt him to be untrustworthy, and we put him on the State Department watch list."

Nonetheless, Mohamed was able to obtain a U.S. visa in 1985 and enlisted in the U.S. Army in 1986 at a relatively advanced age (thirty-four) for army recruits. Apparently no one noticed or cared that he was on a State Department watch list. The army put him to work teaching soldiers about the Middle East.

According to one man who served with him, Mohamed made no secret of his contempt for the United States. "To be in the [enlisted ranks] and have so much training was weird," he said of Mohamed. "And to be in the U.S. military and have so much hate toward the U.S. was odd. He never referred to America as his country."[9]

How did Ali Mohamed get into the country, join the military, and even teach soldiers, while expressing open contempt for the United States and having known connections with its enemies?

Answers have not been forthcoming.

HIZBALLAH IN THE FBI AND CIA

Signs of jihadist infiltration extend past the military into our key intelligence and law enforcement agencies. The most dramatic illustration of this is the case of Nada Nadim Prouty, a Lebanese national who has been employed by both the FBI and the CIA. In November 2007 she admitted that she searched FBI files for information on investigations connected to the jihad terrorist group Hizballah—although, according to her plea agreement, she "was not assigned to work on Hizballah cases as part of her FBI duties and she was not authorized by her supervisor, the case agent assigned to the case, or anybody else to access information about the investigation in question."[10]

Among other subjects, Prouty sought information about two accused Hizballah operatives in the U.S.—namely, her sister and brother-in-law. Talal Chahine, her brother-in-law, owns La Shish, a Detroit-based restaurant chain, and has fled the country to escape indictment for evading taxes and sending $20 million of the restaurant's money to Hizballah. While searching for information on Chahine, Prouty also searched FBI files to see what information the Feds had on herself—an exercise that illustrates stunning weaknesses in our basic national security infrastructure. At the time of her guilty plea, some agents declared their suspicion that Prouty was actually a Hizballah mole.[11]

There is no doubt, meanwhile, that she is a former illegal immigrant who admitted to paying a U.S. citizen to enter into a sham marriage with her to help her obtain U.S. citizenship. She is currently married to a longtime State Department official who has held important positions in the Egyptian and Pakistani embassies.[12] And while working for the CIA, Prouty had access to key al Qaeda detainees in Iraq.[13]

For all that, U.S. District Judge Avern Cohn issued her a $750 fine—and no jail time at all.[14]

If Prouty had been a serial double parker she might have drawn a harsher punishment than that. But at this point, her case is closed. The only thing that U.S. government agencies can do now is try to make sure that there will be no more Nada Nadim Proutys—if they have the will to do so.

How can they do it? To begin with, they should examine the culture that enabled her to rise so high in the first place. Before she was hired by the FBI, Prouty was a waitress at La Shish.[15] That's an impressive career move, but it also suggests that when the Feds hired her, they were primarily motivated not by her outstanding qualifications but by the pleasing thoughts that were dancing in their heads—thoughts about reaching out to Detroit's Arab community so as to deflect the ubiquitous criticism leveled by CAIR, MPAC, and the like, who denounce anti-terror efforts as "racial profiling."

Given the fact that such charges are taken seriously by the mainstream media, it's hard to imagine that when she was hired, Prouty was asked any hard questions about just where she stood on Hizballah, or in general about the jihadist ideology and Islamic supremacism. Few agents, in any case, would even have known how to formulate such questions, or how to evaluate the answers. And if they were being asked of Arab and Muslim applicants, CAIR and its ilk would immediately charge bigotry and demand that the application process be changed.

In today's political climate, they would probably succeed in this. But when you don't ask, of course, and make no effort to investigate in any other way, you don't get answers. If the FBI and CIA don't want the relatives of suspected jihadist fugitives illegally rifling through their family members' case files, they shouldn't hire them in the first place, or should subject them to rigorous screening. The very fact that such an elementary recommendation has to be made indicates how all too many officials in these agencies now prioritize political correctness above national security; apparently it's more important for them not to be accused of being racist than to protect their own agencies from jihadist moles. In fact, in a perverse display of the extent of the multicultural rot within these agencies, several CIA officials have praised Prouty as a great agent and expressed interest in rehiring her.[16]

Prouty's case was not even unique. In April 2008, Muhammad Weiss Rasool, a Muslim police sergeant in Fairfax County, Virginia, admitted that he had searched police databases for information about a member of the mosque Rasool attended who was the subject of a federal terrorism investigation. According to the FBI, Rasool "likely alerted the subject of the FBI investigation which had a disruptive effect on the pending counterterrorism case." When agents eventually arrested the suspect at his home, it was clear he'd been tipped off: he was fully dressed at 6:00 a.m. and was busy destroying evidence.[17]

It came as no surprise that CAIR quickly emerged as one of Rasool's foremost defenders; CAIR Governmental Affairs Coordinator Corey Saylor wrote to the judge, "I have always found Sgt. Rasool eager to promote a substantive relationship between the Fairfax County Police Department and the local Muslim community."[18] In another curiously light sentence, Rasool was given two years' probation.[19]

MR. ISLAM GOES TO THE PENTAGON

As we discussed in chapter three, U.S. Army Reserve Major Stephen Coughlin was a top expert on Islamic law at the Pentagon. He was a courageous, lonely voice warning of the theological underpinnings of Islamic violence, a stand that cost him his job. What's perhaps most disturbing about his removal is that it likely came at the behest of an official with very questionable allegiances.

In late 2007, Coughlin met with Hesham Islam, special assistant for international affairs for the Deputy Secretary of Defense, Gordon R. England. Islam tried to compel Coughlin to soft-pedal his portrayal of the Islamic religion. Coughlin, however, cited Islamic sources to show that he was describing Islamic teaching accurately. According to journalist Bill Gertz in the *Washington Times*, Islam and other Muslims in the Pentagon then began campaigning to have Coughlin fired, calling him a "Christian zealot with a pen."[20] Coughlin, a Joint Staff contractor, was told in January 2008 that his contract would not be renewed when it expired that March.[21]

Coughlin's effective firing wasn't because his work was of poor quality. Retired Air Force Lt. Gen. Thomas McInerney contended that "Steve Coughlin is the most knowledgeable person in the U.S. government on Islamic law," while Marine Corps Lt. Gen. Samuel Helland said that Coughlin "hit the mark in explaining how jihadists use the Koran to justify their actions."[22] LTC Joseph C. Myers, Army Advisor to the Air Command and Staff College, denounced Coughlin's removal as "an act of intellectual cowardice."[23]

In light of Coughlin's sterling record and Hesham Islam's opposition to his message, Coughlin's firing was widely ascribed to Islam's influence, notwithstanding denials from England's spokesmen.[24] The entire episode brought Hesham Islam under public scrutiny, resulting in the emergence of a strange and contradictory account of the background of a man who has quietly risen to a position of prominence in the defense bureaucracy.

Born in Cairo and raised in the Iraq of Saddam Hussein, Hesham Islam came to the U.S. in 1980 and served in the U.S. Navy from 1985 to 2005. He joined England's staff when England was Secretary of the Navy and followed him to the Defense Department. Islam's record was apparently impeccable; England called him "my personal close confidante," and said that Islam "represents me to the international community" and "assists me in my own outreach efforts." England further proclaimed that Islam offers "extraordinarily good advice in dealing with countries and people," and that "I take his advice, and I listen to him all the time."[25]

However, according to terrorism expert Steven Emerson, Islam is "an Islamist with a pro-Muslim Brotherhood bent who has brought in groups to the Pentagon who have been unindicted co-conspirators."[26] Furthermore, Gertz reported that Islam's wrath against Coughlin stemmed from the fact that Coughlin identified numerous groups that are close to Islam as agents of the stealth jihad. Hesham Islam, Coughlin argued, was involving the Muslim Brotherhood in Pentagon community outreach programs. According to Gertz, "Coughlin came under fire from pro-Muslim officials after a memorandum he wrote identified several groups that are being courted by Mr. Islam's community outreach program as front organizations for the pro-extremist Muslim Brotherhood." Islam also prevailed upon England to host members of the Islamic Society of North America at the Pentagon in April 2008, "raising concerns," wrote Gertz, "that the deputy defense secretary does not understand clearly the nature of the Islamist threat he is working against as the No. 2 official."[27]

What's more, there are curious inconsistencies in Islam's story of his early life. A profile published by the Defense Department says that he was caught in an Israeli bombing raid in Cairo during the Six-Day War in 1967—but Israel did not bomb Cairo during that war. It also says that once in Iraq, Islam was a "merchant mariner adrift for three days in the Arabian Sea after an Iranian torpedo sunk his 16,000-ton cargo ship, drowning all but Islam and four of his crewmates." But Pentagon officials could not or would not provide any details of this incident—the name of the ship, the date this happened—to Claudia Rosett of the Foundation for the Defense of Democracies when she inquired about it. And Rosett's research uncovered no such ship torpedoed in those circumstances.

Even more strangely, after Rosett wrote about the inconsistencies in Islam's account of his background and the Pentagon's inability to explain them, the profile of Islam mysteriously vanished from the Defense Department website, without explanation.[28]

Islam, incidentally, has also played the victim card so often invoked by jihadists and their allies and dupes: "Since 9/11," he claimed rather implausibly in 2007, "I no longer have a land line. I only work with my cell phone, because I got a lot of hate messages on the phone."[29]

In any case, the Hesham Islam/Stephen Coughlin affair illustrated most vividly the present situation at the highest levels of the U.S. government. After a public outcry, Coughlin was given a position in the Defense Department, but that did not erase the details of the episode. A highly valued official was effectively fired apparently because the content of his message was opposed by another official. Another was not fired, or even investigated, despite highly questionable assertions in his account of his own past, including a stint in the military of Saddam Hussein's Iraq. Instead, the Defense Department actually covered for him by deleting the suspicious material.

Infiltration? As is often the case, it's hard to tell. But at the very least, we see that some important people are asleep at the wheel. According to Clare Lopez, a professor at the Centre for Counterintelligence and Security Studies (CI Centre) in Alexandria, Virginia, "Muslim Brotherhood organizations such as the Islamic Society of North America (ISNA), the Council on American-Islamic Relations (CAIR), and the International Institute of Islamic Thought (IIIT), all three listed by the Department of Justice as unindicted co-conspirators, have achieved unprecedented access to the Department of Defense and even the White House."[30] So wide is this access that in April 2008 the State Department gave ISNA a grant for a program to bring "young professionals" from the Middle East to the United States.[31]

The price America ultimately pays for this kind of short-sightedness could be beyond astronomical.

WHAT IS TO BE DONE?

"WE WILL DOMINATE YOU"

The stealth jihad is rapidly advancing all over the West, particularly within America's Western European allies, and every day's headlines seem to bring news of a new stealth jihad initiative.

The trajectory of attack, however, is clear, and undoubtedly will proceed along these lines for the foreseeable future: Islamic groups will continue to push for international and domestic bans on "hate speech," by which they mean, among other things, any honest discussion of the elements of Islam that justify violence and Islamic supremacism. These groups, many linked to the Muslim Brotherhood, will continue to work to dominate the public debate by discrediting their critics and intimidating the media into silence on these issues. They will continue to pursue their cause in our schools and universities, in the courts, and in the workplace. The incidents recounted in this book are merely manifestations of a larger effort—and we can see where it is all heading by looking at Europe.

On October 13, 1999, the Roman Catholic Archbishop of Izmir, Turkey, Giuseppe Germano Bernardini, warned the Synod of European Bishops about a "clear program" among Muslims for the "re-conquest" of Europe. "During an official meeting on Islamic-Christian dialogue," he wrote, "an authoritative Muslim person, speaking to the Christians participating, at one point said very calmly and assuredly: 'Thanks to your democratic laws we will invade you; thanks to our religious laws we will dominate you.'"

This domination, he continued, has already begun—"with the 'petrol-dollars,' used not to create work in the poor North African or Middle Eastern countries, but to build mosques and cultural centers in Christian countries with Islamic immigration, including Rome, the center of Christianity. How can we ignore in all of this a clear program of expansion and re-conquest?"

Bernardini also recorded one Muslim's piquant expression of Islamic supremacism: "During another Islamic-Christian meeting, always organized by Christians, a Christian participant publicly asked the Muslims present why they did not organize at least once a meeting of this kind. The Muslim authority present answered the following words: 'Why should we? You have nothing to teach us and we have nothing to learn.'"[1]

Since the stealth jihad is more advanced in Europe than it is in the United States, the situation there is more dire. Through massive immigration and official dhimmitude from European leaders, Muslims are accomplishing today what they have tried but failed to do for over a millennium: conquer Europe. Europe is being Islamized so rapidly that even historian Bernard Lewis, despite having grown increasingly apologetic and disingenuous about Islamic supremacism in the twilight of his long and distinguished career, has nonetheless predicted without hesitation or qualification that "Europe will be Islamic by the end of the century."[2]

It could even happen sooner than that. If current demographic trends continue, France, Holland, and other Western European nations could have Muslim majorities by mid-century. It is a near-certainty that if this demographic transformation does indeed take place, these new Muslim majorities will attempt to impose Islamic law in its entirety upon the states of Europe. The growing Muslim minorities in those states are increasingly assertive, and are ever more insistently demanding accommodation to Islamic law. Recent news from Europe demonstrates the determination of all too many Muslims in Europe to reject European law and impose their own.

For example, Sweden's third-largest city, Malmo, has become an Islamic enclave within that country. A quarter of the city's population is now Muslim, and that proportion is rapidly growing. The city is now essentially autonomous because non-Muslim authorities are afraid to enter it. "If we park our car it will be damaged—so we have to go very often in two vehicles, one just to protect the other vehicle," reported a Malmo police officer. Meanwhile, Swedish ambulance drivers will not enter some areas of the city unless police accompany them.[3]

Such segregated Muslim communities are spreading throughout Europe at an alarming pace. In April 2008, the Rt. Rev. Michael Nazir-Ali, Anglican Bishop of Rochester in England, warned that Islamic jihadists were turning "already separate communities into 'no-go' areas where adherence to this ideology has become a mark of acceptability." He declared that non-Muslims "may find it difficult to live or work there because of hostility to them and even the risk of violence . . . . Attempts have been made to impose an 'Islamic' character on certain areas, for example, by insisting on artificial amplification for the Adhan, the call to prayer. Such amplification was, of course, unknown throughout

most of history and its use raises all sorts of questions about noise
levels and whether non-Muslims wish to be told the creed of a
particular faith five times a day on the loudspeaker."[4]

Indeed. It also raises questions about the supremacist agenda of
those operating the loudspeakers. But no public debate on Islamic
supremacism was forthcoming; instead, it was Nazir-Ali's words
that provoked a furor in Britain, as Muslims vociferously
denounced the bishop. One Muslim leader, Mohammed Shafiq of
the Ramadhan Foundation, fulminated, "Mr. Nazir-Ali is promoting hatred towards Muslims and should resign."[5] Nazir-Ali
soon had to be placed under police protection after receiving
death threats.[6] Despite denials from various Muslim leaders that
such hostile Islamic enclaves really existed in Britain, Nazir-Ali's
account was indirectly confirmed by the British government in
March 2008 when officials forbade British military personnel
from wearing their uniforms in certain parts of the country in
order to avoid abuse from "ethnic minorities."[7]

The spreading of Islamic separatism and the adoption of sharia
law in British communities really should come as no surprise,
since this is the documented agenda of numerous Muslim leaders
in Britain. This was exposed by an undercover investigation of
British mosques by Britain's Channel 4 *Dispatches* program in late
2006, which found Muslim preachers exhorting audiences to create a "state within a state" in Britain. One preacher, Dr. Ijaz Mian,
exclaimed, "You cannot accept the rule of the kaffir [unbeliever].
We have to rule ourselves and we have to rule the others."[8]

In France, meanwhile, Daniel Pipes reported in November 2006
that there are no less than 751 areas in France that are euphemisti-
cally classified as "Sensitive Urban Zones" (ZUS). Pipes explains
that these are "places in France that the French state does not control," and that "a more precise name for these zones would be

Dar al-Islam, the place where Muslims rule."[9] European historian and journalist Paul Belien noted in January 2008 that these areas have also become magnets for mafia groups: "The ZUS are centers of drug trafficking.... Since they operate from within the ZUS the drug dealers are beyond the reach of the French authorities. The ZUS exist not only because Muslims wish to live in their own areas according to their own culture and their own sharia laws, but also because organized crime wants to operate without the judicial and fiscal interference of the French state. In France, sharia law and mafia rule have become almost identical."[10]

There are zones of this kind all over Europe. *Deutsche Welle* TV discovered one in September 2007 in the Molenbeek neighborhood of Brussels when a local Muslim leader threatened its film crew and denied they had a right to film there. Of this man, *Deutsche Welle* remarked, "Belgian laws do not interest him. The man is confident that it is he who controls the neighborhood." It continued, "Many police officers are afraid that the State no longer wields authority here—at least not the sole authority. They know that Islamists view Molenbeek as subject only to Muslim law."[11]

Europe is now reaping what it has long sown. In her book *Eurabia,* Bat Ye'or, the pioneering historian of dhimmitude, chronicles how this has come to pass. Europe, she explains, began thirty years ago to travel down a path of appeasement, accommodation, and cultural abdication in pursuit of shortsighted political and economic benefits. She observes that today, "Europe has evolved from a Judeo-Christian civilization, with important post-Enlightenment/secular elements, to a 'civilization of dhimmitude,' i.e., Eurabia: a secular-Muslim transitional society with its traditional Judeo-Christian mores rapidly disappearing."[12]

If Western Europe does become Islamized, as demographic trends suggest, before too long America will be facing a world that is drastically different and more forbidding than today. And the same process of Islamization will proceed here—unless enough people wake up in time to head it off.

MYRICK'S COUNTERJIHAD PLAN: MCCARTHYISM OR COMMON SENSE?

One of the few who have awakened to the danger is Representative Sue Myrick (R-NC). In April 2008 she unveiled a ten-point plan for fighting against jihadist activity in the United States, including stealth jihad activity.[13] Myrick's plan was unusual for its sheer singularity; few of her colleagues in any branch of government have offered any concrete proposals for resisting the jihad beyond various "counterterrorism" initiatives, and hardly any have noticed the stealth jihad at all.

Myrick's proposals, outlined below, became yet another test case for self-proclaimed moderate Muslim leaders, and again they failed. One might have thought that those Muslims who profess to oppose today's global jihad would have welcomed Myrick's initiative as a way to isolate the Islamic "extremists" they claim to reject, but instead local Islamic leaders roundly denounced Myrick. One Muslim leader from Myrick's district, Jibril Hough of the Islamic Center of Charlotte, charged that "Myrick's latest attempt at fighting terrorism is nothing more than a fear campaign. It is nothing more than a new McCarthyism, or Myrickism. As Muslims, we have become expendable as politicians like Myrick seek political gain."[14]

Myrick responded by inviting the Islamic Center of Charlotte to offer a point-by-point rebuttal to her proposals, but neither Jibril Hough nor any other Muslim leader showed any interest in accommodating her request. Their opposition to Myrick's plan, however, is illuminating in itself.

Myrick's first two proposals were to investigate all military and prison chaplains endorsed by Abdurahman Alamoudi,[15] who is serving twenty-three years in prison, after pleading guilty in a terrorism financing case.[16] Is it not possible that some of the military and prison chaplains he endorsed share his jihadist views? Would Jibril Hough be able to explain why it would not be important to find out?

Myrick then called for an investigation of the selection process of the Arabic translators employed in the Pentagon and the FBI. As we saw in chapter ten, an FBI whistleblower has reported that Arabic translators there cheered the September 11 attacks. Would Hough be able to explain why this should not be a cause for concern?

The remainder of Myrick's plan consisted of the following proposals:

- *Examine the non-profit status of the Council on American-Islamic Relations*

   In light of the information we examined in chapter five, would Hough be able to explain why CAIR's tax-exempt status should not at least be examined?
- *Make it an act of sedition or solicitation of treason to preach or publish materials that call for the deaths of Americans*

   Could Islamic leaders object to this for any reason other than their attachment to the stealth jihad?
- *Audit sovereign wealth funds in the United States*

   If these funds may be used to conduct economic and cultural warfare against the U.S., what exactly could Hough's objection be?

- *Cancel scholarship student visa program with Saudi Arabia until they reform their text books*

  As we saw in chapter eight, it is demonstrably true that Saudi textbooks promote hatred of non-Muslims. Would Islamic leaders like Hough endorse this hatred and violence, or do they prefer for some reason that non-Muslims not know what Saudi-funded Islamic schools are teaching in the United States?

- *Restrict religious visas for imams who come from countries that don't allow reciprocal visits by non-Muslim clergy*

  Is there some reason we can't insist on a modicum of religious toleration from Islamic countries?

- *Cancel contracts to train Saudi police and security in U.S. counterterrorism tactics, and block the sale of sensitive military munitions to Saudi Arabia*

  Given ongoing Saudi financing of the global jihad, this is simple common sense.[17]

After promulgating her plan, Myrick expressed her desire to open a "dialogue" with the Islamic Center of Charlotte, insisting that "the whole point is that we're trying to get people to work together." Yet in response, the leader of Charlotte's Islamic community resorted to the predictable charges of "McCarthyism" and bigotry. And he was not alone; CAIR's Ibrahim Hooper mounted his familiar hobbyhorse to decry Myrick's plan, arguing, "It sounds like your usual laundry list of talking points you can see on anti-Muslim hate sites on the Internet."[18]

As we saw in chapter three, this is a tested and proven strategy. But Americans who are aware of the stealth jihad cannot afford to let it go unchallenged. Myrick's plan should have been discussed on every major news feature show on television, talk radio, and in the newspapers. That her proposals did not receive serious attention is yet another indication of how far the public debate is today from anything resembling an informed discussion on jihadist terrorism.

And that puts us all at a risk greater than the one we already must endure.

OTHER WAYS TO COUNTER THE STEALTH JIHAD

Every one of Myrick's recommendations should be implemented. But opponents of the stealth jihad must first inform the public that her plan exists and explain why it's so vital. Seven years after September 11, raising awareness about the nature and goals of the global Islamic jihad remains the foremost responsibility of all lovers of freedom. We must stand strongly for freedom of speech against those who would strip it away. The core of our struggle is civil rights: will we defend them or let them go, as Europe and Canada in many ways already have?

Many people argue that such a turn of events simply couldn't happen here in America. Well, it never has, because we never let it. But are we too addicted to oil and convenience at this point to resist any longer?

As we campaign to implement the Myrick plan, we should advocate the following additional steps:

- *Enforce existing laws.* Section 2385 of the federal criminal code states that "whoever knowingly or willfully advocates, abets, advises, or teaches the duty, necessity, desirability, or propriety of overthrowing or destroying

the government of the United States or the government
of any State, Territory, District or Possession thereof, or
the government of any political subdivision therein, by
force or violence, or by the assassination of any officer
of any such government . . . shall be fined under this title
or imprisoned not more than twenty years, or both, and
shall be ineligible for employment by the United States
or any department or agency thereof, for the five years
next following his conviction."[19] If this law were
enforced against Islamic groups in the United States, the
stealth jihad could be stopped in its tracks.

- *Reclassify Muslim organizations.* Any Muslim group in
  America that does not explicitly renounce, in transparent and manifest deed as well as word, any intention
  now or in the future to replace the Constitution of the
  United States with Islamic sharia should either be
  closed or, at a minimum, be classified as a political
  rather than a religious organization and made subject
  to all the responsibilities and standards to which political organizations must adhere. Likewise, mosques and
  Islamic schools should be closely monitored, and any
  that preach Islamic supremacism in the United States
  summarily closed.

- *End Muslim immigration into the United States.* This is
  a simple matter of national security. Immigration policy
  must work toward the integration of all immigrants,
  and the all-encompassing societal program of sharia
  makes the integration of pious Muslims ultimately
  impossible. While there are undoubtedly millions of
  Muslims who have no interest in jihad either by violence
  or stealth, no Islamic authorities anywhere in the world

have declared heretical or in any way unacceptable the idea that non-Muslims must be fought against by various means and subjugated under the rule of Islamic law. Unless and until that begins to happen, no one can be sure of the sentiments of any individual believer. Consequently, simply to protect ourselves, there should be an end to Muslim immigration, combined with a clear notice to Muslims in the United States that any action on behalf of sharia supremacism is unacceptable.

But ending Muslim immigration to America must be considered a long-term goal, since such a measure is impossible in today's political climate. The proposal would inevitably be denounced as "racist," despite the fact that jihadist supremacism is not a race. But at the very least, immigration officials should immediately adopt a program to screen Muslims entering the United States for jihadist sentiments. This will provide grounds for deportation if an entrant renounces some aspect of sharia supremacism on his immigration application and then works for it once in the country.

- *Take pride in our own culture.* We must reject the revisionism and self-hatred that dominates the textbook view of U.S. history and Western civilization today, and recognize that Western culture, threatened in many particulars that we take for granted, is worth defending. American schools should rescue their curriculum from the empty rhetoric of inclusion and multiculturalism, and place a greater emphasis on the study of our own country and of Western civilization. We must re-learn our own history, take pride in it, and revere—not find new ways to deride—those who built the political and legal institutions of this country, with its unrivalled freedoms and solicitude for the individual. As far as the study of Islam goes, we must demand that schools eliminate the misinformation deliberately inserted in textbooks by Islamic interest groups.

IN THE END, WILL THE PRICE BE TOO HIGH?

In 1995, speaking at a conference of the Muslim Arab Youth Association in Toledo, Ohio, Muslim Brotherhood Sheikh Yusuf al-Qaradawi declared, "We will conquer Europe, we will conquer America! Not through sword but through Da'wa [Islamic proselytizing]."[20] This is the Brotherhood's agenda for Western countries—to conquer them by stealth. In the years since al-Qaradawi's proclamation, the power and influence of Islam has grown exponentially in America, alongside mounting calls for Americans to adapt to sharia provision. Where will it end? It will not end until America adopts Islamic law—unless enough Americans resist.

But even if America never becomes a full-blown sharia state, how much of our freedoms and rights will we allow to erode before we stand up and call a halt to this attack?

The current signals are disconcerting. Geert Wilders's film *Fitna,* discussed in chapter four, first appeared at an online video uploading site, LiveLeak.com. However, the day after it was originally posted, LiveLeak pulled the film, replacing it with the following announcement:

> Following threats to our staff of a very serious nature, and some ill informed reports from certain corners of the British media that could directly lead to the harm of some of our

staff, Liveleak.com has been left with no other choice but to remove *Fitna* from our servers.

This is a sad day for freedom of speech on the net but we have to place the safety and well being of our staff above all else. We would like to thank the thousands of people, from all backgrounds and religions, who gave us their support. They realised LiveLeak.com is a vehicle for many opinions and not just for the support of one.

Perhaps there is still hope that this situation may produce a discussion that could benefit and educate all of us as to how we can accept one anothers culture.

We stood for what we believe in, the ability to be heard, but in the end the price was too high.

"In the end the price was too high"—that mournful phrase could be the epitaph of the free West, particularly given the fact that the film merely reports—accurately—how jihadists commit and justify acts of violence and supremacism. Truth, as the "hate crime" trial of Mark Steyn and other developments indicate, is no longer a defense.

LiveLeak's concern for its employees was legitimate; they didn't sign up for death threats and violent intimidation. And a few days later, apparently after the company increased its security, it reinstated *Fitna*. But beyond this incident, if Americans, Westerners, and all people who are threatened by the global jihad and Islamic supremacism are not willing to stand up and fight for this cause, then all is lost. Because the jihadists are willing to go all the way— to give up their very lives—in their quest to control ours. For them, no price is too high.

If fighting against jihad is too high a price for a free people, then ultimately we will have to pay a different price: the jizya—the tax specified by Qur'an 9:29 for certain non-Muslims, particularly Jews and Christians, subjugated as inferiors under the rule of Islamic sharia law.

What ever happened to "Give me liberty, or give me death?"

Or "with a firm reliance on the protection of Divine Providence, we mutually pledge to each other our Lives, our Fortunes, and our sacred Honor"?

Will the price that the children and beneficiaries of those heroic sacrifices are willing to pay prove too high?

The answer will become clear sooner than most people think.

ACKNOWLEDGMENTS

Jack Langer is an editor without peer, and I am enormously grateful to him for the shape and clarity he added to this manuscript. I am also indebted (as always) to Jeff Rubin, whose solid good sense and unrivaled precision of insight have been of immense help to me on more occasions than I can count; Harry Crocker, with his exemplary wit and steadiness, and generosity with sound advice; Hugh Fitzgerald, one of the most brilliant men in the world today, who offered many important additions and elucidations for this book; Pamela Geller, a dynamo of energy and a paragon of courage and fearlessness; and a host of others, many of whom I am not at liberty to name publicly, but I trust they know who they are.

NOTES

Introduction

1. Joseph R. Biden, Jr., "Republicans and Our Enemies," *Wall Street Journal*, May 23, 2008.
2. Lawrence Wright, "The Rebellion Within: An al Qaeda mastermind questions terrorism," *The New Yorker*, June 2, 2008.
3. Neil MacFarquhar, "Hizballah's Prominence Has Many Sunnis Worried," *New York Times*, August 4, 2006.
4. "Mufti of Egypt Sheik Ali Gum'a: Wife-Beating Is Permitted by Islam in Muslim Countries, but Is Forbidden in the West," Middle East Media Research Institute, Clip No. 1154, May 26, 2006.
5. Ramadan Al Sherbini, "Top cleric denies 'freedom to choose religion' comment," *GulfNews*, July 25, 2007.

Chapter One

1. Mohamed Akram, "An Explanatory Memorandum on the General Strategic Goal for the Group in North America," May 22, 1991, Government Exhibit 003-0085, U.S. vs. HLF, et al. 7 (21).
2. Aaron Klein, "Soda, pizza and the destruction of America," WorldNetDaily, March 18, 2003.
3. "Sami Al-Arian, in his words," *St. Petersburg Times*, February 21, 2003.

4. "Hamas MP and Cleric Yunis Al-Astal in a Friday Sermon: We Will Conquer Rome, and from There Continue to Conquer the Two Americas and Eastern Europe," Middle East Media Research Institute (MEMRI), Clip No. 1739, April 11, 2008.

5. "New Muslim Brotherhood Leader: Resistance in Iraq and Palestine is Legitimate; America is Satan; Islam Will Invade America and Europe," Middle East Media Research Institute, Special Dispatch Series No. 655, February 4, 2004.

6. Art Moore, "Did CAIR founder say Islam to rule America?," WorldNetDaily, December 11, 2006.

7. *Minneapolis Star Tribune*, April 4, 1993, quoted in Daniel Pipes and Sharon Chadha, "CAIR: Islamists Fooling the Establishment," *Middle East Quarterly*, Spring 2006.

8. Jagan Kaul, "Kashmir: Kashmiri Pundit View-point," *Kashmir Telegraph*, May 2002.

9. Brynjar Lia, *The Society of the Muslim Brothers in Egypt* (Ithaca, NY: Ithaca Press, 1998), 28.

10. Ibid., 68-9, 75-6.

11. Ibid., 79.

12. Shaker El-sayed, "Hassan al-Banna: The leader and the Movement," Muslim American Society, http://www.maschicago.org/library/misc_articles/hassan_banna.htm.

13. Lia., 153-4.

14. Ibid., 155.

15. Jonathan Raban, "Truly, madly, deeply devout," *The Guardian*, March 2, 2002.

16. Martin Kramer, "Fundamentalist Islam at Large: The Drive for Power," *Middle East Quarterly*, June 1996.

17. "New Muslim Brotherhood Leader: Resistance in Iraq and Palestine is Legitimate; America is Satan; Islam Will Invade America and Europe," Middle East Media Research Institute, Special Dispatch Series No. 655, February 4, 2004.

18. "The Project," trans. Scott Burgess, quoted in Patrick Poole, "The Muslim Brotherhood 'Project' (continued)," FrontPageMag.com, http://www.frontpagemag.com/articles/Read.aspx?GUID=61829F93-7A81-4654-A2E8-FOA5EGDD3DC4.

19. Patrick Poole, "The Muslim Brotherhood 'Project,'" FrontPageMag.com, http://www.frontpagemag.com/articles/Read.aspx?GUID=67736123-6864-4205-B51E-BCBDEF45FCDE.

20. Mohamed Akram, "An Explanatory Memorandum on the General Strategic Goal for the Group in North America," May 22, 1991, Government Exhibit 003-0085, U.S. vs. HLF, et al., 7 (21).

21. "Retrial of Hamas Financing Case Begins in Dallas," AP, September 23, 2008.

22. Mohamed Akram, "An Explanatory Memorandum on the General Strategic Goal for the Group in North America," May 22, 1991, Government Exhibit 003-0085, U.S. vs. HLF, et al., 7-8 (21-22).

23. I have rearranged the order of these points in order to group them thematically.

24. "Al-Arian Released After Five Years, Awaits 2nd Trial," AP, September 2, 2008; Robert Spencer, "A Jailed Jihadist's Unhappy Anniversary," *Human Events*, April 9, 2008; Robert Spencer, "The New Alger Hiss," *Human Events*, April 23, 2008.

25. Josh Gerstein, "Islamic Groups Named in Hamas Funding Case," *New York Sun*, June 4, 2007.

26. Art Moore, "Did CAIR founder say Islam to rule America?," WorldNetDaily, December 11, 2006.

27. "Muslim-rights voice indicted in jihad plot," WorldNetDaily, July 9, 2003.

28. Joe Kaufman, "A Night of Hamas 'Heroes,'" FrontPageMagazine.com, March 8, 2004.

29. "The Charter of Allah: The Platform of the Islamic Resistance movement (Hamas)," translated and annotated by Raphael Israeli, The International Policy Institute for Counter-Terrorism, April 5, 1998, http://www.ict.org.il/documents/documentdet.cfm?docid=14.

30. Robert S. Leiken and Steven Brooke, "The Moderate Muslim Brotherhood," *Foreign Affairs*, March/April 2007.

31. "U.S. Reaching Out to Muslim Brotherhood: Report," IslamOnline, April 3, 2005.

32. "U.S. approves contacts with Muslim Brotherhood: 'Region is going Islam,'" *World Tribune*, June 28, 2007.

33. Jonathan Dahoah-Halevi, "The Muslim Brotherhood: A Moderate Islamic Alternative to al Qaeda or a Partner in Global Jihad?," Jerusalem Center for Public Affairs, November 1, 2007.

34. Ibid.

35. Ibid.

36. Noreen S. Ahmed-Ullah, Sam Roe and Laurie Cohen, "A rare look at secretive Brotherhood in America," *Chicago Tribune*, September 19, 2004.

37. Jason Trahan, "Muslim Brotherhood's papers detail plan to seize U.S.: Group's takeover plot emerges in Holy Land case," *Dallas Morning News*, September 17, 2007.

38. Ibid.

39. "IPT Footage Takes Down Omeish," Investigative Project on Terrorism, September 27, 2007, http://www.investigativeproject.org/article/494.

40. "Abdurahman Alamoudi Sentenced to Jail in Terrorism Financing Case," Department of Justice, http://www.usdoj.gov/opa/pr/2004/October/04_crm_698.htm.

41. Steven Emerson, *American Jihad: The Terrorists Living Among Us* (Free Press, 2002), 210-211.

Chapter Two

1. Hasan Al-Banna, "The Message of the Teachings," Young Muslims Canada Online Library, http://www.youngmuslims.ca/online_library/books/tmott/.
2. "Full text: bin Laden's 'letter to America,'" *Observer*, November 24, 2002.
3. "Surat at-Tawba: Repentance, Tafsir," http://ourworld.compuserve.com/homepages/ABewley/tawba1.html
4. Ibn Abi Zayd al-Qayrawani, *La Risala* (*Epitre sur les elements du dogme et de la loi de l'Islam selon le rite malikite*), trans. Leon Bercher, 5th ed. (Algiers, 1960), 165. Cited in Andrew G. Bostom, "Khaled Abou El Fadl: Reformer or Revisionist?," http://www.secularislam.org/articles/bostom.htm.
5. Ibn Taymiyya, "Jihad," in Rudolph Peters, *Jihad in Classical and Modern Islam*, Markus Wiener Publishers, 1996, 49.
6. *Hidayah*, vol. Ii. P. 140, quoted in Thomas P. Hughes, *A Dictionary of Islam* (W.H. Allen, 1895), "Jihad," pp. 243-248.
7. Abu'l Hasan al-Mawardi, *al-Ahkam as-Sultaniyyah (The Laws of Islamic Governance)* (UK: Ta-Ha Publishers, 1996), 60.
8. "Clarifying the meaning of Jihad," *Pakistan Daily*, May 21, 2008.
9. Majid Khadduri, *War and Peace in the Law of Islam* (Johns Hopkins University press, 1955), 51.
10. Imran Ahsan Khan Nyazee, *Theories of Islamic Law: The Methodology of Ijtihad* (The Other Press, 1994), 251-252.
11. Ibid., 253.
12. "Surat at-Tawba: Repentance, Tafsir," http://ourworld.compuserve.com/homepages/ABewley/tawba1.html
13. Ibn Kathir, *Tafsir Ibn Kathir (Abridged)*, Darussalam, 2000. Vol. 4, 406.
14. "Surat at-Tawba: Repentance, Tafsir," http://ourworld.compuserve.com/homepages/ABewley/tawba1.html
15. Bat Ye'or, *The Decline of Eastern Christianity Under Islam: From Jihad to Dhimmitude* (Madison, NJ: Fairleigh Dickinson University Press, 1996), 271–272.
16. Middle East Media Research Institute (MEMRI), "Friday Sermons in Saudi Mosques: Review and Analysis," MEMRI Special Report No. 10, September 26, 2002, www.memri.org. This sermon is undated, but it recently appeared on the Saudi website www.alminbar.net.
17. Ihsan Bagby, *A Portrait of Detroit Mosques: Muslim Views on Policy, Politics, and Religion* (Institute for Social Policy and Understanding, 2004), 37.
18. Daniel Pipes Interview with Ahmed Yusuf, "Ahmad Yusuf: 'Hamas Is a Charitable Organization,'" *Middle East Quarterly*, March 1998.
19. Hassan Nasrallah, Al-Manar, September 27, 2002 (BBC Monitoring). Quoted in Deborah Passner, "Hassan Nasrallah: In His Own Words," Committee for Accuracy in Middle East Reporting in America (CAM-

ERA), July 26, 2006,
http://www.camera.org/index.asp?x_context=7&x_issue=11&x_article=1158

20. Hilary Leila Krieger, "FBI: Hizbullah avoiding attacks on US," *Jerusalem Post*, April 12, 2007.

21. "Pakistan-Based Militant Group Lashkar-e-Islam Vows 'To Spread Islam Across the World,'" Middle East Media Research Institute, Special Dispatch Series No. 1906, April 23, 2008.

22. Jonathan Wynne-Jones and Tom Harper, "The cemetery where all face Mecca," *Telegraph*, September 24, 2006.

23. "Muslim Fundamentalists Attack Xtian Female Students in FUT," *Daily Champion of Lagos*, reprinted at AllAfrica.com, September 24, 2005.

24. Frank Gardner, "Grand Sheikh condemns suicide bombings," *BBCNews*, December 4, 2001.

25. Ahmed ibn Naqib al-Misri, *Reliance of the Traveller ('Umdat al-Salik): A Classic Manual of Islamic Sacred Law*, trans. Nuh Ha Mim Keller (Beltsville, MD: Amana Publications, 1999), xx.

26. *'Umdat al-Salik*, o8.2-3.

27. *'Umdat al-Salik*, e4.3.

28. *'Umdat al-Salik*, m10.3.

29. *'Umdat al-Salik*, r40.1.

30. *'Umdat al-Salik*, o9.8.

31. Douglas Jehl, "Moderate Muslims Fear Their Message Is Being Ignored," *New York Times*, October 21, 2001.

32. George W. Bush, Second Inaugural Address, January 20, 2005.

33. Mark O'Keefe, "Has the United States Become Judeo-Christian-Islamic?," *Newhouse News Service*, May 16, 2003.

34. Michael Novak, *On Two Wings: Humble Faith and Common Sense at the American Founding* (NY: Encounter Books, 2002), 28-29.

35. Joseph J. Ellis, *American Sphinx* (Vintage Books, 1998), 89.

Chapter Three

1. Reihan Salam, "The Sum of All PC: Hollywood's reverse racial profiling," *Slate*, May 28, 2002.

2. Robert Spencer, "CAIR threatens Young America's Foundation over my talk tomorrow," Jihad Watch, August 1, 2007.

3. Bryan Preston, "CAIR threatens Young America's Foundation, seeks to stifle Robert Spencer – Updates," HotAir.com, August 1, 2007.

4. "CAIR Libel Suit Against Anti-CAIR's Andrew Whitehead Dismissed 'With Prejudice,'" Anti-CAIR, http://www.anti-cair-net.org/Dismissed; Daniel Pipes, "CAIR Backs Down from Anti-CAIR," FrontPageMagazine.com, April 21, 2006.

5. Muhammad Hisham Kabbani, "Islamic Extremism: A Viable Threat to U.S. National Security," speech at U.S. Department of State, January 7, 1999.

6. MSNBC, *Nachman*, February 25, 2003.
7. "Imam accused of 'gay death' slur," *BBC News*, October 26, 2006.
8. "US paper distributes free anti-Prophet book: Book is said to contain lies and hate," *Al-Arabiya*, March 16, 2008.
9. Hillel Fendel, "Two-Year-Old Anti-Islam Book Infuriates Moslems," *Israel National News*, March 19, 2008.
10. Muhammed Ibn Ismaiel Al-Bukhari, *Sahih al-Bukhari: The Translation of the Meanings*, trans. Muhammad M. Khan (Darussalam, 1997), Vol. 4, book 56, no. 2977.
11. Bukhari, vol. 5, book 64, no. 4046.
12. Ibn Ishaq, *The Life of Muhammad: A Translation of Ibn Ishaq's Sirat Rasul Allah*, trans. A. Guillaume (Oxford University Press, 1955), 504.
13. Yahiya Emerick, *The Life and Work of Muhammad* (Alpha Books, 2002), 240.
14. Ibn Ishaq, 369; Ibn Sa'd, *Kitab Al-Tabaqat Al-Kabir*, vol. II, trans. S. Moinul Haq and H K. Ghazanfar Kitab Bhavan, n.d., 36.
15. Charles Krauthammer, "The Truth about Torture," *The Weekly Standard*, December 5, 2005.
16. "Incitement Watch: Krauthammer Says Quran 'Inspires Barbarism,'" Council on American-Islamic Relations Chicago office, November 28, 2005, http://chicago.cair.com/actionalerts.php?file=aa_barbarism11282005.
17. Sarah Lemagie, "Muslim civil liberties group seeks FBI probe of school threats," *Minneapolis-St. Paul Star Tribune*, April 14, 2008.
18. "Muslim Group Asks for Inquiry on Alleged Threats Against School," Associated Press, April 27, 2008.
19. Sarah Lemagie, "Muslim civil liberties group seeks FBI probe of school threats," *Minneapolis-St. Paul Star Tribune*, April 14, 2008; "Law Enforcement on Watch for Hate Crimes at Twin Cities Charter School," MyFox9.com, April 14, 2008.
20. Charles C. Haynes, "Separation Of Mosque and State Sparks Death Threats," *North Country Gazette*, May 8, 2008.
21. See, for example, Daniel Pipes and Sharon Chadha, "CAIR's Hate Crimes Nonsense," FrontPageMagazine.com, May 18, 2005.
22. "Infinite Justice, Out – Enduring Freedom, In," BBC News, September 25, 2001.
23. Jake Tapper, "Islam's Flawed Spokesmen," Salon, September 26, 2001.
24. Ibid., Charles Krauthammer, "Voices of Moral Obtuseness," *Washington Post*, September 21, 2001, and "L.A. Area Muslims Disagree with Khomeini's Call to Kill Rushdie," *Los Angeles Times*, February 22, 1989.
25. Bill Gertz, "Inside the Ring: Coughlin sacked," *Washington Times*, January 4, 2008.
26. Stephen Collins Coughlin, "'To Our Great Detriment': Ignoring What Extremists Say About *Jihad*," Unclassified thesis submitted to the fac-

ulty of the National Defense Intelligence College in partial fulfillment of the requirements of the degree of Master of Science of Strategic Intelligence, July 2007, 221-222.

27. Matthew Lee, "'Jihadist' booted from government lexicon," Associated Press, April 24, 2008.

28. Stephen Coughlin, "Analysis Of Muslim Brotherhood's General Strategic Goals For North America Memorandum," The Investigative Project on Terrorism, September 7, 2007.

29. "Al-Qaradawi full transcript," BBC, July 8, 2004.

30. Stephen Coughlin, "Analysis Of Muslim Brotherhood's General Strategic Goals For North America Memorandum," The Investigative Project on Terrorism, September 7, 2007.

31. Email to author, June 25, 2008.

32. Ahmed ibn Naqib al-Misri, 'Umdat al-Salik (Reliance of the Traveller: A Classic Manual of Islamic Sacred Law), trans. Nuh Ha Mim Keller (Beltsville, MD: Amana Publications, 1999), xx, o11.10 (5).

Chapter Four

1. Jonathan Wynne-Jones, "Bishop warns of no-go zones for non-Muslims," Telegraph, April 18, 2008.

2. Rukmini Callimachi, "Defame Islam, Get Sued?," Associated Press, March 14, 2008.

3. Ibid.

4. "Muslims condemn Dutch lawmaker's film," CNN, March 28, 2008.

5. "Iran protests to EU presidency over Dutch anti-Islam film," Islamic Republic News Agency, March 30, 2008; "UN chief condemns anti-Islam film," BBC News, March 28, 2008.

6. "U.N.'s Ban condemns Dutch film as anti-Islamic," Reuters, March 28, 2008.

7. "Louise Arbour condemns the film 'Fitna,'" Kuwait News Agency, March 28, 2008.

8. Jorge Sampaio, Statement of the High Representative on the Wilders film Image, "A call for respect and calm," United Nations Alliance of Civilizations, March 29, 2008.

9. "Muslim countries win concession regarding religious debates," Associated Press, June 19, 2008.

10. "UN Human Rights Council: Any mention of the word '' is now taboo," Jihad Watch, June 19, 2008.

11. Ahmed ibn Naqib al-Misri, Reliance of the Traveller ['Umdat al-Salik]: A Classic Manual of Islamic Sacred Law, trans. Nuh Ha Mim Keller (Beltsville, MD: Amana Publications, 1999), e4.3.

12. Geneive Abdo, No God But God: Egypt and the Triumph of Islam, (Oxford University Press, 2000), 59.

13. "Urgent Action," Amnesty International, February 6, 2008,

http://www.amnestyusa.org/actioncenter/actions/uaa03308.pdf.

14. Ekmeleddin Ihsanoglu, "Speech of Secretary General at the thirty-fifth session of the Council of Foreign Ministers of the Organisation of the Islamic Conference," June 18, 2008.

15. Doudou Diène, "Racism, Racial Discrimination, Xenophobia and Related Forms of Intolerance: Follow-Up To and Implementation of the Durban Declaration and Programme of Action," United Nations Human Rights Council, August 21, 2007.

16. "Al-Qaida claims it attacked Denmark Embassy," Associated Press, June 4, 2008.

17. "Pakistan ambassador: 'Are you satisfied?,'" *Copenhagen Post*, June 4, 2008.

18. Tahir Niaz, "Pakistan to ask EU to amend laws on freedom of expression," *Daily Times*, June 8, 2008.

19. "Religious Speech Debated," *Washington Times*, July 17, 2008.

20. "Pakistan ambassador: 'Are you satisfied?,'" *Copenhagen Post*, June 4, 2008.

21. "Muslims condemn Dutch lawmaker's film," CNN, March 28, 2008.

22. "Over 25,000 Pakistanis Rally Against Anti-Koran Film, Prophet Cartoons," Associated Press, April 6, 2008; "Muslim, UN outrage over Dutch MP's anti-Islam film," *Anatolian Times*, March 28, 2008.

23. Philippe Naughton, "Van Gogh killer jailed for life," *Times Online*, July 26, 2005.

24. Steven Stalinsky, "Dealing in Death," *National Review*, May 24, 2004.

25. Michael Steen, Andrew Bounds, and Ferry Biederman, "Muslim reaction to Dutch film is muted," *Financial Times*, March 29, 2008.

26. "Tunisians Had Planned To Strangle Prophet Cartoonist – Report," Agence France Presse, June 19, 2008.

27. Paula Newton, "Artist defiantly draws Prophet Mohammed," CNN, October 16, 2007.

28. Bryan Preston, "Larry O'Donnell admits he's afraid to criticize Islam publicly," HotAir.com, December 11, 2007.

29. Jana Winter, "Iranian Artist Fights to Have Muhammad Art Displayed in Dutch Museums," FOX News, May 3, 2008.

30. "Swiss Muslims File Suit Over 'Racist' Fallaci Book," *IslamOnline*, June 20, 2002.

31. Margaret Talbot, "The Agitator: Oriana Fallaci directs her fury toward Islam," *The New Yorker*, June 5, 2006.

32. "Oriana in Exile," *American Spectator*, July 18, 2005.

33. "Swiss Muslims File Suit Over 'Racist' Fallaci Book," *IslamOnline*, June 20, 2002.

34. "Prophet of Decline," *Wall Street Journal*, June 23, 2005.

35. "Bardot Fined Over Racial Hatred," BBC News, June 3, 2008.

36. Syed Soharwardy, "Why I'm withdrawing my human rights complaint against Ezra Levant," *Toronto Globe and Mail*, February 15, 2008.

37. "Neocon Book Offends Canada Muslims," *IslamOnline*, January 1, 2008.

38. "Clueless Would-be Censors Attack Mark Steyn Again," Western Standard blog, Mark Steyn, "The future belongs to Islam," *Macleans*, October 20, 2006.

39. Jim Henley, "Sympathy for the Devil," *Unqualified Offerings*, December 8, 2007, http://www.highclearing.com/index.php/archives/2007/12/08/7517

40. Lorenzo Vidino, "Forceful Reason," *National Review*, May 4, 2004.

41. "Leading Sunni Sheikh Yousef Al-Qaradhawi and Other Sheikhs Herald the Coming Conquest of Rome," Middle East Media Research Institute Special Dispatch Series No. 447, December 6, 2002.

42. James Slack, "Government renames Islamic terrorism as 'anti-Islamic activity' to woo Muslims," *Daily Mail*, January 17, 2008.

43. Ibid.

44. Demetri Sevastopulo, "Security chief decries 'war on terror,'" *Financial Times*, May 28, 2008.

45. Stephen Glover, "Stephen Glover on The Press: Judges' decisions need careful scrutiny to protect a free Press," *The Independent*, May 20, 2007.

46. "Governor Paterson Signs Legislation Protecting New Yorkers Against Infringement Of First Amendment Rights By Foreign Libel Judgments," New York State Governor's Office, May 1, 2008.

47. Mark Steyn, "The vanishing jihad exposés," *Orange County Register*, August 5, 2007.

48. Http://www.binmahfouz.info/faqs_2.html.

49. "Profile: Muwafaq Foundation," *CooperativeResearch.org*, http://www.cooperativeresearch.org/entity.jsp?entity=muwafaq_foundation; Mark Steyn, "The vanishing jihad exposés," *Orange County Register*, August 5, 2007.

50. "La note de la DGSE sur les ressources d'Oussama bin Laden," Geopolitique.com, http://www.geopolitique.com/terrorisme/la-note-de-la-dgse-sur-les-ressources-financieres-d-oussama-bin-laden.html

51. Conversation with the author, June 15, 2007.

Chapter Five

1. "What They Say about CAIR," Council on American-Islamic Relations, www.cair.com.

2. "CAIR-Chicago, Muslims, Meet With U.S. Customs & Border Protection at O'Hare Airport," *CAIR-Illinois*, June 26, 2006, http://www.cairchicago.org/ournews.php?file=on_airportvisit06262006.

3. Daniel Pipes and Sharon Chadha, "CAIR: Islamists Fooling the Establishment," *Middle East Quarterly*, Spring 2006.

4. "Our Vision, Mission, and Core Principles," Council on American-Islamic Relations, www.cair.com.

5. Josh Gerstein, "Islamic Groups Named in Hamas Funding Case," *New York Sun*, June 4, 2007.
6. "HLF's Financial Support of CAIR Garners New Scrutiny," The Investigative Project on Terrorism, October 12, 2007.
7. "Terror Suit Award Tossed Out; Judge: No Hamas Tie to Teen Slaying Shown," *Chicago Tribune*, December 29, 2007; Joseph Kaufman, "Death of a Terror Lobby," FrontPageMagazine.com, February 3, 2006.
8. "Islamic Association For Palestine (IAP)," DiscoverTheNetwork.org, http://www.discoverthenetworks.org/printgroupProfile.asp?grpid=6215
9. Ibid.
10. Ibid.
11. Daniel Pipes and Sharon Chadha, "CAIR: Islamists Fooling the Establishment," *Middle East Quarterly*, Spring 2006.
12. Frederic J. Frommer, "Muslim Convert Running For Congress," Associated Press, September 22, 2006.
13. "Islam Subway Ads Cause Stir in New York," CNN.com, July 22, 2008. Daniel Pipes, "The Danger Within: Militant Islam in America," *Commentary,* November 2001.
14. "Islam's Flawed Spokesmen," Salon, September 26, 2001.
15. Peter Ford, "Listening for Islam's silent majority," *Christian Science Monitor*, November 5, 2001.
16. Liza Porteus, "US Airways Passengers Who Reported 'Suspicious' Imam Activity May Be Sued," FOX News, March 19, 2007. Omar Mohammedi was identified as the President of CAIR-NY in the Speaker Biographies published at the National Association of Muslim Lawyers conference, "Advancing Justice & Empowering the Community," March 31-April 2, 2006.
17. Major Garrett, "Congress to Protect Citizens Who Report 'Flying Imams'-Type Suspicions," FOX News, July 25, 2007.
18. Sarah Downey and Michael Hirsh, "A Safe Haven?," *Newsweek*, September 30, 2002. Cited in Daniel Pipes and Sharon Chadha, "CAIR: Islamists Fooling the Establishment," *Middle East Quarterly*, Spring 2006.
19. "An Interview with Muslim Brotherhood's #2, Mohammed Habib," Pajamas Media, http://pajamasmedia.com/blog/an-interview-with-the-muslim-brotherhoods-2/2/.
20. Steven Emerson, "Re: Terrorism and the Middle East Peace Process," testimony before the U.S. Senate Foreign Relations Committee, Subcommittee on Near East and South Asia, March 19, 1996. Cited in Daniel Pipes and Sharon Chadha, "CAIR: Islamists Fooling the Establishment," *Middle East Quarterly*, Spring 2006.
21. Steven Pomerantz, "Counterterrorism in a Free Society," *The Journal of Counterterrorism & Security International*, Spring 1998. Cited in Daniel Pipes and Sharon Chadha, "CAIR: Islamists Fooling the Establishment," *Middle East Quarterly*, Spring 2006.

22. Evan McCormick, "A Bad Day for CAIR," FrontPageMagazine.com, September 24, 2003.

23. Cinnamon Stillwell, "Savage vs. CAIR: The battle over free speech," *San Francisco Chronicle*, December 19, 2007.

24. "9/11 Families' Suit Thrown Out Again; U.S. Appeals Court Rules Relatives of Sept. 11 Victims Can't Seek Damages From Saudi Arabia," *Newsday* (New York), August 15, 2008; *John P. O'Neill vs. Al Baraka*. Cited in Daniel Pipes and Sharon Chadha, "CAIR: Islamists Fooling the Establishment," *Middle East Quarterly*, Spring 2006.

25. "Teacher Sentenced for Aiding Terrorists," *Washington Post*, August 26, 2006; Daniel Pipes and Sharon Chadha, "CAIR: Islamists Fooling the Establishment," *Middle East Quarterly*, Spring 2006.

26. Daniel Pipes and Sharon Chadha, "CAIR: Islamists Fooling the Establishment," *Middle East Quarterly*, Spring 2006.

27. "Urban Legends," Council on American-Islamic Relations, January 19, 2007.

28. Ibid.

29. Daniel Pipes and Sharon Chadha, "CAIR: Islamists Fooling the Establishment," *Middle East Quarterly*, Spring 2006.

30. "Urban Legends," Council on American-Islamic Relations, January 19, 2007.

31. Ibid.

32. Nicholas K. Geranios, "Second man with ties to University of Idaho arrested," Associated Press, March 14, 2003. For Khafagi's position with CAIR, see Carol Eisenberg, "A Troubling Year For Muslims in America," *Newsday*, September 2, 2002.

33. Daniel Pipes and Sharon Chadha, "CAIR: Islamists Fooling the Establishment," *Middle East Quarterly*, Spring 2006.

34. "Urban Legends," Council on American-Islamic Relations, January 19, 2007.

35. "Historic Display of Unity: Fiqh Council of North America presents Fatwa denouncing terrorists to Cardinal McCarrick and other religious leaders," Bridges to Common Ground, November 28, 2007, http://www.bridgestocommonground.org/sp.html

36. Fiqh Council of North America, "U.S. Muslim Religious Council Issues Fatwa Against Terrorism," http://islam.about.com/od/terrorism/a/terrorism_fatwa.htm.

37. "Historic Display of Unity: Fiqh Council of North America presents Fatwa denouncing terrorists to Cardinal McCarrick and other religious leaders," Bridges to Common Ground, November 28, 2007, http://www.bridgestocommonground.org/sp.html

38. "The Killings of Non-Muslims is Legitimate," November 24, 2006, http://www.youtube.com/watch?v=maHSOB2RFm4.

39. Suzanne Goldenberg, " 'It's gone beyond hostility,' " *The Guardian*, August 12, 2002.

40. "Arab Liberals: Prosecute Clerics Who Promote Murder," *Middle East Quarterly*, Winter 2005.
41. "Al-Qaradawi full transcript," BBC News, July 8, 2004.
42. "Director of London's Al-Maqreze Centre for Historical Studies Hani Sibai: There are No 'Civilians' in Islamic Law; The Bombing is a Great Victory for Al-Qa'ida, Which 'Rubbed the Noses of the World's 8 Most Powerful Countries in the Mud,'" Middle East Media Research Institute Special Dispatch Series No. 932, July 12, 2005.
43. Christopher Goffard, "Controversy follows Dennis Prager to Yorba Linda," *Los Angeles Times*, January 24, 2007.
44. "MPAC Condemns London Bombings," Muslim Public Affairs Council, July 7, 2005.
45. "MPAC Challenges Steve Emerson to Release Full Recording," Muslim Public Affairs Council, July 12, 2005.
46. George Melloan, "Making Muslims Part of the Solution," *Wall Street Journal*, March 29, 2005.
47. "Fight Terrorism: Campaign Mission," Muslim Public Affairs Council, http://www.mpac.org/ngcft/campaign-mission/index.php
48. "Al-Qaradawi full transcript," BBC News, July 8, 2004.
49. "Fight Terrorism: Frequently Asked Questions About MPAC's National Anti-Terrorism Campaign Campaign Mission," Muslim Public Affairs Council, http://www.mpac.org/ngcft/faqs/.
50. "Fight Terrorism: Mosque Guidelines Recommendations," Muslim Public Affairs Council, http://www.mpac.org/ngcft/mosque-guidelines/.
51. "Fight Terrorism: Frequently Asked Questions About MPAC's National Anti-Terrorism Campaign Campaign Mission," Muslim Public Affairs Council, http://www.mpac.org/ngcft/faqs/.
52. "Fight Terrorism: Mosque Guidelines Recommendations," Muslim Public Affairs Council, http://www.mpac.org/ngcft/mosque-guidelines/.
53. "A Response to Criticism of 'Counterproductive Counterterrorism,'" Muslim Public Affairs Council, February 15, 2005, http://www.mpac.org/article.php?id=210.
54. Muhammad Hisham Kabbani, "Islamic Extremism: A Viable Threat to U.S. National Security," speech at U.S. Department of State, January 7, 1999.
55. "Arab American Organizations Call for Administrative Action," May 20, 2004. http://www.arableague-us.org/palestinians_targeted.html.
56. "Apologists or Extremists: Salam al-Marayati," Investigative Project on Terrorism, http://www.investigativeproject.org/profile/114.
57. Daniel Pipes, "Needed: Muslims against Terror," *Forward*, July 16, 1999.
58. Daniel Pipes, "The Rochester Institute of Technology and My Unwillingness to Be 'Balanced' at Campus Talks," DanielPipes.org, December 31, 2004. Updated April 15, 2005.
59. Lee Green, "CAMERA Alert: *LA Times* Mum on Al-Marayati's

Record," Committee for Accuracy in Middle East Reporting in America, June 26, 2000.

60. "ZOA Urges State Dept. To Rescind Invitation To Muslim Extremist Who Has Praised Terrorist Groups," Zionist Organization of America, January 23, 2002.

61. Robert Spencer, "The Muslim Public Affairs Council's War on Steve Emerson," FrontPageMagazine.com, January 12, 2005.

62. "Counterproductive Counterterrorism: How Anti-Islamic Rhetoric is Impeding America's Homeland Security," Muslim Public Affairs Council, December 2004.

63. Zachary Block, "One Man's War on Terror," *Brown Alumni Magazine*, November/December 2002.

64. Daniel Pipes, "A Slick Islamist Heads to Jail," FrontPageMagazine.com, August 3, 2004.

65. "Official: Terrorism suspect attended White House meeting," CNN, February 23, 2003.

66. Steven Emerson, *American Jihad: The Terrorists Living Among Us*, Free Press, 2002. Pp. 210-211.

67. Muzaffar Iqbal, "The American Calamity," *The Minaret*, May 2002.

68. Hassan Hathout, Maher Hathout, and Fathi Osman, "About the Authors," *In Fraternity: A Message to Muslims in America* (The Minaret Publishing House, 1989).

69. *The Minaret*, March 1998, p. 41.

70. Daniel Pipes, "MPAC, CAIR, and Praising Osama bin Laden," Front Steven Emerson, "MPAC in Denial About Radicalization of Muslim Youth?," Counterterrorism Blog, May 23, 2007.

72. Steven Emerson, "Ms. Lekovic...A Dozen Printing Mistakes?," Counterterrorism Blog, May 30, 2007.

73. "Fight Terrorism: Frequently Asked Questions About MPAC's National Anti-Terrorism Campaign Campaign Mission," Muslim Public Affairs Council, http://www.mpac.org/ngcft/faqs/.

Chapter Six

1. "Bart Simpson becomes Badr Shamssoon," *Ya Libnan*, November 5, 2005.

2. "Disney's Piglet banned in Middle East!," QatarLiving.com, January 28, 2007, http://www.qatarliving.com/blog/camper/disneys-piglet-banned-in-middle-east

3. Alfred de Montesquiou, "Sudan president pardons British teacher," Associated Press, December 3, 2007.

4. Justin McCarthy, "'View' Co-Hosts Blame Woman Persecuted by Sudan," *NewsBusters*, November 30, 2007.

5. "Grudge sparked teddy bear crisis," CNN, December 3, 2007.

6. Christopher Dickey and Rod Nordland, "The Fire That Won't Die Out," *Newsweek*, July 22, 2002, 34-37.

7. Martin Edwin Andersen, "For One Diplomat, the High Road Is a Lonely One," *WorldNetDaily*, February 11, 2002.
8. "American Woman Jailed in Saudi Arabia for Sitting With Man at Starbucks," FOX News, February 7, 2008.
9. Thomas Landen, "Police Protection for 'Mohammed Pulpit,'" *Brussels Journal*, May 13, 2008.
10. "Woman Fired For Eating 'Unclean' Meat," Local6.com, August 4, 2004.
11. Sarah Karush, "Hamtramck vote a victory for those in favor of allowing mosques to broadcast Islamic call to prayer," Associated Press, July 20, 2004.
12. "Muslim Dunkin' Donuts Owner Can Sue Over Pork, Appeals Court Says," Reuters, July 10, 2007.
13. Roger Yu, "Airport Check-in: Fare refusals in Minnesota," *USA Today*, September 18, 2006; Patrick Condon, "Muslim cabbies tell airport they won't bend in alcohol dispute," Associated Press, February 27, 2007.
14. Keith Oppenheim, "If you drink, some cabbies won't drive," CNN, January 26, 2007.
15. Roger Yu, "Airport Check-in: Fare refusals in Minnesota," *USA Today*, September 18, 2006.
16. Katherine Kersten, "Airport taxi flap about alcohol has deeper significance," *Minneapolis-St. Paul Star Tribune*, October 26, 2006.
17. Roger Yu, "Airport Check-in: Fare refusals in Minnesota," *USA Today*, September 18, 2006.
18. "Target shifts Muslims who won't ring up pork," Associated Press, March 18, 2007.
19. Erin Dostal, "Muslims to get floor sinks at airport by fall: New, sanitary facilities for ritual foot-washing will serve taxi drivers," *Indianapolis Star*, April 4, 2008.
20. Francesca Jarosz, "Airport's sinks to help Muslims carry out rituals," *Indianapolis Star*, September 16, 2007.
21. "Sky Harbor installs cleanup station to Muslim taxi, limo drivers," Associated Press, May 20, 2004.
22. Erin Dostal, "Muslims to get floor sinks at airport by fall: New, sanitary facilities for ritual foot-washing will serve taxi drivers," *Indianapolis Star*, April 4, 2008.
23. Katherine Kersten, "'Accommodations' could open door to more demands," *Star Tribune*, April 18, 2007.
24. Karen Bouffard, "College's foot bath plans spark backlash: Project for Muslim students draws accusation U-M Dearborn is giving faith favored treatment," *The Detroit News*, June 7, 2007.
25. Andrea Billups, "School to provide Muslim students with foot baths," *Washington Times*, August 29, 2007.
26. Erin Dostal, "Muslims to get floor sinks at airport by fall: New, sanitary facilities for ritual foot-washing will serve taxi drivers," *Indianapolis*

Star, April 4, 2008.

27. "Public Minnesota College to Install Foot-Washing Basins for Muslim Students," FOX News, April 13, 2007.

28. Yoav Gonen, "Islam Gains A 'Foothold' At NYU: Students To Get Ritual Baths For Prayer," *New York Post*, October 3, 2007.

29. "Some say schools giving Muslims special treatment," *USA Today*, July 25, 2007.

30. Ibid.

31. Andrea Billups, "School to provide Muslim students with foot baths," *Washington Times*, August 29, 2007.

32. Angela Caputo, "First Jell-O, now Santa," *Chicago Sun-Times*, September 28, 2007.

33. "School Keeps Christmas, Halloween; Adds Ramadan," CBS News, October 4, 2007.

34. Elizabeth Stuart, "The End of Religious School Holidays? A Florida School District Is Not Alone as It Struggles to Accommodate Religious Holidays for all Students," ABC News, April 9, 2007.

35. Naheed Mustafa, "Holidays and Halal food: Two examples of universities' accommodation of Muslims," SoundVision.com, http://www.soundvision.com/info/education/university/university.asp.

36. Benjamin Sarlin, "Mayor: Muslim Holy Days Shouldn't Be School Holidays," *New York Sun*, March 7, 2008.

37. "Georgia public schools to accommodate Friday prayers," United Press International, October 28, 2004.

38. Helen Gao, "S.D. elementary at center of dispute," *San Diego Union-Tribune*, July 2, 2007; "Islamic prayers finally dropped," *WorldNet-Daily*, August 1, 2007.

39. "Jihad In Schools?," *Investor's Business Daily*, July 9, 2007.

40. Dan Packard, "Muslim prayer time new legal issue at Swift plant," Morris News Service, November 14, 2007.

41. Oskar Garcia, "Swift offers partial accommodation for Muslim prayers," Associated Press, August 23, 2007.

42. Sean O'Sullivan, "Muslim former employees at I-95 service station sue Exxon," *Wilmington News Journal*, November 7, 2007.

43. Susan Jones, "Muslims Settle 'Prayer in the Workplace' Dispute," CNSNews.com, March 18, 2005.

44. Muhammad Ridha, "Islam in the Workplace - suggested practice for HR personnel," http://www.kwintessential.co.uk/cultural-services/articles/islam-in-the-workplace.html.

45. "Missing Prayers at Work," *IslamOnline*, March 27, 2004.

46. Chris Penttila, "Prayer meeting: can employers meet Muslims' requests in the workplace?," *Entrepreneur*, August, 2005.

47. "Questions And Answers About The Workplace Rights Of Muslims, Arabs, South Asians, And Sikhs Under The Equal Employment Opportunity Laws," Equal Employment Opportunity Commission, May 14,

2002.

48. Amy Griffith, "Southern Hills sued for religious discrimination,"
   Nashville City Paper, October 4, 2007.

49. Chris Casey, "Facing protests, Swift vows to 'balance needs of all
   employees,'" *Greeley Tribune*, September 6, 2008.

50. Eric J.S. Townsend, "Update: Quran can be used in courtrooms,"
   Greensboro News-Record, May 24, 2007.

51. Amy Argetsinger and Roxanne Roberts, "But It's Thomas Jefferson's
   Koran!," *Washington Post*, January 3, 2007.

52. Dennis Prager, "America, Not Keith Ellison, decides what book a congressman takes his oath on," Townhall.com, November 28, 2006.

53. Eugene Volokh, "Oh Say, Can You Swear on a Koran?," *National
   Review*, November 29, 2006.

54. Ibn Kathir, *Tafsir Ibn Kathir* (Abridged), volume 2 (Darussalam, 2000),
   142.

55. "Al-'Imran 28," *Tafsir al-Jalalayn*, trans. Feras Hamza,
   www.altafsir.com.

Chapter Seven

1. "Some say schools giving Muslims special treatment," *USA Today*, July
   25, 2007.

2. Katherine Kersten, "Normandale's 'meditation room' is home to a single
   faith," *Minneapolis-St. Paul Star Tribune*, December 18, 2007.

3. "School Keeps Christmas, Halloween; Adds Ramadan," CBS News,
   October 4, 2007.

4. Sarah Dallof, "Dispute over airport breakroom leads to lawsuit,"
   KSL.com, January 30, 2008.

5. Jessica Ravitz, "Deep Tensions Arise Over Prayer Space at Salt Lake
   City International Airport," *Salt Lake Tribune*, February 22, 2008.

6. Jaya Narain, "You can swim, but you have to wear Muslim dress,"
   Daily Mail, December 9, 2006.

7. Colin Fernandez and Nick McDermott, "Public pool bars father and
   son from its 'Muslim-only' swimming session," *Daily Mail*, April 18,
   2008.

8. Abbie Ruzicka, "To accommodate Muslim students, Harvard tries
   women-only gym hours," *The Daily Free Press*, February 25, 2008.

9. Colin Fernandez and Nick McDermott, "Public pool bars father and
   son from its 'Muslim-only' swimming session," *Daily Mail*, April 18,
   2008.

10. Richard Kerbaj and Milanda Rout, "Muslims want unis to fit prayer
   time," *The Australian*, February 25, 2008.

11. Http://www.msanational.org/taskforces/matf/.

12. Katherine Kersten, "Ritual-washing Area for Muslims at MCTC May
   be Only the Beginning," *Minneapolis-St. Paul Star-Tribune*, April 16,

2007.

13. "United States: The Jamaat al-Fuqra Threat," Stratfor, June 3, 2005.

14. Ibid.

15. Ibid.

16. Paul L. Williams, op. cit.

17. David Kennedy Houck, "The Islamist Challenge to the U.S. Constitution," *Middle East Quarterly*, Spring 2006, 21-28.

18. Ibid.

19. Nina Bernstein, "In Secret, Polygamy Follows Africans to N.Y.," *New York Times*, March 23, 2007.

20. Lewis Smith, "Muslim men use law loophole to get a harem of 'wives,'" *The Times*, October 21, 2004.

21. Nicholas Hellen, "Muslim second wives may get a tax break," *The Times,* December 26, 2004; "Polygamous husbands can claim cash for their harems," *Evening Standard*, April 17, 2007.

22. Maryclaire Dale, "Pa. bigamist slain hours before trip," Associated Press, August 8, 2007.

23. Noor Javed, "GTA's secret world of polygamy," *Toronto Star*, May 24, 2008.

24. Barbara Bradley Hagerty, "Some Muslims in U.S. Quietly Engage in Polygamy," National Public Radio, May 27, 2008.

25. Allison Engel, "Conversation With Timur Kuran," *University of Southern California News*, December 18, 2006.

26. "Unicorn Capital Sponsors Islamic Finance Conference In Istanbul," Press Release, May 26, 2008.

27. "$4 Trillion in Middle Eastern Capital Available for Investment," Press Release, May 26, 2008.

28. "Allianz Global Investors opens Middle Eastern office and launches two sharia-compliant equity funds," Press Release, May 28, 2008.

29. Christopher Holton, "Financial Jihad: What Americans Need to Know," Center for Security Policy, May 11, 2008.

30. James Fontanella, "U.K. the Global Center for Islamic Finance?," OhMyNews, June 14, 2006.

31. Alyssa A. Lappen, "Congress should outlaw shari'a finance," *The Examiner*, June 2, 2008.

32. Rachel Ehrenfeld and Alyssa A. Lappen, "America for Sale," *Human Events*, April 1, 2008.

33. Alyssa A. Lappen, "Congress should outlaw shari'a finance," *The Examiner*, June 2, 2008.

34. Michael Nazir-Ali, "Extremism flourished as UK lost Christianity," *Telegraph*, January 11, 2008.

35. Rachel Ehrenfeld and Alyssa A. Lappen, "America for Sale," *Human Events*, April 1, 2008.

36. Abdul Malik Mujahid, "Riba: The Personal Dilemma: 5 Ways to Deal with it," SoundVision.com,

http://www.soundvision.com/Info/life/riba.asp.

37. Christopher Holton, "Financial Jihad: What Americans Need to Know," Center for Security Policy, May 11, 2008.

38. Alex Alexiev, "Jihad Comes to Wall Street," *National Review*, April 3, 2008.

39. "Al-Qaradawi full transcript," BBC, July 8, 2004.

40. Christopher Holton, op. cit.

41. "Islamic sharia-based firms on the rise worldwide," Kuwait News Agency, May 26, 2008.

Chapter Eight

1. Gilbert T. Sewall, "Islam in the Classroom: What the Textbooks Tell Us," American Textbook Council, June 2008, 6.

2. Ibid., 19–20.

3. Ibid., 20.

4. "Judge rules Islamic education OK in California classrooms," WorldNetDaily, December 13, 2003.

5. Sewall, op. cit., 18.

6. Ibid.

7. Ibid.,19.

8. "Colorado Congressman Tom Tancredo Speaks Out on Education," *Yorktown Patriot*, April 1, 2004.

9. Sewall, op. cit., 15–16.

10. Ibid., 23.

11. Scott Galupo, "Progress and Islam: The mini-enlightenment that was Andalusia," *National Review Online*, May 30, 2002.

12. María Rosa Menocal, *The Ornament of the World: How Muslims, Jews, and Christians Created a Culture of Tolerance in Medieval Spain* (Little, Brown Co., 2002), 72-3.

13. Kenneth Baxter Wolf, *Christian Martyrs in Muslim Spain* (Cambridge University Press, 1988), 9–10.

14. Sewall, op. cit., 21–22.

15. Ibid., 24.

16. "Islam and the Textbooks: A Report of the American Textbook Council," *Middle East Quarterly*, Summer 2003.

17. Sewall, op. cit., 31–32.

18. Ibid., 32.

19. Ibid., 34.

20. Ibid., 35.

21. Ibid., 41.

22. Ibid., 37.

23. Ibid., 42.

24. Ibid., 9.

25. Samana Siddiqui, "Profile: Council On Islamic Education," SoundVi-

sion.com,
http://www.soundvision.com/Info/education/pubschool/pub.cie.asp.

26. Paul Sperry, "Look who's teaching Johnny about Islam: Saudi-funded Islamic activists have final say in shaping public-school lessons on religions," WorldNetDaily, May 3, 2004.

27. Patrick Poole, "Georgetown University - Wahhabi Front," FrontPageMagazine.com, February 22, 2008.

28. Sewall, op. cit., 18.

29. Ibid., 48.

30. Nick Schou, "Pulling His Cheney," *Orange County Weekly*, October 25, 2001.

31. President Bill Clinton, "Memorandum on Religion in Schools," July 12, 1995, http://www.cofc.edu/~whitel/ClintonSchoolReligion.htm.

32. "How to get religious accommodation in the public school system: a 6-step guide," SoundVision.com, http://www.soundvision.com/Info/education/pubschool/pub.guide.asp.

33. Matthew Barakat, "Review: Troubling passages in texts at Va. School," Associated Press, June 12, 2008.

34. *Sahih Bukhari*, trans. Muhammad Muhsin Khan, Vol. 4, book 53, no. 394. *USC-MSA Compendium of Muslim Texts*, http://www.usc.edu/dept/MSA/fundamentals/hadithsunnah/bukhari/.

35. *Bukhari*, vol. 1, book 2, no. 24.

36. *Bukhari*, vol. 4, book 52, no. 260.

37. Sperry, op. cit.

38. Eric Lichtblau, "American Accused in a Plot to Assassinate Bush," *New York Times*, February 23, 2005; Caryle Murphy, "Facing New Realities as Islamic Americans," *Washington Post*, September 12, 2004.

39. "Ahmed Omar Abu Ali Sentenced To Prison On Terrorism Charges," Department of Justice Press Release, March 29, 2006.

40. Susan L. Douglass and Nadia Pervez, "Hirabah, not Jihad," Council on Islamic Education, 2003.

41. "Islam and the Textbooks: A Report of the American Textbook Council," *Middle East Quarterly*, Summer 2003.

42. Stanley Kurtz, "Saudi in the Classroom," *National Review*, July 25, 2007.

43. Cinnamon Stillwell, "Islam in America's public schools: Education or indoctrination?," *San Francisco Chronicle*, June 11, 2008.

44. " 'Open tent' at Amherst Middle School," *The Cabinet*, May 31, 2007.

45. Sperry, op. cit.

46. Ibid.

47. "Judge rules Islamic education OK in California classrooms," WorldNetDaily, December 13, 2003.

48. Alexis Amory, "Muslim Re-Education," FrontPageMagazine.com, October 20, 2004.

49. Bob Unruh, "Texas children roped into Islamic training," WorldNet-

Daily, May 30, 2008.

50. Bob Unruh, "Islam-promoting principal defied order to protect kids: Students required to attend CAIR indoctrination event," WorldNet-Daily, May 30, 2008.

51. Ericka Mellon, "Principal has new job after 'Islam 101' controversy: Parents outraged over assembly allowed by Friendswood Junior High leader," *Houston Chronicle*, June 5, 2008.

52. Sarah Garland, "New Brooklyn School To Offer Middle East Studies," *New York Sun*, March 7, 2007. Cited in Daniel Pipes, "On New York's 'Khalil Gibran International Academy,'" DanielPipes.org, March 7, 2007, updated through May 22, 2008.

53. "Broadcast Exclusive... Ousted NYC Arabic School Principal Debbie Almontaser Speaks Out on the New McCarthyism & Rightwing Media Attacks," *Democracy Now!*, April 29, 2008. Cited in Daniel Pipes, "On New York's 'Khalil Gibran International Academy,'" DanielPipes.org, March 7, 2007, updated through May 22, 2008.

54. "Brooklyn Arabic School," *New York Sun*, May 8, 2007. Cited in Daniel Pipes, "On New York's 'Khalil Gibran International Academy,'" DanielPipes.org, March 7, 2007, updated through May 22, 2008.

55. Chuck Bennett and Jana Winter, "City Principal Is 'Revolting,'" *New York Post*, August 6, 2007. Cited in Daniel Pipes, "On New York's 'Khalil Gibran International Academy,'" DanielPipes.org, March 7, 2007, updated through May 22, 2008.

56. Andrea Peyser, "Shirting the Issue," *New York Post*, August 7, 2007. Cited in Daniel Pipes, "On New York's 'Khalil Gibran International Academy,'" DanielPipes.org, March 7, 2007, updated through May 22, 2008.

57. "Joel Klein's Choice," *New York Post*, August 7, 2007. Cited in Daniel Pipes, "On New York's 'Khalil Gibran International Academy,'" DanielPipes.org, March 7, 2007, updated through May 22, 2008.

58. Debbie Almontaser, Letter to Joel Klein, August 10, 2007, http://www.danielpipes.org/rr/2007-08-10-almontaser-kgia.pdf. Cited in Daniel Pipes, "On New York's 'Khalil Gibran International Academy,'" DanielPipes.org, March 7, 2007, updated through May 22, 2008.

59. "Danish Cartoons - on display at NYU THIS WEEK!," HAhmed.com, March 26, 2006, http://www.hahmed.com/blog/2006/03/26/danish-car-toons-on-display-at-nyu-this-week.com

60. Beila Rabinowitz, "New York set to open Khalil Gibran 'Jihad' School—connected to Saudi funded ADC—principal won CAIR award," PipeLineNews.org, March 10, 2007. Cited in Daniel Pipes, "On New York's 'Khalil Gibran International Academy,'" DanielPipes.org, March 7, 2007, updated through May 22, 2008.

61. "About Amana," Amana Academy, http://www.amanaacademy.org/about.htm

62. Akhtar H. Emon, "Bringing Arabic to U.S. / Canadian High Schools:

Growing Number of Organizations Seek to Introduce Arabic Curriculum," http://www.hadi.org/ALIF/proposal/arabic-to-highschools.htm. Cited in Daniel Pipes, "Does Learning Arabic Prevent Moral Decay?," DanielPipes.org, November 26, 2004.

63. Sara G. Levin, "Arabic lessons to begin near ground zero high school," *Downtown Express*, September 9-15, 2005. Cited in Daniel Pipes, "Other Taxpayer-Funded American Madrassas," DanielPipes.org, March 8, 2007.

64. Patrick Poole, "CAIR Goes Back to School," FrontPageMagazine.com, August 23, 2007.

65. "Tarek Ibn Ziyad Academy Charter School Enters Teacher Performance Pay Program," Minnesota Department of Education, December 7, 2006.

66. Sarah Lemagie, "Charter school getting threats for Islamic ties," *Minneapolis-St. Paul Star Tribune*, April 12, 2008.

67. Http://www.tizacademy.com/.

68. Katherine Kersten, "Are taxpayers footing bill for Islamic school in Minnesota?," *Minneapolis-St. Paul Star Tribune*, March 9, 2008.

69. "Furor over Islam taught at US public school," Agence France Presse, April 16, 2008.

70. Noreen S. Ahmed-Ullah, Sam Roe and Laurie Cohen, "A rare look at secretive Brotherhood in America," *Chicago Tribune*, September 19, 2004.

71. "Tarek Ibn Ziyad," *IslamOnline*, May 23, 2004.

72. Nicole Muehlhausen, "News crew confronted at school," KSTP.com, May 19, 2008.

73. "Our Pledge," Bureau of Islamic and Arabic Education, http://www.biae.net/pledge.html.

74. "Islamic teachers suspended for praising essay on killing Jews," *The Telegraph*, March 28, 2005.

75. "Saudi Publications On Hate Ideology Invade American Mosques," Center for Religious Freedom, 2005. P. 12.

76. Marc Fisher, "Muslim Students Weigh Questions Of Allegiance," *Washington Post*, October 16, 2001.

Chapter Nine

1. David Horowitz, *Indoctrination U: The Left's War Against Academic Freedom* (NY: Encounter Books, 2007), vii.

2. Omid Safi, "Islam and Modernity (Religion 329)," http://omidsafi.com/index.php?option=com_content&task=view&id=15&Itemid=34. Robert Spencer, "Spencer makes the Enemies' List at Colgate U," Jihad Watch, April 11, 2004. Robert Spencer, "Omid Safi clarifies his enemies' list," Jihad Watch, February 7, 2005.

3. Carl W. Ernst, *Following Muhammad* (North Carolina: University of North Carolina Press, 2003), 27.

4. For a full list of these attacks, see www.thereligionofpeace.com.

5.   Carl W. Ernst, "Notes on the Ideological Patrons of an Islamophobe, Robert Spencer,"
     http://www.unc.edu/~cernst/courses/2004/026/001/spencer.htm.
6.   "UNC Grad in Court on Alleged Hit and Run," Associated Press, March 6, 2006.
7.   "Mohammed Taheri-Azar's letter to police," *The Herald-Sun*, March 29, 2006.
8.   Robert Spencer, "Letters from a mujahid," Jihad Watch, May 12, 2006.
9.   Thomas Hegghammer, "Jihadi studies: The obstacles to understanding radical Islam and the opportunities to know it better," *Times Literary Supplement*, April 2, 2008.
10. Richard Landes, "Tenure in Middle Eastern Studies," InsideHigherEd.com, October 23, 2007.
11. Matt Korade, "Lack of Openness Makes Scholarly Discussion of Islam Dangerous, Says Bernard Lewis," *Congressional Quarterly's Homeland Security News and Analysis*, April 27, 2008.
12. Ibn Warraq, "Edward Said and the Saidists, Or, Third World Intellectual Terrorism," in Robert Spencer, editor, *The Myth of Islamic Tolerance*, Prometheus, 2005, 475.
13. Ibn Warraq, "Edward Said and the Saidists, Or, Third World Intellectual Terrorism," in Robert Spencer, editor, *The Myth of Islamic Tolerance*, Prometheus, 2005, 511-512.
14. "American prof's book on Islam wins award in Cairo," *Outer Banks Sentinel*, August 2, 2004.
15. Karen W. Arenson, "Saudi Prince Gives Millions to Harvard and Georgetown," *New York Times*, December 13, 2005.
16. John J. Miller, "Clash of Cultures: How donors can increase understanding of the Middle East," *Philanthropy*, August 6, 2007. Of course, it was ultimately established that the death toll at the Towers was slightly less than 3,000, but Giuliani's point still holds.
17. Karen W. Arenson, "Saudi Prince Gives Millions to Harvard and Georgetown," *New York Times*, December 13, 2005.
18. Richard Garner, "Saudi prince gives universities £16m for study of Islam," *The Independent*, May 8, 2008.
19. "Saudis purchasing UK universities? Extremism in academia follows millions in donations," *WorldNetDaily*, April 14, 2008.
20. "Q & A with W.D. Mohammed," *Los Angeles Times*, May 15, 1999. Reprinted at http://www.sunnah.org/publication/salafi/WDMuhammad_saudi.htm.
21. Ahmad Faiz bin Abdul Rahman, "Esposito: Do not be too Quick to Draw the Bid'a Gun Against the Sheikh al-Azhar," *Ireland On-Line*, September 19, 1997, http://www.iol.ie/~afifi/BICNews/Afaiz/afaiz40.htm.
22. Martin Kramer, *Ivory Towers on Sand*, Washington Institute for Near East Policy, 2001. P. 56.

23. Ibid., 51.
24. John L. Esposito, *The Islamic Threat: Myth or Reality?* (Oxford University Press, 1999), 30. Quoted in David Cook, *Understanding Jihad* (University of California Press., 2005), 42.
25. David Cook, *Understanding Jihad* (University of California Press., 2005), 42.
26. John L. Esposito and Dalia Mogahed, *Who Speaks For Islam?: What a Billion Muslims Really Think* (Gallup Press, 2008).
27. Robert Satloff, "Just Like Us! Really?," *The Weekly Standard*, May 12, 2008.
28. Hillel Fradkin, "Who does speak for Islam?," Middle East Strategy at Harvard, April 10, 2008, http://blogs.law.harvard.edu/mesh/2008/04/who_does_speak_for_islam/
29. Jacob Gershman, "Saudis Funded Columbia Program At Institute That Trained Teachers," *New York Sun*, March 10, 2005.
30. Adam Daifallah, "Said Chair At Columbia Also Backed By Saudis," *New York Sun*, July 23, 2003.
31. Jacob Gershman, "Saudis Funded Columbia Program At Institute That Trained Teachers," *New York Sun*, March 10, 2005.
32. Aaron Klein, "Obama worked with terrorist: Senator helped fund organization that rejects 'racist' Israel's existence," *WorldNetDaily*, February 24, 2008.
33. Http://www.msanational.org/.
34. "The Constitution of The Muslim Student's Association of the United States and Canada," http://www.msanational.org/about/constitution/
35. David Horowitz, "My Encounter With the Enemy in Milwaukee," FrontPageMagazine.com, May 13, 2008.
36. Aaron Klein, "Obama worked with terrorist: Senator helped fund organization that rejects 'racist' Israel's existence," *WorldNetDaily*, February 24, 2008.
37. Hamid Algar, *Wahhabism: A Critical Essay*, Islamic Publications International, 2002, 52-3.
38. "The Muslim Students Association and the Jihad Network," Terrorism Awareness Project, David Horowitz Freedom Center, 2008, 4-5.
39. Ibid., 5-6.
40. Ibid., 7.
41. Ibid., 31.
42. Ibn Sa'd, *Kitab Al-Tabaqat Al-Kabir*, vol. II, trans. S. Moinul Haq and H K. Ghazanfar, Kitab Bhavan, n.d. 136-37.
43. Ibid., 142.
44. David Horowitz Freedom Center, op. cit., 7-8.
45. "The Spirit of Jihad," *Al-Talib*, July 1999.
46. David Horowitz Freedom Center, op. cit., 9.
47. Ibid., 14.
48. Ibid., 19.

49. Ibid., 20.
50. Ibid., 24.
51. Ibid., 28.
52. Jagan Kaul, "Kashmir: Kashmiri Pundit View-point," *Kashmir Telegraph*, May 2002.

Chapter Ten

1. Paul Sperry, "FBI: Jews need not applyfor Arabic linguist jobs: Despite shortage, loyalty issues, bureau snubbed 90 N.Y. applicants," WorldNetDaily, October 9, 2003.
2. Jeff Karoub, "Recruiting Arabs Still Tough for Army," Associated Press, March 20, 2008.
3. Jamie Glazov, "Infiltration," Interview with Paul Sperry, FrontPageMagazine.com, April 12, 2005.
4. Chris Gourlay, Jonathan Calvert, and Joe Lauria, "For sale: West's deadly nuclear secrets," *The Sunday Times*, January 6, 2008.
5. Paul Sperry, "Arab translators cheered Sept. 11: FBI whistleblower: 'Questions of loyalty' taint interpretation of al-Qaida chatter," WorldNetDaily, January 7, 2004.
6. Chris Gourlay, Jonathan Calvert, and Joe Lauria, "For sale: West's deadly nuclear secrets," *The Sunday Times*, January 6, 2008.
7. Joseph Goldstein, "Mystery Deepens Over WMD Documents," *New York Sun*, February 6, 2008.
8. Joseph Goldstein, "Translator Who Took Classified Iraq Maps Is Sentenced," *New York Sun*, May 20, 2008.
9. Joseph Neff and John Sullivan, "Al Qaeda terrorist duped FBI, Army," *News and Observer*, October 21, 2001.
10. Philip Shenon, "C.I.A. Officer Admits Guilt Over Hizballah Files," *New York Times*, November 14, 2007; James Gordon Meek, "FBI appalled at CIA veterans's defense of agent Nada Nadim Prouty's lies," *New York Daily News*, November 18, 2007.
11. James Gordon Meek, "FBI appalled at CIA veterans's defense of agent Nada Nadim Prouty's lies," *New York Daily News*, November 18, 2007.
12. Susan Edelman and Jill Culora, "Jihad Jane's 'State' of Bliss," *New York Post*, November 18, 2007.
13. Andrea Mitchell and Robert Windrem, "How big a role did disgraced CIA officer have?," NBC News, November 15, 2007.
14. David Ashenfelter, "Woman spared jail, fined in conspiracy case," *Detroit Free Press*, May 13, 2008.
15. James Gordon Meek, "FBI appalled at CIA veterans's defense of agent Nada Nadim Prouty's lies," *New York Daily News*, November 18, 2007.
16. James Gordon Meek, "Busted illegal alien was great spy, say sources,"

New York Daily News, November 16, 2007.

17. Tom Jackman, "Probation For Sergeant Who Misused Databases," *Washington Post*, April 23, 2008.
18. Paul Sperry, "CAIR's Traitorous Cop Ally," FrontPageMagazine.com, June 25, 2008.
19. Tom Jackman, "Probation For Sergeant Who Misused Databases," *Washington Post*, April 23, 2008.
20. Bill Gertz, "Coughlin backed," *Washington Times*, January 11, 2008.
21. Bill Gertz, "Coughlin sacked," *Washington Times*, January 4, 2008.
22. Bill Gertz, "Coughlin backed," *Washington Times*, January 11, 2008.
23. "The termination of Stephen Coughlin on the Joint Staff is an act of intellectual cowardice," Jihad Watch, January 5, 2008.
24. Bill Gertz, "Coughlin sacked," *Washington Times*, January 4, 2008.
25. Claudia Rosett, "Questions for the Pentagon: Who is Hesham Islam?," *National Review*, January 25, 2008.
26. Ibid.
27. Bill Gertz, "Muslim pressure," *Washington Times*, December 28, 2007.
28. Claudia Rosett, "And Now, Hesham Islam's Amazing, Disappearing Profile. What's the Pentagon Trying to Tell Us?," Pajamas Media, January 28, 2008.
29. Claudia Rosett, "Questions for the Pentagon: Who is Hesham Islam?," *National Review*, January 25, 2008.
30. Clare M. Lopez, "Score one for the Muslim Brotherhood," *Middle East Times*, April 28, 2008.
31. Beila Rabinowitz and William Mayer, "State Department Funding ISNA's Propagation Of Islam," PipeLineNews.org, April 25, 2008.

Conclusion

1. "We Will Dominate You," *Middle East Quarterly*, December 1999.
2. "Europa wird am Ende des Jahrhunderts islamisch sein," *Die Welt*, July 28, 2004.
3. Steve Harrigan, "Swedes Reach Muslim Breaking Point," FOX News, November 26, 2004.
4. Michael Nazir-Ali, "Extremism flourished as UK lost Christianity," *Telegraph*, January 11, 2008.
5. Caroline Gammell, "Muslims call for 'no-go' CoE bishop to resign," *Telegraph*, April 18, 2008.
6. "British bishop says he faces threats after comments on Islamic extremism," Associated Press, February 3, 2008.
7. Michael Evans, "Military uniforms in public 'risk offending minorities,'" *Times of London*, March 8, 2008.
8. Jamie Doward, "Revealed: preachers' messages of hate: Muslim worshippers are being urged by radical clerics to ignore British law," *The Observer*, January 7, 2007.
9. Daniel Pipes, "The 751 No-Go Zones of France," DanielPipes.org,

November 14, 2006.

10. Paul Belien, "'Sensitive urban areas,'" *Washington Times*, January 16, 2008.

11. "Belgian laws do not interest him. The man is confident that it is he who controls the neighborhood," Jihad Watch, September 5, 2007.

12. Bat Ye'or, "How Europe Became Eurabia," FrontPageMagazine.com, July 27, 2004.

13. Lisa Zagaroli, "N.C. congresswoman releases 10-point list to tackle radical Islam threats," McClatchy Newspapers, April 18, 2008.

14. Jim Morrill, "Muslim condemns Myrick plan: Senator says she welcomes dialogue on anti-terrorism proposal," *Charlotte Observer*, April 29, 2008.

15. Zagaroli, op. cit.

16. "Abdurahman Alamoudi Sentenced To Jail In Terrorism Financing Case," Department of Justice, October 15, 2004.

17. "Treasury Designates Three Key Terrorist Financiers," U.S. Department of the Treasury, October 10, 2007.

18. Zagaroli, op.cit.

19. United States Code Title 18, Part I, Chapter 115, Section 2385: "Advocating overthrow of Government."

20. "Apologists or Extremists: Yusuf al-Qaradawi," Investigative Project on Terrorism, http://www.investigativeproject.org/profile/167.

INDEX